# GACE

## Early Childhood Special Education General Curriculum Part 1 of 2

# SECRETS

## Study Guide
### Your Key to Exam Success

GACE Test Review for the
Georgia Assessments for the
Certification of Educators

Dear Future Exam Success Story:

Congratulations on your purchase of our study guide. Our goal in writing our study guide was to cover the content on the test, as well as provide insight into typical test taking mistakes and how to overcome them.

Standardized tests are a key component of being successful, which only increases the importance of doing well in the high-pressure high-stakes environment of test day. How well you do on this test will have a significant impact on your future, and we have the research and practical advice to help you execute on test day.

The product you're reading now is designed to exploit weaknesses in the test itself, and help you avoid the most common errors test takers frequently make.

## How to use this study guide

We don't want to waste your time. Our study guide is fast-paced and fluff-free. We suggest going through it a number of times, as repetition is an important part of learning new information and concepts.

First, read through the study guide completely to get a feel for the content and organization. Read the general success strategies first, and then proceed to the content sections. Each tip has been carefully selected for its effectiveness.

Second, read through the study guide again, and take notes in the margins and highlight those sections where you may have a particular weakness.

Finally, bring the manual with you on test day and study it before the exam begins.

## Your success is our success

We would be delighted to hear about your success. Send us an email and tell us your story. Thanks for your business and we wish you continued success.

Sincerely,

Mometrix Test Preparation Team

**Need more help? Check out our flashcards at: http://MometrixFlashcards.com/GACE**

# TABLE OF CONTENTS

# Top 20 Test Taking Tips

1. Carefully follow all the test registration procedures
2. Know the test directions, duration, topics, question types, how many questions
3. Setup a flexible study schedule at least 3-4 weeks before test day
4. Study during the time of day you are most alert, relaxed, and stress free
5. Maximize your learning style; visual learner use visual study aids, auditory learner use auditory study aids
6. Focus on your weakest knowledge base
7. Find a study partner to review with and help clarify questions
8. Practice, practice, practice
9. Get a good night's sleep; don't try to cram the night before the test
10. Eat a well balanced meal
11. Know the exact physical location of the testing site; drive the route to the site prior to test day
12. Bring a set of ear plugs; the testing center could be noisy
13. Wear comfortable, loose fitting, layered clothing to the testing center; prepare for it to be either cold or hot during the test
14. Bring at least 2 current forms of ID to the testing center
15. Arrive to the test early; be prepared to wait and be patient
16. Eliminate the obviously wrong answer choices, then guess the first remaining choice
17. Pace yourself; don't rush, but keep working and move on if you get stuck
18. Maintain a positive attitude even if the test is going poorly
19. Keep your first answer unless you are positive it is wrong
20. Check your work, don't make a careless mistake

# English Language Arts

## Technological content

A curriculum that is project-based begins with explicit questions meant to stimulate the curiosity of students and serve as a basis for launching various research ideas and directions. Teachers can see that curricular units provide a valuable advantage in motivating students with regard to developing hypotheses, finding research information in many sources of data in order to confirm or argue the hypotheses, and in developing arguments which are based upon understanding certain intended concepts. The Internet can provide a wealth of information but can also provide challenges for teachers. Students with literacy challenges have difficulties finding information, identifying relevant information and then reading that which they find. These challenges may at times be linked to the inability of a student to draw conceptual parallels in content and then translate them into an Internet search.

## Culturally-relevant approaches

Teachers should develop learning environments that are reflective of their students' social, cultural and linguistic experiences. These serve as instructors, mediators, guides, consultants and advocates for students in helping them to find a way that is most effective to connect their cultural and community-based knowledge to their learning experiences in the classroom. A key criterion for teaching that is culturally relevant is nurturing and supporting competence in cultures both at school and at home. Teachers should use the student's home cultural experience as a base on which to build skills and increase knowledge. Content that is learned in this manner becomes more significant to the student and helps facilitate a transfer of school learning to real-life.

## Peer influence

Peer influence on children's behavior as well as on learning is well recognized in psychological literature. Peer influence can operate both ways, positive and negative. Teachers will try normally exploit the positive influence on peers and promote many of the learning experiences the children may have by organizing them into small groups in which they can become involved in learning. The negative aspects of peer influence are obvious when parents of children expect him and her to show interest in school work and spend time on homework but many of the children's peers do not have the same goals on their agendas. It is under such circumstances that it might become necessary to have the child discontinue his or her association with those peers who are negative influences.

## Terms

### Phonological awareness
A conscious sensitivity to the structure of language by sound. It includes the ability to distinguish between parts of speech such as syllables and phonemes.

### Phonemic awareness
A part of phonological awareness in which listeners may understand and distinguish between phonemes.

### Alphabetic principle
An assumption which underlies systems of alphabetic writing, in that each speech sound or phoneme of a particular language requires its own distinctive representation graphically.

<u>Decoding</u>
Willingness and ability to sound out words through generation of sounds into recognizable words, known as a phonological recording.

<u>Sight vocabulary</u>
That stable of words a reader can automatically identify.

Phonics - a methodical approach to reading and spelling which emphasizes the basic relationships between symbols and sounds; often used with beginning readers or with people who are new to a language.

Grapheme - a letter or combination of letters in the written language which represents a meaningful sound (phoneme) in the spoken language.

Syntax – the rules which govern the grammatical relationship between words and other units within a sentence.

Grammar – rules for syntax, inflection and word formation which govern how sentences are formed.

Semantics – the study of linguistic meaning in a language, including words, phrases, and sentences.

Dialect – a language variation occurring in a certain region or social class; differs from the standard language in pronunciation, grammar or vocabulary.

## Systems of language

Before a child enters school, he has already developed language at home.  Language is defined as a system of expressing and taking in information in a meaningful way.  Speech is the verbal expression of language. Four language systems have been identified:

1. Phonological (sound) system – refers to the meaningful sounds of a language (phonemes) and their corresponding letters of the alphabet.
2. Syntactic (structural) system – refers to the structural organization (grammar) of a language which dictates how words are combined into sentences; components of syntax include word order, capitalization, punctuation, and morphemes.
3. Semantic (meaning) system – refers to vocabulary, including synonyms, antonyms, and idioms.
4. Pragmatic (social & cultural) system – refers to the social and cultural aspects of usage, such as how language varies among different social classes, ethnic groups, and geographic areas.

## Literacy differences across content areas

Studies have shown that it is impossible to separate practices in the classroom such as strategies for activating prior knowledge from the larger cultural and social contexts in which the practices exist. Researchers say that a need exists for adolescent literacy that includes the adolescent's literacy practices beyond the confines of the classroom setting, their expanded conceptions of text such as the Internet, and the relationship that exists between the development of identity and literacy. However, the need for additional research in the teaching and learning of context in secondary schools still exists. For instance, more study is needed on the interactions between student and teacher, and between student and student;

also on how students perceive themselves as readers, what their interests are at a particular time, and how institutional configurations affect the daily events occurring both in and out of school.

**Teaching Vocabulary**

Teaching specific words

Here is an example of how to teach specific words in class. A teacher might have his class read a novel. The novel may have a concept that is important to the plot so the teacher might try several ways to ensure the students understand what that concept means. For instance, the teacher might have students discuss the concept and read a sentence from the book that contains the concept. He might then ask students to use context and prior knowledge to try and determine what the concept means. The teacher might ask students to use the concept word in their own sentences to help deepen the understanding of the word. Students must develop word-learning strategies such as using dictionaries or using knowledge about word parts to determine what a word in text means.

Extended and active engagement

Extended and active instruction can be used to better learn words. For example, a first-grade teacher wants their student to understand the concept of work. Over time, the teacher has the students do exercises in which they repeatedly use the meaning of the concept of work. The students have many opportunities to see and use the word in different contexts that will reinforce its meaning. The teacher will ask them what they already know about work and have them give example of the type of work their parents perform. The class could have a discussion about the work that is done at school. The teacher can find a simple book about work that introduces ideas about specific work that should be done. The teacher can ask students to make up sentences describing the work their parents do.

Repeated exposure to words

Repeated exposure to words can be taught in a manner such as this: A second-grade class is reading about George Washington. The story talks about his role as a farmer. The teacher wants to ensure that the students understand the meaning of "farm" and "farmer," not only because these words are an important part of the book, but also because they are words that students need to know in school and in their everyday lives. The teacher calls the students' attention to the words farm and farmer when mentioned in textbooks and reading selections. The teacher has students use the word in their own writing. The teacher asks the students to find the words in print in newspapers. Upon reading the book, the teacher discusses George Washington's role as a farmer and how farms were different from today.

Using word parts

Knowing common prefixes and suffixes along with base and root words can help students learn the meanings of many words. Just learning the most common English prefixes (un-, re-, in-, dis-) gives students clues to more than half of all the English words with prefixes. Prefixes are relatively easy to learn because their meanings are clear. For instance, un- means "not" and re- means "again." They are usually spelled similarly from word to word and they are always at the word's beginning. Suffixes can be more challenging to learn because their meanings are more abstract than prefixes. For instance, -ness means "the quality or state of" something. Other suffixes are easier to figure out such as -less which means "without." Teachers should teach word roots as they occur in texts as well as teaching those root words that are most likely to be encountered.

Using dictionaries and other reference aids

Here is an example of how dictionaries and other reference material can be used to teach vocabulary. A second-grade teacher finds that many of his students do not know the word "might" as it is used in the sentence, "The children moved the rock with all their might." The teacher shows them how to find the word "might" in the classroom dictionary and shows that there are five definitions for the word "might." The teacher reads each definition and discusses with the class whether each definition would fit in the sentence's context. The students eliminate the definitions of might that do not work in the sentence. The teacher then has students substitute the most likely definition for "might" into the original sentence to ensure that it makes sense.

Using context clues
Here is an example of how to use context clues to determine the meaning of a vocabulary word. A student reads the sentence, "The birds were chirping loudly and the cat was quickly tiring of the racket. The cat quickly became unhappy with the birds. The cat finally solved the problem when it accidentally stuck its head into a bowl and was not able to hear a thing." The teacher tells the students that the context of the paragraph helps to determine what racket means. There is chirping and it is loud. The cat was unhappy. When the cat got its head stuck in a bowl, it could no longer hear the chirping. These are all clues that the birds are being noisy and that racket means loud noise.

## Reading disorder

Students who have a reading disorder have problems with their reading skills. Their skills are significantly below that which is normal for the student's age, intelligence, and education. The poor reading skills can cause problems with the student's academic success and in other areas of life. Signs associated with reading disorders include poor word recognition in reading, very slow reading, or making many mistakes. They may also show poor comprehension. Students who suffer from reading disorders normally have low self-esteem, social problems, and a higher drop-out rate in school. Reading disorders may be associated with conduct disorder, attention deficit disorder, depression, or other learning disorders. Reading disorders are usually brought to the attention of a child's parents in kindergarten or the first grade, when reading instruction becomes a very important facet of teaching.

## Bias in selecting tests

When selecting tests, care should be taken to ensure the test is not biased or offensive with regard to race, sex, native language, geographic region, or ethnic origin, as well as other factors. Those who develop tests are expected to show sensitivity to the test-takers' demographic. Steps can be taken during test development and documentation to minimize the influence of cultural factors on the test scores. These may include evaluating the items for offensiveness and cultural dependency, and using statistics to identify differential item difficulty. Questions to ask include: "Were the tests analyzed statistically for bias?" "What method was used?" "How were the items selected for the final version?" "Should the test be used with non-native English speakers?"

## "Scaffolding" in reading-writing

As proposed by Lev Vygotsky as part of his Social Cultural learning model, scaffolding is the process in which an adult/teacher provides help to a child, then decreases the level of assistance as the child masters the skill or topic. Scaffolding ties in with what Vygotsky termed the Zone of Proximal Development (ZPD), which is the gap between what an individual knows about a topic and what he does not. In children, ZPD refers to the range of tasks a child can do with help from a parent or teacher but which he cannot accomplish on his own. A teacher can use scaffolding and awareness of ZPD in planning lessons involving reading, writing, speaking, and listening. Specifically, a teacher reading out loud provides students with an opportunity to model that behavior, and then to write and read further about the topic, perhaps through the utilization of a KWL chart.

# Literacy

## Social class and family background variables

The social class and family background variables are prominent in emergent literacy research. Numerous studies have addressed links between parental occupation, income, and children's achievements. One finding is that there are wide variations in children's achievements, regardless of social class in relation to a child's early literacy experiences. Specific factors in family environments such as parental interest, positive attitudes, and modeling have been identified as major predictors of academic success despite social class or educational levels. There is considerable variation among family environments in the status and value given to books, the presence of materials for writing, and the time that is spent reading and writing. Studies have shown that early readers tend to come from homes with more pencils, paper, and books, and that have mothers who read more often.

## Sociocultural theory and the genetic analysis aspect

Sociocultural approaches to literacy developed out of more general sociocultural theory which came from the theories of Soviet psychologist L.S. Vygotsky. The three central planks of sociocultural theory that have contributed to a new interpretation of literacy are the concepts of genetic analysis, social learning, and mediation. Genetic or developmental analysis suggests that it is possible to understand mental functional aspects by understanding their origin and transitions. From genetic analysis it is understood the futility of seeing literacy as something that is isolated. Rather, a proper understanding of the emergence of literacy has to take into account the broad cultural, social and historic factors that relate to the significance of reading and writing for human communication and cognition.

## Social learning and mediation aspects

Along with genetic analysis, social learning and mediation are the three major components of a sociocultural approach to literacy. Social learning refers to the social origin of mental functioning. Vygotsky said that every function in the child's cultural development appears first on the social level and later on the individual level. The first development is between people and the second is inside the child. Vygotsky also believed the development occurred through such means as apprenticeship learning, or interaction with teachers and peers. This view looks at learning not as an isolated act of cognition but rather a process of gaining entry to a discourse of practitioners. Mediation is the notion that all human activity is mediated through signs or tools. It is not so much the tools, such as computers or writing, by themselves as it is how they transform human action in a fundamental way.

# African-Americans and "acting white"

Dr. John Ogbu has argued for years that the blacks have developed an oppositional cultural identity because of discrimination developed by their own culture. This stems in part from the times when blacks were asked to have the same behavior and speech as whites, such as after emancipation. With the Black Power Movement of the 1960s, an oppositional cultural identity was in place where racial pride was expressed. Regardless, Ogbu believed that blacks still try to enter white culture. A resulting behavior, derided by some, especially younger blacks, called "acting white" can be stressful for blacks. They are accused of being an Uncle Tom or being disloyal to the black community. Speech, in particular, is one activity in which blacks may be labeled as acting white.

# Concept of multiliteracies

A great deal of interest has risen around the world in the future of literacy teaching through so-called "multiliteracies." The multiliteracies argument is that our personal, public, and working lives are currently changing in some very significant ways and that these changes have the effect of transforming cultures and the ways in which we communicate. The ramification of this is that the way literacy is now taught will become obsolete and what counts for literacy must also change. Multiliteracies has at its heart two major and closely related changes. First is the growing significance of cultural and linguistic diversity. This is reinforced every day by modern media. Each day, both globally and in our local communities, we have to negotiate differences that are interconnected with our working and community lives. As this happens, English is becoming a world language. The second major shift is the influence of new communications technologies.

## Home vs. school literacy experience

Studies have shown that a positive relationship exists between children's literacy experiences at home and their ease in transitioning to school. Family literacy environments do differ in some aspects. While the development of print awareness appears to be common across cultures, major differences occur in the quantity of exposure children have had to the written language, storybooks in particular. There also is a difference in the perception of the roles that parents have in their children's literacy experiences. Studies have found that such family characteristics relating to reading achievement include parental aspirations for the child, academic guidance, attitude toward education, and having reading materials in the home.

## Advantages of literacy starting at home

Children's school readiness is influenced by their parents' educational levels. The higher the parents' education, the more likely the child will succeed in school. Children who are raised in literate homes are likely to enter first grade with several thousand hours of 1-to-1 pre-reading experience. Children have a better chance of becoming fully literate adults if they are encouraged to read at home. Studies have shown that improving parents' skills positively affects their children's language development. Without parental support, the cycle of under-education will continue in families from generation to generation. With support from family literacy programs, children who may have otherwise been educationally and developmentally behind their peers came into school on par with their peers.

## Places literacy is learned

Literacy does not just come from going to school. It is learned everywhere, from reading bus stop signs and cereal boxes to listening to family stories in the language of the home. Caregivers as well as parents have a profound impact on their children's readiness upon entering school. Each year, the influence grows and changes form. The positive influence of the family continues to be important as the children develop through elementary, junior high, and high school. It can be enhanced through meaningful involvement in ways such as engaging parents, having parents and children participate in literacy activities together, and helping parents through adult education. Likewise, peers and community members will all play a significant part in mutually developing literacy.

## Metacognition process

In the simplest terms, metacognition is the process of thinking about thinking. The concept is most often associated with John Flavell, a developmental psychologist at Stanford University. As applied to reading and writing, students can use metacognition to develop specific plans of action to enable a better understanding of the material. The three key elements of this process are: 1) designing the plan of action; 2) monitoring it; and 3) assessing its effectiveness. The process can be facilitated by encouraging students to ask a series of questions. For instance, when developing the plan, a student should ask questions such as "Why am I reading this?" and "How much time do I have?" Questions for the monitoring phase include

"What information is most important?" and "What should I do if I don't understand?" Finally, the assessment phase prompts questions such as "How did I do?" and "What could I have done differently?"

## Reading-writing connection

Reading and writing are generally viewed as two sides of the same coin. Reading leads to writing and vice-versa. When a child reads, he learns structure, punctuation, and vocabulary, all of which can make him a better writer and a better reader. To help make the connection, a teacher may require a student to keep a journal in which he writes about what he reads. The process of writing will help the student analyze and question what he has read. Therefore, a journal can also be a vital tool for enhancing metacognition. For older students, a classroom debate would require students to read pertinent material and write position papers. Another metacognitive approach to making the reading-writing connection is the KWL chart. Before reading new material, students will be asked to write down what they Know about the topic and what they Want to know. Afterwards, they will write down what they Learned.

## Phonemic awareness

Different levels of phonemic awareness in terms of abilities include:
1. Hearing rhymes and alliteration as measured by knowing nursery rhymes.
2. Doing tasks such as comparing and contrasting the sounds of words for rhyme and alliteration, also known as oddity tasks.
3. Blending and splitting syllables.
4. Performing phonemic segmenting such as counting out the number of phonemes contained in a word.
5. Performing tasks of phoneme manipulation such as adding or deleting a particular phoneme.

Instruction in phonemic awareness might include:
1. Engaging preschool children in activities that direct their attention to sounds in words, such as rhyming games.
2. Teaching segmentation and blending.
3. Combining letter-sound relationship instruction with segmentation and blending.
4. Sequencing examples systematically when teaching blending and segmentation.

### Phonological recoding
Phonological recoding refers to the use of systematic relationships between letters and phonemes in order to produce the pronunciation of a printed string that is unknown or to spell words. Phonological recoding includes regular word reading, irregular word reading, and advanced word analysis. Regular word reading includes beginning recoding such as the ability to read from left to right words that are regular and unfamiliar, generation of sounds for letters, and blending sounds into recognizable words. Beginning spelling is translating speech to print through phonemic awareness. Irregular word reading is reading those words that cannot be decoded because either the letter sounds are unique to the word or a few words or the letter-sound correspondences in the word have not yet been learned. Advanced word analysis is knowing those words needed for fluency.

### Important phonemic awareness skills
Children of kindergarten age require development of phonemic awareness by hearing, identifying, and manipulating phonemes or individual sounds within spoken words. Once children acquire knowledge of letters, they can be taught to perform activities to isolate phonemes and achieve phoneme segmentation by pointing to or manipulating letters along with sounds. Blending and segmentation in phonemic awareness is important because they provide a foundation for skills such as spelling. Studies have shown

that phonemic awareness can be acquired with as little as 20 hours of instruction, although some children might require more instruction in order to accurately segment words. The individual students should be assessed to verify that the instruction was successful. More instruction might be required for some children than others.

Sing-songs and phonemic awareness
Rhyme is a prominent feature of many songs. Listening to and singing songs helps make children aware of the phonemic nature of spoken language. Songs that help children to manipulate sounds in words are most effective in having children pay attention to a language's sound structure. Manipulating sounds in words can be challenging for those children in the early stages of phonemic awareness development, so children should be given many opportunities to learn the songs before they start trying to manipulate the sounds. One way this can be done is to play tapes of such songs during transitional activities such as snack time or clean-up time in order to help children become more familiar with sound play.

## Onset-rime blending

Children can be encouraged to think about words as sounds when someone is able to break the words down into smaller parts. One particular way in which a syllable can be broken down is into onset and rime. Onset is everything that comes before the vowel, while rime refers to the vowel and everything that comes after it. For instance, truck could be broken down into /tr/ and /uck/. Rhyming is blending a new onset onto an old rime. Children must have a great amount of experience recognizing rhymes before they are able to produce rhymes. Among the daily activities that help early childhood classes gain these skills are by listening to rhyming stories, reciting poetry that rhymes, and singing rhyming songs.

## Orthographic analogies

Orthographic analogies are word families that can be generated from knowing onsets and rimes. Using orthographic analogies can help students rapidly build their reading and writing vocabularies. For instance, if a child knows the word "man," they could use a rime analogy to read or write any word that rhymes such as "tan," "fan," "can," etc. There have been studies that question the effectiveness of using orthographic analogies for young children. These studies indicate that children do not see the orthographic similarities but rather hear a word from an adult that functions as a clue. The studies indicate that using analogies in teaching reading may not always be helpful if an adult is required to be there to give the word clue to a child.

## Body-coda blending

Vowels are the loudest parts of syllables, or the peak if you will. One may always stretch the vowel and say it out loud. Children can break syllables on either side of the loud vowel, with relative ease. For example, they might break "ship" into "sh-ip" or "shi-p." In discussing the body of a syllable, the reference is to all of the phonemes within the vowel. Those consonants that are found after the vowel are called codas. For instance, in the word dream, /dre/ is the body of the syllable and the coda is /m/. The reward for body-coda blending is that it is easier than onset-rime blending because some distortion frequently occurs during onset-rime blending.

## Understanding alphabetic principle

Sound analysis training
Children can understand that the letters in printed words represent the sounds in words that are spoken. Children can change single consonants at the start or end of one-syllable words upon a teacher's request,

such as changing "cat" to "rat." Sound analysis alone has been found to be effective in developing alphabetic principle skills. But teaching sound analysis along with the relationships between sounds and letters that give practice in using these letter-sound relationships in reading and writing provides the greatest benefit. Alphabetic mapping is also useful. When children know sounds of four or five consonants, they can start to develop an understanding of how the alphabetic principle works. Using movable letters to show switched letters can help highlight different sound combinations.

<u>Word families</u>
Knowing that words containing the same sound pattern will often share spelling patterns is important for a child to know. When a child learns that a number of frequently occurring patterns of spelling occur and has learned that these spelling patterns can be generalized, the child will be able to analyze and identify unfamiliar words more efficiently. The major value of word families, also known as phonograms, in kindergarten is that they give the student the opportunity to practice decoding the beginning letters in a word. It should not be expected that the children will learn to use the word families in generative ways. In other words, they are not expected to learn word families as a means of independently decoding new words. Word families give children more practice with the application of the alphabetic principle.

**Constructivist theory and learning**

A major portion of constructivist theory is the idea that learning is an active process in which those who learn build new ideas or concepts based upon their current and past knowledge. Those who learn select and transform information, build a hypothesis, and make decisions that rely on a cognitive structure in order to make it work. Cognitive structures such as mental models or schema provide meaning and organization to experiences. This lets the individual go beyond the information that is given there. In constructivist theory, instruction should address:
1. A predisposition towards learning,
2. The different ways knowledge can be built so that the learner most readily grasps it,
3. The most effective sequences in which material can be presented, and
4. The nature as well as pacing of rewards and punishments.

**Increasing prior knowledge**

Accretion is one form of increasing prior knowledge. Each time something new is taught or referred to in a class, there are traces of it that are left in a student's memory. Tuning happens when students modify and reshape information they receive until it fits their needs. Reconstruction occurs when students learn something that goes against what they previously thought was true. Students can build on what they already know when they can expand on terms and information they understand. Increased background information on more in-depth ideas about a topic also helps the student better understand what is being read. Students can also provide real-life experiences to help with understanding.

**Schemas and stages of reading**

Prior knowledge and experience are common to the various stages of reading transactions. Readers build meaning before, during, and after a reading transaction based upon their interest in and prior knowledge about:
1. Facts relating to a particular topic
2. Concepts and vocabulary that is related to those concepts and
3. The underlying principles and generalizations.

Readers have schemas, or organized networks of prior knowledge and experiences, about certain topics which foster expectation whenever they read about those topics. When students are reading, they add to or adjust their schemas as they boost their comprehension of what is being read.

## Reading aloud to children

Storybook reading at home is a key component of early reading acquisition, according to several studies. Studies have documented the relationship between reading to children and their later success on reading readiness tasks. Children who are read to have also been found to acquire concepts about the function of written language in books. Findings show that most successful early readers have had contact at home with written material. When poor readers enter school they have had much less experience with books and reading than those who become better at reading. In short, children learn how to attend to language and apply that knowledge to literacy situations by interacting with others who model functions of language.

## Social constructivism

Social constructivism is a variant of cognitive constructivism that puts an emphasis on the collaborative nature of learning. This theory was developed by Soviet psychologist Lev Vygotsky. He was a cognitivist but he rejected postulations by other cognitivists such as Piaget and Perry which said that separating learning from its social context was possible. Vygotsky theorized that all cognitive functions originate and must be explained as products of social interactions and that learning was not simply the accommodation and assimilation of new knowledge attained by those learning. Instead, he felt it was the process by which learners were integrated into a community of knowledge. Vygotsky believed that the cultural development of children appears first on the social level and only later inside the child. This applies equally in voluntary attention to logical memories and forming concepts. Higher functions come from actual relationships between people, Vygotsky postulated.

## Cultural constructivism

Cultural constructivism is a theory asserting that knowledge and reality are products of their cultural context. This means that two independent cultures will likely form different methodologies of observation. Western cultures usually utilize objects for making scientific descriptions, while Native American cultures use events to describe phenomena. Beyond social environments for learning are wider cultural influences such as custom, language, religion, biology, and tools. The tools such as language and symbols that people use can have an effect on the way they think, according to this theory. There are some schools of thought which hold that tools redistribute the cognitive load of some task between the people and the tools being used. For instance, a telephone can change a conversation's nature.

## Culturally responsive teaching

One goal of effective teaching is to make learning a meaningful endeavor for children. In order to fully comprehend their experience, children must see connections between what they know and what they experience in schools and other settings. Increasing the congruence and continuity between children's home and school environments is a crucial aspect in achievement for children who come from diverse cultures and varied social classes. Recognizing and fostering the cultural knowledge of children from culturally and linguistically diverse backgrounds can help bridge the gap between home and school. Creating a culturally responsive learning situation takes a lot of work. This includes effective partnerships between schools and families where each is treated as a full partner in attaining a successful outcome.

## Sapir-Whorf hypothesis

The Sapir-Whorf hypothesis says that a systematic relationship exists between grammatical categories of the language a person speaks and how the person thinks and behaves in it. The hypothesis was actually an axiom developed by anthropologist Edward Sapir and his student and colleague Benjamin Whorf. The hypothesis is also known as the principle of linguistic relativity. There are arguments to the version of this idea that thought is constrained by language. One argument is that all people have occasional problems expressing themselves due to the language being inadequate for what they are meaning to say. Thus, thought is not a set of words because a concept can be understood without it being expressed in words. Arguments also exist for the extreme opposite—that language does not at all influence thought.

## Fluency

Fluency is key to becoming competent as a reader. It involves getting words right as well as phrasing and proper intonation. Children who are younger readers engage in stop and start reading. These children are spending most of their time decoding text. But studies have shown that the more time children give to text decoding, the less they will comprehend the text. Studies also show that higher-order skills such as synthesizing, analyzing, and summarizing require fluency in reading. A lack of comprehension in reading affects all content areas. Because students cannot read fluently, their time is spent decoding the words rather than taking in the text from which they should be learning.

### Fluency and development of meaning
Fluency and reading comprehension are closely related. By learning to read accurately, children are able to comprehend text. Also, research shows that students who score low on fluency tests also tend to score low on reading comprehension assessments. Fluency is not the same as automaticity which refers to a reader's ability to recognize words automatically, accurately, and rapidly. Fluency involves reading connected passages with little effort and with expression. Automatic word recognition is important, but is insufficient as a skill for developing fluency. Fluent readers are able to read grade-level text with 90 percent accuracy and a rate of about 90 words per minute. They are also able to demonstrate comprehension of text when they read aloud.

### Developing fluency in reading
Developing fluency requires extensive practice and exposure to reading. Research indicates that repeated oral reading is particularly effective for readers who are both beginning and struggling. This practice can help improve accuracy, word recognition, speed, and fluency. It may also lead to an increased reading comprehension. Students benefit from reading the same story aloud several times until they are fluent enough to read the passage independently. The number of required repetitions is often three or four, but varies depending on the student. Practicing by reading aloud sight words from lists is not sufficient in improving fluency. This is because the student may be able to recognize a sight word in isolation but still be unable to read it.

## Stages of reading for young children

Children gain literacy through emergent, beginning, and fluent stages. The emergent stage is marked by children noticing environmental print, showing interest in books, pretending to read, and using picture cues and predictable patterns in books in order to retell a story. They also can identify some letters, reread books with patterns that are predictable, and recognize up to 10 familiar words. The beginning stage will show the child identifying letter names and sounds; matching written and spoken words; using the beginning, middle, and ending sounds to decode words; recognizing as many as 100 high-frequency words; reading slowly, word by word; and self-correcting while they are reading. The fluent stage features automatic identification with most words, reading with expression, reading at about 100 words per minute or more, preferring to read silently, recognizing up to 300 high-frequency words, and often reading independently making inferences.

## Reading proficiency at a young age

There is strong evidence that young people who are not fluent readers and writers by the end of the third grade may never catch up with their peers. One study found that first graders who were not on grade level by the end of the year stood a 1-in-10 chance of never having proficiency at grade level in reading. A governor of Indiana indicated that the determination of how many new prison beds to build was based, in part, on the number of second graders who do not read at second grade level. The number of future prison beds in California depends on numbers of children who do not go past the fourth grade reading level.

## Orthography

The orthography of a language refers to the set of rules of how to write correctly in the writing system of a language. The term comes from the Greek ortho-, meaning correct, and graphos meaning "that writes." In the modern sense of the word this includes spelling and punctuation, as well as the rest of the writing system of a language. For instance, English has 26 letters in an alphabet for both consonants and vowels, but no glyph or specific symbols that represent a semantic or phonetic unit of definitive value for emphasis. But each letter in the English alphabet may represent more than one sound and each sound may be written by more than one letter, as demonstrated by "f" and "ph." Orthography entails certain rules on how letters are used such as "i before e except after c."

## Inflection and word formation

It is possible to distinguish between two kinds of morphological rules. Some rules relate different forms of the same lexeme. Other rules relate two lexemes that are different. Rules that relate to the different forms of lexeme are called inflectional rules. Those rules relating to multiple lexemes are word formation rules. The plural for dog, dogs, is an inflectional rule. Compounds such as cowboy or firefighter are examples of word formation rules. Word formation informally forms new words while inflection provides more forms of the same word. A distinction also exists between two kinds of word formation, derivation and compounding. Compounding involves combining complete word forms into compounds. Derivation involves prefixes or suffixes that are not independent words.

## Allomorphy and morphophonology

The one-to-one correspondence between meaning and form hardly ever holds in language and this is one of the largest sources of complexity in morphology. There are words in English such as deer/deer, goose/geese where the differences between singular and plural forms are signaled differently from a regular pattern or are not at all signaled. Even the cases considered normal are not that simple. For example, consider that the -s in cats and the -s in dogs are not pronounced the same way. In plural like dishes there is another vowel before the -s. The cases where the same distinction is affected by different changes of form for different lexemes are known as allomorphy. The study of allomorphy resulting from the interaction of morphology and phonology is called morphophonology.

# Morphology

Morphology - a sub-discipline of linguistics, or the study of word structure. Words are accepted as being the smallest syntactical units, but in most languages words can be related to other words by rules. Those who speak English recognize that these relationships can be formulated as rules applying to many other pairs of words. For example, fire is to firefighter, as cow is to cowboy. Morphology is the linguistic branch that studies such rules across and within languages.

## Morpheme-based morphology

There are three primary approaches to morphology that attempt to capture the distinctions in different ways. They are morpheme-based morphology, lexeme-based morphology, and word-based morphology. Morpheme-based morphology is where word forms are analyzed as sequences of morphemes, or the minimal meaningful unit of language. Words such as independently have in-, depend, -ent, and -ly as morphemes, with the root word being depend. The other morphemes are derivational affixes, or morphemes that attach to words. In words such as cats, cat is the root and -s is an inflectional morpheme. Analyzing word forms as if they were composed of morphemes that are put after one another like a string of pearls is called "item and arrangement morphology."

## Lexeme-based morphology

There are three primary approaches to morphology that attempt to capture the distinctions in different ways. They are morpheme-based morphology, lexeme-based morphology, and word-based morphology. Lexeme-based morphology normally follows an "item and process" approach. Rather than analyzing word forms as sets of morphemes that are arranged in sequence, the word form is a result of applying rules that alter word forms or stems in order to produce new ones. An inflectional rule takes a stem, makes changes to it, and outputs a word form. Unlike the item and arrangement process, one may take a word such as geese and not consider it a zero-morph. Instead, while the plural of cat is made by adding -s to the end of the word, the plural of goose is made by changing the vowel stem.

## Word-based morphology

There are three primary approaches to morphology that attempt to capture the distinctions in different ways. They are morpheme-based morphology, lexeme-based morphology, and word-based morphology. Word-based morphology is considered a "word and paradigm" approach to morphology. This theory takes paradigms as a central notion. Rather than stating rules to combine morphemes into word forms, or generate word forms from stems, word-based morphology has generalizations that hold between inflectional paradigm forms. A main point behind this approach is that many generalizations are hard to state with either morpheme-based or lexeme-based morphology. An example is where a piece of a word is given. In a morpheme-based theory it would be called an inflectional morpheme and correspond to a combination of grammatical categories. A word and paradigm approach treats these as whole words related to one another through analogy rules.

# Lexical affixes

Lexical affixes, also known as semantic affixes, are bound elements that appear as affixes, but function as incorporated nouns within verbs and as elements of compound nouns. In other words, they are similar to word roots or stems in function, but are similar to affixes in form. Although they are similar to incorporated nouns, lexical affixes differ in that they never occur in freestanding nouns. They always appear as affixes. Such affixes are relatively rare. Lexical suffixes often bear little or no resemblance to free nouns with similar meaning. When used, lexical suffixes usually have more general meanings. For instance, a language may have a lexical suffix that means water in a general sense, but not have a noun equivalent referring to water in general. Instead it may have several nouns with more specific meanings, such as saltwater or groundwater.

## Form function of oral language

The form function of oral language consists of phonology, morphology, and syntax. Phonology is the system of phonemes or sounds in language. Morphology is the system of rules governing word structure and organization. Many sounds have no meaning by themselves; these are phonemes. Every morpheme, however, has meaning on its own, as a root word, or attached to a root word as a prefix, suffix, or word ending. In English, the normal sentence is structured as subject + verb + object. Syntax refers to the way in which words are combined into sentences. Students with an understanding of syntax can comprehend how the various parts of a sentence relate to one another other.

## Ausubel's theory

The major idea in Ausubel's theory of meaningful learning is the hierarchical organization of knowledge, or the idea that new information is meaningful only in that it can be related to that which is already known. Consequently, the theory stresses a hierarchical type of learning rather than rote learning or memorization, as well as emphasizing received knowledge instead of discovery learning. Ausubel postulated four processes which are environments for meaningful learning. Derivative subsumption describes a situation in which new information learned is an example of something one has already learned. Correlative subsumption is a process by which new information may be accomodated, such as a when one is accustomed to seeing blue skies, but instead encounters gray. Superordinate learning classifies information such as learning different types of clouds. Finally, combinatorial learning describes a process in which a new idea stems from another idea but has neither a higher nor lower hierarchy.

## Areas that help boost readers

Specific instruction in writing for different reasons and audiences as well as instruction in strategies to help clarify and enrich language expression is crucial. Language mechanical skills such as usage, capitalization, and grammar can be taught and integrated into the students' own writing through the process of editing. For instance, students might study the use of adjectives and adverbs, and then write descriptive compositions. Cooperative learning can be a very effective upper elementary reading and writing instruction if used properly. Students should generally work in groups of four or five members that stay together for six-to-eight weeks. Each group might be presented a lesson on main idea and the students can work in groups to practice such a skill.

## Group reporting student assessment

Group reporting is a fun way for students to show the teacher and their peers what they have learned. In this assessment method, students interact with one another in small groups. The students are able to learn from one another and practice social skills. Groups that work together consistently may create a portfolio of the group work. This could include self-assessments in which the students can comment on what they have learned while creating the portfolio. A group skit is a creative way to demonstrate almost anything the students have learned. A mini-fair is another activity where, after a small group project, the students can share their learning, using booths in a location where other class members can see it.

## Word identification approach

The identification or recognition of words is the ability of students to develop an automaticity when reading isolated words. Automaticity refers to the speed and accuracy with which students are able to read these isolated words. Automatic words recognition is an important part of literacy because the level of students' abilities to recognize known words and decode or determine unfamiliar words can affect how fluently the students may read, and fluency is essential for comprehension. It should be remembered that building meaning is the goal of any literacy endeavor. Developing strong word recognition skills is also critical for students who, for whatever reason, did not develop strong phonological awareness in early childhood. These students may need to rely more heavily on their vocabularies and less on decoding skills.

## Critical questioning vs. critical thinking

Critical thinking requires a systematic monitoring of thought. Ideas must not be accepted at face value, but should be analyzed for accuracy, clarity, breadth, logicalness, and depth. Critical thinking also requires that reasoning occur within various points of view and frames of reference, that it stem from goals and objectives, and that it have an informational base. When data are used for reasoning, it is vital to remember that the data are interpreted and that the interpretation involves concepts containing assumptions, all of which may have implication. The result of critical thought is that the basic questions of Socrates can be more focally framed and used, leading to questions regarding:
1. ends and objectives,
2. wording of questions,
3. sources of information and fact,
4. method and quality of information collected,
5. assumptions that are behind the concepts being used.

## Role of the newspaper

Students learn when they are motivated and the topics they study hold interest and relevance to their lives. Many classrooms are using newspapers as a source for motivational and timely resources. It is a concept that dates back to 1795 when the Portland Eastern Herald in Maine published an editorial that put forth the role that newspapers can play in helping to deliver, extend, and enrich the curriculum. Classrooms around the world are using newspapers to complement text books and other relevant resources for a variety of disciplines. Newspapers featuring articles, editorials, and advertising help students apply literacy and numeracy skills as well as appreciate the importance of studying history and current affairs. Studies have shown that students who use newspapers score higher on reading comprehension tests and develop stronger critical thinking skills.

## First grade reading comprehension

The process of learning to read is not a linear one. Students need not learn decoding before they learn to comprehend. Both skills should be taught at the same time, beginning at the earliest stages of instruction for reading. Comprehension strategies can be taught using both material that is read to children and material that they read for themselves. Before reading, teachers can delineate the reason for the reading: reviewing vocabulary, encouraging children to predict what stories are about, or activating background knowledge. Teachers can direct children's attention to subtle or difficult portions of the text during reading, point out difficult words and ideas and ask children to find problems and solutions. After reading, children can be taught particular metacognitive strategies such as asking themselves regularly whether what is being read makes sense.

# Reciprocal teaching

In many ways, reciprocal teaching is the aggregation of four separate comprehension strategies: summarizing, questioning, clarifying, and predicting. Summarizing presents the ability to identify and integrate the information that is most important in a text. Text can be summarized across sentences and paragraphs, and also across passages. When students start the reciprocal teaching procedures they are usually focused on sentences and paragraphs. Questioning reinforces the strategy of summarizing. When students identify questions, they identify a kind of information that is important enough to provide substance for a question, then post the information in question form. Clarifying is important for students with comprehension difficulty. They are taught to be alert to the effects of comprehension impediments and to take the necessary measures to restore meaning. Predicting is when students predict what the author will discuss next in the text.

## Rationale behind reciprocal teaching
What is most important in reading education is turning out readers who can understand the meaning in texts. Reciprocal teaching is a scaffolded discussion technique for instilling some of the methods that good readers can use to comprehend text through questioning, clarifying, summarizing, and predicting. Teaching students the four strategies gives them the tools that great readers use in meeting their text-reading goals. Thus, it is the four strategies that are taught rather than reading skills. These multiple strategies help students to read by giving them a choice of strategies to be used in reading. The scaffolding gives support to help the students connect what they know and can do with what they need to do in order to be successful at learning a particular lesson. This also gives the students a chance to support each other and foster a sense of community among classmates.

## Goals of reciprocal teaching
The word "reciprocal" in reciprocal teaching is somewhat misleading in that it does not entail students doing the teaching. But the students use a set of four strategies—summarizing, clarifying, predicting, and questioning—to improve reading comprehension. That improvement is the ultimate goal. Other aspects of the method include:
1. The teacher scaffolds instruction of the strategy by guiding, modeling, and applying the strategies.
2. It guides students to become metacognitive and reflective in the use of strategies.
3. It helps students monitor their comprehension of reading.
4. It uses the social nature of learning in order to improve and scaffold the comprehension of reading.
5. The instruction is presented through different classroom settings including whole group, guided reading groups, and literature circles.

## How reciprocal teaching works
The order of the four stages of reciprocal teaching is not of great importance. A teacher will want to try out various ways to employ the strategy in order to see which particular sequence best fits a teaching style and the students' learning style. The teacher should also carefully choose text selections so that they all fit in with the four stages of reciprocal teaching. In order to successfully implement reciprocal teaching, the students must be taught the four strategies and have ample opportunities to use them. One approach could be having students work from a chart with four columns. Each column will be headed by the different comprehension activity that is involved. The students could then be placed in groups of four and each given one of the four roles: summarizer, questioner, clarifier, and predictor.

<u>How reciprocal teaching exercise operates</u>
The students would have their defined role on a note card. The students could then read several paragraphs of the assigned text passage. They should be encouraged to use note-taking strategies such as selective underlining or sticky notes in helping for their role in the discourse. At a given stopping point, the summarizer will give the key ideas up to this particular point in the text. The questioner will then ask questions about the text such as unclear parts, puzzling information, connections to concepts that have already been learned, or motivations of the characters or actors. The clarifier will try to clear up the confusing parts and answer questions that were asked. The predictor may then make guesses about what the author might tell next. The roles would then rotate one person to the right as another selection is read.

**Two-column note taking strategy**

Two-column note taking will find a student drawing a lengthwise line down the middle of a piece of paper. As the student reads or listens, the major concepts or headings are noted in the left-hand space and the supporting details are recorded in the right column. Only one side of the paper is used. When it is time to study, the paper is folded down the center so that either the main ideas or the details can be seen, but not both. This helps a student studying for an essay test recall details while looking at main ideas. For multiple choice tests, the student tries to recall main ideas while looking at the details. The notes are a memory device that is more efficient than either recalling from memory or rereading.

<u>Challenges of student note-taking</u>
Reading for certain information and then taking notes are perhaps the most challenging steps in the process of solving information problems. Students in grades 3-8 require many developmentally-appropriate chances to locate information before the techniques are mastered. Note-taking consists of identifying keywords and related words, skimming and scanning, and extracting needed information. These steps begin after students define and narrow the task, construct researchable questions, and find the right sources. After students build researchable questions from the information needed to finish a task or solve an information problem, the questions can be transferred to graphic organizers or data charts. This can allow them to focus on the key words. Skimming and scanning will help them make use of the text with less time and effort. Information may be extracted and recorded with different forms of note-taking, including citation, summary, quotation, and paraphrasing.

**Test-taking strategy**

A reason for test anxiety and poor performance on tests is often a lack of preparation. Children often know about a test in advance. Some teachers also tell parents when tests will be given. Knowing when the test is scheduled and what will be covered can help give the child a study schedule to prepare for the test. One schedule is for the student to study nightly for several nights before the test. Teachers may encourage parents to determine how long the child can be expected to concentrate at a given sitting. The parent should also be encouraged by the teacher to ask the child what material might be on the test and to go over questions at the end of chapters and sections. Maps, charts, and diagrams should receive special attention. A sample test can be developed from this information, which can even make studying fun.

**Intermediate school student pre-test strategy**

Before a test students should:
Begin to study the material a few days before the test and take study breaks every 20-30 minutes.
1. Take time to do some kind of physical activity that will help reduce tension and stress.
2. Eat a good breakfast the morning of the test and get a good night's sleep the night before the test.

3. Skim the material and determine which parts are best understood and which ones are still difficult.
4. Read a sentence or two and reread what they don't understand.
5. Pick out main ideas or key terms and think up possible test questions by themselves.
6. Read aloud and study with a partner or parent. While reading, the students should listen to themselves.
7. Think about what important points the teacher talked about during class.
8. Remain motivated and positive.

## Elementary school student pre-test strategy

Students should follow directions carefully. Have the student listen and read the directions to the test so they understand what is expected of them. Teachers need to make sure the students understand vocabulary words and concepts in the directions. Words appearing in the test directions that are common should be introduced to students as part of the process of test preparation. Ensure that the students understand what they are to do. If students have questions, they should be encouraged to ask the teacher before the test starts. Listening and reading activities that will provide practice for following directions can be incorporated into the classroom. Students must know how to budget their time for the test. They should work fast but comfortably. Students can practice this.

## "High interest, low vocabulary" books

Books that have a high interest and low vocabulary are materials with controlled vocabulary and reading difficulty levels, but which also contain plot and topics appropriate to older students. These give an older student, such as a young teen, the opportunity to read without having to read something that might be embarrassing for the teen because it is intended for much smaller children. These high interest and low vocabulary books must also provide supports for those with reading problems, just as the early picture books do. This includes illustrations that support text, vocabulary that is carefully chosen, an appropriate vocabulary load, simple sentences, characters that interest the reader, and compelling stories.

## Reading apprenticeship model

The reading apprenticeship model was developed from the reconceptualization of content reading. This instructional platform is centered on the dual ideas of literacy as complex social and cognitive processes and of teaching as a cognitive apprenticeship. For adolescents to move from beginners to experts in certain content area practices, the subject matter teacher, as the expert practitioner, must guide, make explicit, model, and support the apprentice in his or her development. Because ways of thinking, speaking, reading, and writing differ from subject matter to subject matter, some believe the most appropriate source for students to learn these specific practices is teachers who already have expertise in these fields. A reading apprenticeship involves student and teacher as partners of a collaboration that inquires into reading and reading processes as content area texts are engaged.

## Exploring dimensions of classroom life

There are four integrated dimensions of classroom life that are explored together by student and teacher in a reading apprenticeship: social, personal, cognitive, and knowledge building. The social dimension is based on constructing a community of readers using literacy as a way to connect with their interests, each other, and the social world that they are learning about. The personal dimension involves building students' awareness of themselves as readers, of why they are reading, and of what they hope to accomplish. The cognitive dimension is part of the structure that includes instruction in and use of strategies for comprehension, monitoring tools, and reading flexibility. Knowledge-building is centered on areas such as building schemata, or content knowledge, the vocabulary of the subject matters, and the structures of text and language.

## Literacy in content areas

Attention should be paid to literacy in content areas for several reasons. The 2003 National Assessment of Educational Progress Reading Report shows that general test scores have improved over recent years, but very few young people in the United States can read at proficient or advanced levels. Most can decode and answer simple comprehension questions, but few can synthesize ideas, interpret the information they receive, or critique the ideas they read about, especially when they work with expository texts. Also, literacy in content areas has consequences that go beyond the ability to understand a subject-matter text. Advanced or specialized literacy forms are tools that signify success, both academically and socially, and can be important for economic, social, and political success beyond school.

## Background knowledge

In order for students to ask the right questions about a subject, they need background knowledge. Activating prior knowledge and then building upon that knowledge is a big concern for teachers. Teachers can use language arts strategies to help students find ways to know what they know and what they should know, and to help them visualize content. With such a perspective, teachers can connect the focus on content in the curriculum in order to gain more general literacy strategies that students experience elsewhere. Teachers are also concerned with a lack of comprehension. Students often show a lack of deep conceptual understanding. One challenge is to design ways to help students become more skillful in what they do not know, so that understanding can be used in supporting learning.

## Cubing

Cubing is a literacy strategy in which students are able to explore topics from six separate dimensions or viewpoints. The student can:
1. Provide a description of the particular topic.
2. Compare the topic to a different topic.
3. Associate the topic with something else and provide specific reasons for the choice.
4. Analyze the topic and tell how the topic came about.
5. Give an explanation of what the topic comprises after analysis.
6. Provide an argument for or against the topic.

The teacher chooses a topic related to the thematic unit and students are divided into six groups. Students brainstorm about their dimension ideas and then use a quick write or quick draw. These are shared with the class and are attached to the sides of a cube box. This strategy can be applicable to subjects such as social studies.

## History frames/story map

A history frames/story map strategy is used in helping a student think on the major points of a history story by:
1. Identifying the important individuals who are a part of the story.
2. Succinctly summarizing the story by highlighting its main events.
3. Putting the story into context and realizing the problem that was to be overcome or the goal to be achieved.

4. Explaining the outcome.
5. Relating the story to history, to themselves, and to the world.

Four graphic organizers are used: the history frame, the story map, the story pyramid, and the framed character. The history frame can be used by students who choose main events from a chapter and fill in varying sections for participants, goals, summary, and resolution. The story map can be used for individual articles, for excerpts from oral histories and biographies, or to help understand motives of key historical players.

## Writing prompts

Such a strategy could include a four-step process to help students in decision-making on their writing. It helps the students consider:
1. The writer's role or voice.
2. The audience to whom the piece is written.
3. The format used for writing the piece.
4. The topic to be written about. The teacher can give examples for subjects such as social studies.

The students look over the four questions and consider the topic; then individually, and in small groups, they use the process to plan their writing. Students can have various roles, formats, and audiences. For a unit on World War II, a role might be offered for an American, German, or Japanese soldier, or a French resistance fighter. An audience might be self, community, government, or home. Format could include letters, diary, speeches, news articles, or editorials.

## Debate strategy

Debate practices oral language skills and higher order thinking skills through a structured argument, while discussing knowledge of content. The teacher must choose a topic represented by a single question that can be answered with a yes or no. Alternatively, the topic may be stated as a resolution. The teacher may also choose one of several debate formats. They may be in the Webster-Hayne format in which students are divided into two teams of unlimited size with each side taking turns to speak. The Lincoln-Douglas, Kennedy-Nixon, and academic debate formats are more formal, allowing two speakers each, a specific time period, a designated order, and a time limit for speaking. Students are given a side to argue and they must research material to support their side.

## Technical vocabulary

A strategy for technical vocabulary and language development is a word category exercise requiring thinking on an interpretive level. A teacher will establish sets of four words in which three of the words are related. Students circle the word that is not related. On a line at the top of the set, they write a word or phrase that defines the relationship of the three remaining words. This is a way to comprehend historical terms in a manner other than memorization of definitions and facts, and it forces the student to employ higher-level thinking. It can help to review and show a vocabulary understanding, as well as knowing information from a chapter or unit. It may also be used to mark periods with sets of historical people, places, ideas, and events.

## Value box reading

Value boxes help students change from thinking to writing with graphic organizers that prepare them to build written arguments. It categorizes and notes values that are associated with an idea in three areas:

positive, negative, and interesting. Partners or small groups can meet to discuss ideas and add to lists which are then used to formulate writing. This strategy can be used to help answer higher level thinking questions that need reflection on historical decisions or the impact of historical events. After writing positive, negative, or interesting, students would then write an expository essay with a thesis that evaluates the impact and argues points written in the value boxes.

## Four-way sharing group

A four-way sharing group may be used for any content area. It encourages students to listen to and generate oral language. The four-way sharing helps provide equal access to all students and helps to manage the talk in the classroom, especially after a charged issue. Four students sit on the floor facing each other from the positions of the cardinal directions. The teacher directs the "North" to speak for a full five minutes and the rest of the group will listen. Each of the other directions also get five minutes. It might be helpful to start with a much shorter time period until the students are comfortable doing the circuits. Teachers can find out how effective students use speaking and listening time in this strategy as well.

## Charts

A student can use charts to help develop a thesis when writing about history papers using charts that list the key events during a particular time period. The student would imagine how the story would seem in a movie and list scenes and locations that are crucial to the plot. He would then work with others to develop a list of key events in those locations and of the moments and factors that contribute to how characters or situations evolve. This also may be displayed, compared, and discussed as a continuing aid for understanding the story. The students will generate different hypotheses about the information found on the charts. All of the hypotheses are listed and students pick one or two that might help them in writing. Students also share ideas in peer feedback groups.

## Comic books

Children have been reading comic books since before the middle of the 20th century. Researchers investigated using comic books in stimulating students in language arts classes because of their popularity. One pair of researchers, Wright and Sherman, suggested that teachers should use comic strips in language arts classes for three reasons.
1.  Their students showed a high level of interest in the particular genre.
2.  The wide circulation of comic strips makes them a very viable source of material economically.
3.  Most comic strips have readability levels that are low, with words and sentences that are linguistically apt for readers of elementary and middle school levels.

Comics, TV, drama, and other multimedia formats may provide a way to reach even more language arts students and keep them engaged in the study of literacy skills.

## Media literacy

Media literacy includes both reading (or decoding) and writing (or encoding) media messages. It is a communication that is a basic for the traditional idea of literacy. The skills or competencies involved in media literacy also enter many content areas and can be integrated across the curriculum in the same manner that writing and reading are required skills beyond language arts and English curricula. Some state educational curricula have begun to incorporate media literacy, requiring students in some states to understand the selection of all media in news coverage, draw conclusions about the media's reports and the public's response, and recognize propaganda. While misuses of television and videotape have taken place in some classrooms, there is a much better recognition of the value of media literacy.

## Multimedia literacy

Multimedia literacy is an aspect of literacy that is being recognized as technology expands how people communicate with each other. Literacy, as a concept, emerged as a measure of how one can read or write. It means today that someone reads or writes at a level that is adequate to communicate. Multimedia calls for a more fundamental meaning of literacy when looked upon at a societal level. Multimedia is the use of several different media to send or receive information. These include text, audio, graphics, animation, virtual reality, computer programming, and robotics. The basic literacy of reading and writing is often handled by computer these days and provides a foundation for more advanced levels of multimedia literacy.

## Film and television

Television and film can help students explore cultural context and are easily integrated into the curriculum. They are entertaining media and allow for a great deal of flexibility in techniques of teaching and material. Surveys indicate that more teachers than ever are integrating television and videotapes into their curricula. Teachers are seeking quality programming with the appropriate structure and length, as well as advance information that allows them to preview the programming. Also found in the surveys was that both teachers and students are becoming more media savvy as they use camcorders and other video production equipment with increased frequency. That effect is likely to grow even further with such mobile video platforms as digital cameras and cell phones.

Television news and documentaries have long been used in secondary and postsecondary classrooms for writing instruction. There have been suggestions that the structure and content of news presentations mirror the writing of essays and can help in serving as effective writing instruction. A selected TV program can be viewed in one class period with time for students to ask questions and give comments. Student can also produce outlines for the news report, to be collected at the end of the class period. Advertising images, magazines, and television series may also help promote critical thinking during the writing process.

## Trade books

Language arts can be infused into content areas such as mathematics and science by using trade books. This includes picture books, fiction, and nonfiction books other than text books. Studies have shown that trade books appeal to a student's imagination and curiosity even more than text books. They also help students understand concepts by showing them in language that is familiar. Literature can help students make personal connections to ideas in math and science by putting these subjects into contexts that are meaningful and familiar. Some of these trade books may not be specifically about math or science, but they may show characters who engage in activities involving math and science. Such strategies help students gain confidence in such subjects and develop perseverance in solving problems.

## Electronic textbooks

Technology is commonly used in learning situations, such as elementary science students watching a video of an experiment being performed, middle school students manipulating commercial software that helps them prepare for a rapidly-changing technological workplace, and high school students playing interactive chemistry games on the Internet that score their manipulations of chemical equations and

- 23 -

formulas such as those used to solve problems in real life. Technology can help a child who is blind to hear audible descriptions that allow him or her to understand procedures and participate in a particular portion of class. Students who are physically impaired can complete computer activities with commercial software that has adaptive devices to permit the student to independently complete a task. Students who are hearing impaired can use CD-ROM or Internet video with captions.

### Lifelong learning

Lifelong learning is important in the lives of people in general, and specifically in the lives of teachers. The rapid change in the social, technological, and economic world have required people to prepare for a second or even third career and to keep themselves abreast of new developments that impact their goals, both personally and socially. Lifelong learners keep their senses active and think of new ideas. Much of the learning is self-directed. Skill for lifelong learning include the ability to ask questions, form hypotheses, use the right resources to answer questions, read with comprehension, and take in and evaluate information. Preparing students to be lifelong learners will require that the teacher possess the skills to continually seek knowledge as well.

### Mediating children's literature

The model of mediation is a general and dynamic framework that is meant to guide problem solving for teachers. It does not serve as a guide to analyze particular tasks or a list of steps. It is dynamic because it both evolves and guides through the social interaction that takes place in learning. When the teacher is interacting with a student, he or she must continually analyze how the student thinks and examine the strategies the student uses in problem solving. The analysis tells the teacher both what type of support to provide and how much should be given. The goal of instructional mediation is to help learners develop their own self-directed system of mediation, to become self-directed and independent readers. The decision-making process for the teacher looks at the purpose, the strategies, and the reflection.

### Multicultural literature

There are a number of considerations in selecting multicultural literature for children. They include:
1. Accuracy. Books should have current and accurate information. Stories should acknowledge events that are recent.
2. Stereotypes. Books should reflect the lives of individual people rather than giving general behaviors or personality traits to an entire group of people.
3. Setting. The settings in books should be accurate and, again, avoid stereotypes.
4. Language. Be careful in selecting books that might separate characters into groups of those who speak standard English and those who do not.
5. Epithets. Some books may contain racial or ethnic epithets.
6. Illustrations. The illustrations should show that those in ethnic groups look different from one another.

### Adolescent literature

A number of reasons exist why adolescent literature is important. These reasons include:
1. It helps adolescents understand various concerns and issues.
2. It is a safe place to read real-world experiences. Reading in a medium that is open-ended and not threatening allows students to empathize with others, as well as to consider and understand a wide variety of circumstances and the consequences of what takes place.
3. It helps students discover their place in the world and helps them to discover themselves.

4. It provides models that assist them in dealing with the problems that they may face every day. Adolescents with troubles may identify with the characters and the literature may help them in solving the problems that they have.

## Computers

There is a potential for students to engage in behavior with computers that is not intended, such as "surfing the 'net." Many schools have written guidelines for the use of computers in school and also have teachers sign statements acknowledging the rules for using the computers. Teachers should adopt management schemes that limit problems and ensure that the computers are used appropriately. These are some possible considerations that teachers may opt for when using computers in class:
1. There is zero tolerance for misusing laptops.
2. A "lids down" or "think time" should be designated to ensure that the students' attention is directed at the teacher.
3. Planning should be done ahead for recharging batteries.
4. Identical software packages should be installed.
5. Software shortcuts should be set up.
6. Students should save files to specific directories.

A classroom which is equipped with computers for all students might resemble a computer lab to some students, so teachers should make attendance rules well known to get the class off to a better beginning. A routine may also need to be established for students who are put off by the non-traditional roles that computer technology has them assume. Pacing is also a concern in a classroom with computers. Fewer activities exist for students to work on at their own pace than those that are carefully-timed activities during class periods. Teachers who set goals and activities for a class at the beginning of the class and then let students work at their own pace are usually more comfortable with computers in the classroom.

## One-computer classroom

It can be a challenge to have multimedia activities with only one computer in class but it can be done using strategies to get the most student access. The computer can accordingly be used as a presentation platform for both teacher and student, such as through the use of Power Point-style programs. A single computer may also function as a learning or research center or as a small-group development station. A projection unit or TV converter can be used to turn the computer into a presentation platform. The teacher can demonstrate, provide, and use teaching techniques that are technologically-enhanced. Students can also show their projects to the class. As a learning or research center, computers can be set up where students can find multimedia encyclopedias, the Internet, and various application software such as word processors.

## Making use of technology

Various lessons can be enriched by the use of technology. This includes:
1. Digital presentations. Students can show their learning in a digital presentation. They might create a Web site or create a stand-alone presentation. Students should cite their sources of information as with any research project. They should also be taught the importance of seeking permission for copyrighted matter.
2. Have students read books online. Thousands of books are available online at Web sites such as Online Books Page.
3. Have Web quests. This is an activity that is good for language arts and exploration of literature. The quests list sets of questions and tasks on which students can perform Internet research.

4. Word processing. Word processing programs are good for projects that would require having multiple drafts.

Technology can be used in lessons for a host of content areas. Some examples include:
1. Language arts. The Internet can be used to look at photos described in novels and can provide information about the social fabric of the community, helping students to learn the context.
2. Mathematics. Spreadsheets can be used to calculate distance, speed, and travel time between two cities. The data can be exposed in several forms to help foster the understanding of variables.
3. Science. The Internet can be used to view topographic and satellite maps to help determine an area's rock formations.
4. Physical education. The Internet can be used to watch basketball techniques in slow motion to help improve shooting form.

## Benefitting from technology

Even young children can benefit from using technology. Technology can be a resource for teachers, students, and parents. Research has shown that students using technology have higher achievement levels and enhance their basic skills in reading, writing, and math if they can practice those skills with the use of technology. Students are engaged for longer time periods with the use of technology. It intensifies their basic tasks in learning. Technology can motivate students to learn which helps increase their desire to go to school and continue on to college. It can give students a chance to explore other lands through the internet. Instruction can be enhanced through the use of visual aids and lessons on the internet to boost comprehension.

## Reporting the news

Students are told to be reporters and report the news for their school. They are told that they will need to report on local news, world news, national news, sports, entertainment, and weather. The reporter should visit various news websites to gather information for the stories. The stories must be accurate, informative, and interesting. The audience is the students' fifth grade class so it must be in language they can understand. The teacher functions as the editor. In this exercise, the student learns the parts of the newspaper: the headline, the lead, quotes, body, and ending. There should be pre-writing planning and collection of information. The student gets a "beat" to cover, finds a story, and writes about it.

## Composing texts

The framework for composing texts includes invention, drafting, revision, and editing. Many recursive strategies lie inside these components. Invention refers to the ways in which a writer might think about what he or she wants to do and how it could be done. It involves using outlines, seeking other opinions and perspectives, and research. It is recursive in that writers invent throughout the act of writing, planning, revising, and editing. Drafting refers to the different versions of a text before closure. Writers discover as a result of writing a draft, and then draft some more. Some view revision as a way to see the text from different perspectives. Revision is also rethinking ideas and how they may be conveyed. Editing refers to decisions that writers make to produce writing in which the words and punctuation are correct, along with flowing sentence structure and diction.

## Developmental stages of writing

Writing develops in stages from being dependent to becoming independent. The first stage is a novice who has little, if any, individual style. He or she is dependent on the teacher and seeks approval from the teacher. Stage 2 is a transitional writer. The writer needs support and coaching in order to develop. is the writer learns from modeled behaviors. Stage 3 is the willing writer, who is able to collaborate with others and can learn from criticism. This writer enjoys practicing the craft and develops an appreciation for the audience. Stage 4 is the independent writer. This writer is autonomous, has developed a sophisticated personal style, has developed a writer's voice, is self-aware, and is self-motivating.

## Supporting the writing process

Students who are at an intermediate writing level respond well to a classroom structure that is predictable while offering some choice and flexibility. It is important to develop an environment in which students are encouraged to feel safe in taking risks in order to develop a community of writers, sharing with and supporting each other. The teacher is part of the community. The teachers should let students help to set rules and guidelines. Desks can be arranged in groups and tables can be used for several students. Resources can be provided on a specified shelf. These resources include dictionaries, language texts, literature for models, and samples of writing by class members. Information on the writing process can be displayed on bulletin boards. The teacher can designate certain classroom areas for specific activities connected with writing.

## Class publications

There are several ways of creating publications for students within their classes including the use of the Internet along with developing hard-copy publications. This includes:
1.  Dividing classes into groups to produce a newsletter or similar publication. Newsletters are relatively simple to produce using the templates that come with many word processing programs.
2.  Assigning and electing an editorial board to be responsible for publishing.
3.  The teacher can be the editor who selects what will be published. Students submit their work to the teacher which he or she can organize to reflect goals of the class or topics that are covered.

The copies of these publications can make the student proud.

## Vocabulary

A vocabulary is a set of words that a person or other entity knows that are a part of language. A person's vocabulary is defined either as the set of all words that person understands or the set of all words the person is likely to use when constructing new sentences. The richness of a person's vocabulary is most times thought of as a reflection of intelligence or level of education. Increasing the size of one's vocabulary, or vocabulary building, is an important part of learning and improving one's skill in a language. Students in school are taught new words as part of a particular lesson. Many adults find vocabulary building enjoyable. Words help derive meaning from a text, which is the main goal in reading. Reading comprehension is needed for all subjects that a person learns. A deep vocabulary helps all readers better understand what is read.

### Language expansion

Language expansion is the process of taking a verbalization used by a child and adding to it. Language modeling is the process of talking to children and narrating what occurs in their immediate environment. This involves the pairing of actions or objects with simple words in order to explain the purpose of those words. Language modeling and expansion give the child an opportunity to hear and learn language by allowing the child to hear the appropriate articulation and attempt to imitate sounds and combinations of sounds. Modeling and expansion involves the use of simple words or basic sentences that are easy to understand and have complex structures that are reduced. Most words are learned during everyday experiences with language. Interactions between children and adults are the best way for children to expand their vocabularies.

## Direct instruction of vocabulary
While much vocabulary is learned indirectly, some vocabulary needs to be directly taught. Direct instruction helps student learn words that are difficult such as those words representing concepts that are not part of the everyday experience of a student. The direct instruction of vocabulary in the case of a text leads to better comprehension. Direct instruction includes giving students specific word instruction and teaching students strategies for learning words. Specific word instruction can help expand a student's knowledge of word meanings. A deeper knowledge can help students understand what it is they are writing or speaking. Before having students read a text, the teacher should teach them specific words that will appear in the text.

## Extended instruction
Extended instruction promotes active interaction with vocabulary which improves learning words. Children learn words best when instruction is provided over an extended time period and when the instruction has them working actively with the words. The more that the students use those new words, the more they will be used in different contexts which leads to the students being more likely to learn the words. Repeated exposure to vocabulary in many contexts helps word learning. Students learn new words better when they see them often and in different contexts. The more that children hear, see, and work with specific words, the better they can learn them. Students are given repeated exposure to new words when extended instruction is provided.

## Indirect instruction
Indirect instruction of vocabulary can be encouraged in two major ways. First, students should be read to, no matter what grade level. Students of all ages can learn words from hearing texts being read to them. Reading aloud is most efficient as a means of indirect teaching when the teacher discusses the selection with the class before, during, and after the selection is read. The teacher should talk with students about the new vocabulary words and concepts, and help them relate the words to their prior experiences and knowledge. Another way to indirectly teach vocabulary words is to encourage students to read expansively on their own. The students should be encouraged to read on their own during independent work sessions.

## Word selection
A teacher will most likely have the ability to teach perhaps eight to ten new words per week, so the words that are to be taught must be chosen carefully. The focus should be on teaching:
1. Important words. When words are taught before students read a text, the words that are important to understanding concepts in the text should be taught directly. The students may not know several other words in the selection, but there will not be time to teach them all.
2. Useful words. Words that the student will likely see and use many times should be taught.
3. Difficult words. Some instruction should be given on words that are difficult for the students. Particular challenges include words with multiple meanings depending on the context in which they are used.
4. According to need. Plan and implement instruction addressing strengths and needs.

## Three levels of word knowledge
Knowledge of words by a student is not simply a matter of them knowing or not knowing those words. Instead, the words are known to certain degrees. They may not have seen or heard a word before. They may have heard it or seen it but only vaguely know what that word might mean. Or they may be very familiar with a word meaning and be able to accurately use it in speech and writing. The three levels of

word knowledge are known as unknown, acquainted, and established. At the unknown level, the word is completely unfamiliar and the meaning is not known. At acquainted, the word is somewhat familiar and there is some idea of meaning. At the established level, the word is very familiar, can be easily recognized, and can be used correctly.

<u>Four types of word learning</u>
There are four different types of word learning that have been identified: learning a new meaning for a known word; learning the meaning of a new word that represents a known concept; learning the meaning of a new word that represents an unknown concept; and clarifying and enriching the meaning of a known word. These different kinds of word learning have varied levels of difficulty. Perhaps one of the most common and most challenging is learning the meaning of a new word that represents an unknown concept. This type of word learning is necessary for learning in content areas. Learning words and concepts in mathematics, social studies, and science can be particularly challenging because each concept is often associated with other concepts.

<u>Dictionary game</u>
A dictionary game is a team activity that can help students build their vocabularies and improve their dictionary skills. In the game, the student teams first compete against one another to find word definitions in the dictionary. The team that is the fastest reads the word definition, tells what part of speech the word is, and correctly uses the word in a sentence. Other teams can challenge the team's response. Points are given for correct answers or challenges. The value of this game is in demonstrating the difference between the primary definition of a word and its specific use in the context of a particular content area or in reading. Students should quickly learn that the primary definition of a word is not necessarily going to be its meaning in all contexts.

<u>Word analogies</u>
Word analogies can be used to let students connect familiar words and concepts with new ideas and prior experiences with new information. In such a strategy, the student is confronted by two words which are related and is then challenged to explain the nature of their relationship. Next, the students apply the same relationship to other pairs of words. The form for a word analogy exercise is typically: "Term A is to Term B as Term C is to what word?" Students display critical thinking on two levels using this exercise. First, they describe the relationships between the first pair of words and then suggest new word pairs with similar relationships.

**Student appreciation**

Assignments that make learning personal are often very effective in helping students appreciate studying and completing those assignments. Such work often lets students look into their family, community, and cultural experiences and gain a better appreciation of both their own and their peers' backgrounds. Family tree projects in social studies classes are an example because of the great diversity of most American schools. These projects or others such as historical ones in which family members are sought out may often bring out values that the students might not otherwise appreciate and can also foster closer family relationships. Making assignments personal and valuable gives students a great incentive to appreciate studying about a subject and to find learning as a quest.

**Immigrant students**

American schools have been a major agent for helping those children and youth who recently arrived in this country with adapting to the civic and social demands of their new homes. Classroom lessons and socialization on the school yard take place. But sometimes the home culture teachings and expectations are contrasted with those of American schools. This can lead to labeling children as disabled when no disability actually exists. These students do have issues with psychosocial stress as they attempt to adapt. A transition that is successful to one's new country requires a secure cross-cultural identity. How much of each culture forms this identity depends on the person's needs, skills, experience, education, and support. Recognition of these transitioning needs and support are among the strategic help that can be given to these children.

## Culture capsule

A culture capsule is a biliteracy activity that is usually prepared outside class by students, but presented during class for about five or 10 minutes. It consists of a paragraph or two and explains one minimal difference between an American custom and that of another culture's custom. It also includes several photos and other information that is relevant. These capsules can be used in addition to role playing. Students may act out a part of another culture. Essentially the capsule is a brief description of some aspect of the target culture followed by contrasting information from the students' native language culture. These are done orally with teachers giving a brief talk on the chosen cultural point and then leading a discussion on cultures.

## Teaching culture

A framework for teaching and learning culture includes:
- Knowing about getting information. The nature of content and getting information. Facts about the United States and important facets of its culture.
- Learning objectives—demonstrating a mastery of information.
- Techniques and activities—cultural readings, films, videotapes, cultural artifacts, and personal anecdotes.
- Knowing how culture is traditionally taught. Are students given information and asked to show that they know it.
- Knowing how to develop behaviors—knowing about what facts you learned and acting upon them.
- Learning objectives—demonstrating ability, fluency, expertise, confidence, and ease.
- Techniques—dialogs, role playing, simulations, and field experiences.
- Knowing where communicative competence in the language occurs. Students know both what to say and how to say it in an appropriate manner.

## Goals for teaching culture

The following are goals that should be attained in teaching culture:
- Interest. The student shows a curio
- sity about the target culture and also shows empathy toward its people.
- Who. The student understands that effective communication requires the discovery of the culturally conditioned images that are seen in the minds of people when they think, act, and react to the world that is around them.
- When and where. The student recognizes that situational variables and convention mold behavior significantly. He or she should know how people in the target culture act in both normal situations and crisis situations.
- Why. The student knows that people generally act the way they do because they are using options for satisfying basic physical and psychological needs and that cultural patterns are interrelated and tend to mutually support the satisfactions of needs.

## Attitudes over foreign cultures

Ways to measure the change in attitudes about foreign cultures include:
- Social distance scales. This is to measure the degree to which one separates oneself socially from members of another culture. For instance: Would you marry, have as a close friend, have as an acquaintance, or work with someone from another culture?
- Semantic differential scales. This is to judge the defined culture group in terms of a number of traits that are bipolar. For instance, are people from this culture clean? Are they dirty? Are they good? Are they bad?
- Statements. This is to put a check in front of statements the student agrees with. Is the person you know envious of others? Self-indulgent? Quick to understand? Tactless?
- Self-esteem change. This is to measure self-esteem changes in the primary grades. For instance, am I happy with myself?

## Importance of learning various cultures

Students may display behaviors in their cultures that are different from those in the American mainstream; thus, they are at risk for being labeled by uninformed educators as having behaviors that are "wrong." Teachers should familiarize themselves with a student's home culture's values and practices. There should be an awareness of differences that promotes understanding, tolerance, acceptance, and celebration of others and their ways. Information on other cultures can be found in many textbooks and travel books, and on various Web sites. Another way to develop familiarity with a student's cultural background is the use of a "cultural informant." This is someone who might be familiar with the group and their ways, such as teachers or other successful members of that cultural group.

## Actions of immigrant students

Immigrant students are often under a great deal of anxiety and stress as they learn English and cope with new surroundings. The pressure can result in feelings of being overwhelmed, confused, or frustrated. If this is the case, support services such as counselors or social workers may be needed to help relieve this stress. At times, the way a student responds to a perplexing situation may be misinterpreted by educators. Humans tend to use behaviors that have worked for them before and students are likely to use behaviors reinforced by their home and home culture. These misunderstandings have sometimes resulted in immigrant children being labeled as emotionally disturbed and being placed in special programs.

## Relationships with immigrant stundents

Students need to feel welcomed and valued by their teacher. A direct verbal communication may not be feasible, but there are other methods of showing acceptance and personal warmth toward students. This will help relieve anxiety and can promote an enthusiasm to learn academics and American patterns of behavior. Smiles are a good way to reach different cultural, ethnic, and linguistic groups. Also, teachers should take time to talk with the youngsters, even through an interpreter. Having students talk about their prior life will help the teacher become more familiar with their concerns and enable the teacher to emotionally support the new students. The teacher may also answer questions about schools and what is needed to live here in America. The teacher may also discuss how he or she can help make the transition easier.

## Learning culture

Students learning culture should be taught to react appropriately in social situations. They should be able to describe a pattern in the culture and recognize a pattern when it is illustrated. Additionally, they should be able to explain these patterns and predict how a pattern is likely to apply in a given situation. Students learning culture should describe or manifest an attitude that is important for making oneself acceptable in a foreign society. They should evaluate the form of a statement concerning a culture pattern and describe or demonstrate defensible methods of analyzing a sociocultural whole. They should identify basic human responses which signify that that which is being taught is understood.

## High expectations for immigrant students

It is common for some teachers to become frustrated upon seeing that they are unable to reach one or more of their students. Becoming more culturally informed can help enhance the teaching repertoire. This information can also help teachers realize that these students may have trouble under the teaching of any skilled instructor. But the belief that is expressed in a student helps to create persistence and motivation on their part. Linguistic as well as academic achievements in the United States are often only realized because of the patience, tolerance and encouragement which American teachers display. Effort is promoted by teachers who are supportive and who create a valuing, welcoming and accepting educational setting.

## Support services for immigrant students

Schools can help recent immigrants feel welcome and supported while developing positive identities that are cross-cultural. Schools have many ways to assist their students in learning the curriculum and adapting to American culture and habits. For example, a recent arrival can be partnered with another student who speaks his or her language or dialect, even if they are not necessarily of the same nationality or heritage. Cross-age tutoring is also an option that might be considered. Candidates include someone from the student's culture or region, other recent immigrants, or an accepting and helpful American youngster. Hiring paraprofessionals who speak the student's language can also be helpful.

## Becoming acquainted with strengths and needs

An important part of planning and organizing for instruction is acquiring an understanding of the students. It is useful, early in the school year, to learn as much as possible about the students, what their interests, learning abilities, and learning styles are. As a teacher talks directly with each student, information is provided about how that student perceives himself or herself as a learner. Also useful is:
- Give oral or written diagnostic questionnaires or surveys to assess the students' current abilities, interests, and attitudes.
- Consult other personnel, student portfolios, and the students' records from previous years.
- Consider the potential for using previously successful adaptations with each student, and plan other adaptations to address the specific needs for learning.

## Inventory of learning styles

A teacher wants to know what types of learning styles a student has as well as answers to other questions. These are the answers teachers must use to determine how instruction may be personalized for the students. This can also be surprising information for the students as well. An inventory of student learning styles can build self-esteem by helping the student to discover his or her strengths, learn about the areas in which more effort is required, and appreciate the differences among fellow students. A number of published inventories are available to help students determine their learning strengths. Inventories may also be found for free on the Internet.

## Terms

### Research
Tends to support within-class ability grouping, grouping those with like abilities, as helping most students learn. It is generally flexible and not as stigmatizing as other groups. If such groups are considered, teachers might want only two such groups to make management of the grouping process easier.

### Cooperative learning
an instructional strategy in which students are put into heterogeneous groups. It is perhaps one of the best researched innovations in recent times and can have dramatic student achievement effects when implemented properly.

### Individualized instruction
The best way to deal with individual student difference, but it is very difficult to accomplish. Computer-assisted instruction may change that.

## Grouping formats

Small group reading instruction has been shown in a number of studies to be more effective than instruction of the class as a whole. Most of these studies did not include students who were disabled. Having teacher-led groups of three to 10 students helps the students learn much more than when they are taught using instruction of the whole class. Smaller groups of three to four are usually more efficient than larger groups in terms of time, peer interaction, and improved skills. Combinations of formats also produce reading benefits that are measurable, especially for those children with disabilities.  For instance, students who work in pairs for two days and in small groups for two days can be combined with whole-class instruction for a part of a period.

## Nongraded or ungraded grouping

Nongraded and ungraded grouping usually refers to grouping children in classes without designation of grade levels and with age spans of more than one year. The original rationale was to increase the heterogeneity of class compositions and liberate children and teachers from rigid achievement expectations that are based on the age of a student. But research later found that implementing these classes tended to result in homogeneous grouping of children based on ability and achievement level, despite age. In many instances of nongraded groups, children in classes are put in regular or temporary groups for specific instruction, regardless of age. In such approaches, the main goal is to increase homogeneity of ability of groups rather than interaction across ability group lines.

## Progress with respect to class groupings

Continuous progress generally means that children remain with their classroom peers in an age cohort, despite having met or surpassed specific grade-level achievement expectations. This term is usually associated with an emphasis on the individualized curriculum, so that teaching and learning tasks are responsive to previous experience, and on the rate of progress of the child despite age. This practice is sometimes referred to as social promotion. The main reason for this practice is that there might be a stigmatizing effect on children if removed from their age cohort. Like ungraded approaches, the programs that are focused on continuous progress are not aimed at maximizing the educational benefits of children of different abilities and ages being together. Instead their goal is to let the children progress without being made to meet expectations of achievement.

## Age grouping schemes

Grouping practices might seem to have slight distinctions but there are significant implications in practice. Ungraded or nongraded approaches indicate that age is not a good indicator of what children are ready to learn. It emphasizes regrouping children for class based on perceived readiness to acquire skills and knowledge instead of age. Its main goal is of homogenizing children for instruction based on achievement rather than age. Combined grade groupings and continuous progress practices do not intend to increase a sense of family within class or to encourage children to share knowledge and experience, but mixed-age grouping does take advantage of heterogeneity of experience and skills in a group of children.

## Valuing correct answers

One of the most effective ways to establish a safe learning environment for students is to help them learn that errors are friends rather than faults. Students often apologize for not knowing something. They can be reassured that no one knows everything and that everyone has something to learn. Teachers can teach them to value their correct answers rather than dwelling on their errors. Students have learned to count errors, but they can be taught to instead count the number they got right, thus offering positive reinforcement. Even if a student gets one item correct and the remainder incorrect, the student can be told that they have already learned something. Patterns of errors can be pointed out as well.

## Conflict resolution

The numerous, well-publicized instances of violence in schools, and in society as well, have prompted many schools to consider making violence prevention and conflict resolution a part of the curriculum. These programs rely on instruction that is ongoing and discussion that helps change the perceptions, skills, and attitudes of children. A number of these curricula have been available since the 1980s. These include conflict resolution, violence prevention, and curricula for solving social problems. These curricular approaches are typically integrated into a broader program that has other components such as peer mediation, cooperative learning, and programs that address school wide behavior management and anger management.

## Safe learning environment

Most incidents of school violence or serious disruption begin as less serious behavior that has escalated to the point of requiring attention. Many aggressive or disruptive behaviors that spiraled out of control could have been prevented by early and appropriate classroom responses. A well-documented knowledge base exists on how to prevent misbehavior escalation in the classrooms. A number of those programs that integrate those findings into classroom management packages have become available. Most rely on principles of effectively managing the classroom including:
- Multiple options that rely on various strategies and responses for maintaining an effective learning environment.
- Emphasizing the positive.
- Teaching responsibility.
- Decelerating emotional conflict.
- Consistently communicating appropriate behavior.

- Early responses that let the student know what the school and classroom rules are and that they will be enforced.

## Bullying prevention

Many of those involved as perpetrators in the well-publicized school shootings in recent years had been picked on or persecuted by their peers. This highlights why addressing bullying in school is essential. Studies show that almost one-third of elementary students are bullied. About 10 percent of secondary school students have reported being bullied. But studies have also shown that school personnel persistently underestimate the extent of bullying that takes place in their school. Students also worry that no action will be taken. A whole-school approach may be needed to combat bullying rather than individual interventions. This could include awareness programs for teachers, parents, and students. Also, a strict enforcement of school and classroom policies helps to send a clear message that there is no tolerance for bullying.

## Preventing school violence

There are three assumptions underlying most of the methods schools use to reduce the risk that minor incidents and disruptions will turn into life-threatening violence. These assumptions are:
- Violence is preventable. Serious violent incidents seem unpredictable, but prevention programs can make a difference. No guarantee exists that schools with comprehensive programs will be violence free, but schools that implement violence prevention components do see fewer incidents of disruption, which can lower the chance of serious violence.
- There is no one quick fix. Many schools have begun using metal detectors in the wake of school shootings or have instituted no tolerance suspensions and expulsion, but no data exists to show the effectiveness of these measures.
- Prevention requires continuous planning and commitment. Effective school safety must have ongoing planning, commitment, and partnerships among the school staff, parents, and community.

## Intrinsic and extrinsic motivation

Intrinsic motivation can be seen when people take part in an activity for its own sake, without some obvious external incentive present. An example is a hobby. Extrinsic motivation is the desire to perform a behavior based on the potential external rewards that the activity might bring. It was once thought that both intrinsic and extrinsic behavior were additive and could not be combined to form higher motivation levels. Some scholars believe that students are more likely to experience intrinsic motivation if they:
- Attribute their educational results to internal factors that they can control.
- Believe that they can be effective agents in reaching their goals.
- Are motivated by the deep mastery of a topic rather than rote learning just to get a grade.

## Reading due to motivation

Motivated readers are those who generate their own literacy learning opportunities, and thus, determine their own literacy learning destiny. This places motivation in part of an engagement process. An engaged reader reads for different purposes, participates in meaningful social interactions focused around reading, and scaffolds knowledge that helps construct new learning. Motivation can take place at any time with any young reader. Teachers can suggest to parents ways to motivate children to read at home, even when the parent is busy and cannot drop what they are doing. One way to get the child another reading audience is to suggest that the child read to a few dolls or stuffed animals. This kind of activity can help both prereaders and beginning readers.

## Book clubs

Student-organized and student-driven book clubs help to build a community in the classroom and to encourage students to read independently. They are in effect taking responsibility for their learning of literacy. Book clubs let students choose what they want to read, where they read, how they read, and with whom they read. The choice is valued by students. Students must work together to negotiate places and times to meet, along with the pacing and discussion of their books in order to have successful book clubs. They learn to value one another as readers and learners. Teachers can allow book clubs to meet in small-group times during reading in order to give the students freedom in operating their own club.

## Building activities for book clubs

Activities in which school book clubs can grow together as a group include:
- Letting the group name themselves. Let them decide on a club mascot.
- Allowing each club to keep a group reading notebook or journal where they track their readings. Perhaps they might decorate the journal if they so wish.
- Allowing groups to decide upon projects that are inquiry-based. For example, a group might decide to explore something of specific interest to them and search for the information. After these steps are taken, teachers should explain the process and allow some class time so that students may discuss the activities and establish their first groups. Those students who are not interested in this voluntary activity can read on their own.

## Learning development problems

Some primary organic conditions are associated with developing learning problems as secondary symptoms. The child's reading and more general learning are thought to result from cognitive or sensory limitation that follow from the diagnosis. These include:
- Cognitive deficiencies. Children with severe cognitive deficiencies usually develop very low, if any, reading achievement. Factors associated with this include very low birth weight, fetal alcohol syndrome, lead poisoning, or nutritional deficiency.
- Hearing impairment. Hearing impairment is another condition associated with reading difficulty. This may be caused by chronic ear infections that lead to hearing loss.
- Early language impairment. Some children are so clearly behind by age 3 that it arouses concerns of parents, neighbors, preschool teachers, or others. Delayed language development is often the first indication of a broader primary condition, including developmental disability, autism, or hearing impairment.
- Attention deficits. Those with reading problems often have attention deficits.

## Nature of reading difficulties

The foundations of good reading for children are all the same. All readers need to develop fluency, comprehension, and motivation to read in order to become successful readers. This is true regardless of the reader's age, aptitude, or gender. Children who have reading difficulties are no different. They must also develop the basic foundations for reading and they also require the same type of learning experiences in order for that to happen. Most young children with reading difficulties have problems with development of fluency. The rate at which they read is slow, their word identification is hesitant, and they rely too much on contextual clues. Since most of their mental or cognitive effort is spent trying to identify words, their comprehension falters.

## Biologically related reading disability

A reading disorder is often presumed to be a dysfunction of the central nervous system, or a biological defect. But the actual role of biology is much more complex than such an assumption implies. Biological differences can play some role with reading disabilities and in learning to read as they do for a variety of cognitive abilities in humans. But little evidence exists that most children identified in school as reading disabled actually have a biologically-based problem. Evidence that factors such as genetics actually keep children from learning to read is also lacking. However, evidence does exist that labeling children as poor readers and assuming they have an intrinsic disorder caused by biology may create lower teacher expectations.

## Unexpected reading failure

Reading disorders have historically been looked at as unexpected or unexplained reading failures in contrast to failures from low intelligence, poor listening comprehension, poverty, or sensory impairment. Such a concept came about at a time when significantly less was known about the cognitive processes used in learning to read. It is now known that learning to read uses many different abilities and not all correlate to IQ. Someone may have serious problems with word decoding, yet still score high in IQ testing. Reading problems are not unexpected for children if there is monitoring of their cognitive abilities such as phonological awareness. The idea of unexpected failure is no longer useful in conceptualizing problems with reading.

## Symptoms of dyslexia

Typical symptoms of dyslexia include the terms "dysphonetic" and "dyseidetic." A person who is dysphonetic has problems connecting sounds to symbols and may have difficulty sounding out words. Spelling mistakes would show a very poor phonics understanding. This is also sometimes known as "auditory dyslexia" because of its relation to the way a person processes language sounds. On the other hand, a dyseidetic person usually understands phonics concepts but has great problems with word recognition and spelling. This is also known as "surface dyslexia" or "visual dyslexia." Words are usually spelled in a way that can easily be deciphered phonetically, but may be far from correct. One might also see transpositions and reversals in spelling, but the letters that correspond to the right sounds are there. Most remedial programs use phonics.

## Language disorders

- Stuttering is an interruption in the rhythm or flow of speech that is characterized by hesitations, repetitions, or prolongation of sounds, syllables, words, or phrases.
- Articulation disorders are difficulties with the way sounds are formed and put together. They are usually characterized by substituting one sound for another (wabbit for rabbit), omitting a sound (han for hand), or distorting sounds.
- Voice disorders are characterized by pitches that are inappropriate, such as being too high, too low, never changing or breaking, excessive or inadequate volume, or vocal qualities such as harsh, hoarse, nasal, or breathy.
- Aphasia is the loss of speech and language abilities as a result of a head injury or stroke.
- Delayed language is characterized by a marked slowness in grammar and vocabulary development that is needed to express and understand ideas and thoughts.

## Manifestations of dyslexia

Dyslexia involves a brain difference that is not a defect but does make it excessively hard to learn language. A child with dyslexia will have problems from the very beginning in learning to understand speech and being understood. The child might need to describe what he or she wants, might have trouble sequencing words, or may speak words in an incorrect order. A child may have problems positioning letters when he or she enters school. Dyslexia is difficult to recognize because many of its manifestations are part of the natural maturing process of young children. When children get stuck in these stages and it lasts for an abnormally long period, parents and teachers should recognize this as a possible problem. But a dyslexic mind may have exceptional ability for singing or playing a musical instrument at an early age.

## Traumatic brain injury

Traumatic brain injury may be of the following types:

1. Closed head injury, or bruising. This is common at the point of impact and on the opposite side of the brain. It is also common where the brain is adjacent to the rough and bony surfaces of the skull.
2. Shearing. This is commonly seen in the brain stem from severe head injury and is commonly in the frontal and temporal lobes where the brain surface rubs against bony skull ridges.
3. Hematoma, or bleeding. This occurs in areas that receive the brunt of the injury. These injuries are associated with specific deficits that are related to a particular brain area.
4. Frontal lobe damage. Deficits in regulating behavior including social and cognitive behavior.

## Results of traumatic brain injury

Traumatic brain injury causes the following results:
- Difficulty concentrating
- Weak orientation to task and difficulty in shifting from task to task
- Relatively slow performance
- Difficulty organizing tasks or information
- Difficulty with abstract thinking
- Difficulty thinking strategically
- Difficulty remembering new information or assignments
- Lower academic performance than before the injury
- Poor awareness of cognitive limitations
- Impulsive or inappropriate behavior in class
- Conflicts with teachers or peers
- Excessive moodiness
- Exaggerated responses to stress
- Excessive tiredness
- Depression and withdrawal
- Limited safety judgment
- Anxiety
- Anger and acting out
- Apathy
- Difficulty starting tasks without being prompted to do so

## Student assessment systems

Assessment system types include norm-referenced, criterion-referenced, and individual or alternative assessments. Criterion-referenced systems are those in which an individual's performance is compared to a certain learning objective of performance standard rather than the performance of other students. Norm-referenced systems are those in which student performance is compared to a "norm group," which may be a national sample that represents a diverse cross-section of students. These tests usually sort students and measure achievement based on some performance criterion. An individual assessment is one focusing on the individual student, such as a portfolio assessment. This is a portfolio of the student's classroom work. Alternative assessments are those requiring students to respond to a question rather than a set of responses.

## Wide-Range Achievement Test

The Wide-Range Achievement Test is one of a number of standardized achievement assessments to determine a child's cognitive ability. It is designed for individuals ages 5-75. It contains scoring for reading, spelling, and math. It provides up to 30 minutes for each of the three forms. The test uses a single-level format as well as alternative forms. These alternative forms may be used individually or with one another in order to provide a more qualitative assessment of academic skills. The reading subtest includes letter naming and word pronunciation out of context. The spelling subtest asks the student to write his or her own name, and then write words as they are directed. The mathematical portion includes counting, reading problems, number symbols, and written computation.

## Informal reading inventory

The informal reading inventory is an individually administered survey that is designed to help determine a student's needs in reading. The student's performance on the informal reading inventory will help to determine the instructional level and the amount and type of support the student is likely to need. Specifically, using the informal reading inventory will help teachers assess a student's strengths and needs in the areas of word recognition, word meaning, reading strategies, and comprehension. While an informal reading inventory is a suitable tool for determining a student's reading ability and needs, it is not infallible. An educator should use information from the inventory along with other tests and information to make decisions about instructional plans.

## Student reading inventory

To administer a student reading inventory certain materials would be needed such as a stop watch to time the student, a copy of all readings for both the student and the teacher, and comprehension questions for scoring purposes. Steps to be taken when administering the inventory include:

1. Explain to students that this is not a test. Tell them that this inventory is really to tell how the teacher can teach them better.
2. Set the timer.
3. Begin the timer as the student reads the first excerpt aloud.
4. Score errors on the teacher's copy.
5. Stop the timer when the student stops and record the total time. 6) Give the comprehension questions and record the answers.

## On-demand, direct writing assessment

An on-demand writing assessment for a ninth-grader might embed stages of the writing process into defined time periods. Students write about events from their past. The prompt focuses on some aspect of the social or intellectual development of the students. The topic is meant to encourage ninth grade students to be reflective. An example topic might be when the student got into a new interest, or a book or TV show that had a particularly strong effect on what they did or thought. The assessment includes the task introduction, a short reading selection that serves as a model, some discussion questions, one or more planning suggestions, a prompt, and a checklist of revision and editing questions.

## Formative assessment

A formative assessment is a diagnostic use of assessment to provide feedback to teachers and students over the course of instruction. That is in contrast to a summative assessment, which usually happens after a period of instruction and requires making judgments about the learning that has occurred, such as with a test score or paper. Assessments in general include teacher observation, classroom instruction, or an analysis of student work, including homework and tests. Assessments are formative when the information is used to adapt teaching and learning to meet the needs of the students. When teachers know how students are progressing and where they are having difficulties, they can use this information to make needed instructional adjustments, such as reteaching, alternative instruction approaches, or offering more practice opportunities.

The goal of formative assessment is to gain an understanding of what students know or don't know in order to make responsive changes in teaching and learning. So techniques such as teacher observation and classroom discussion have an important place along with analyzing tests and homework. Questioning and classroom discussion is a good way to increase the students' knowledge and improve understanding. The teacher does need to make sure to ask thoughtful, reflective questions instead of simple factual ones and give students sufficient time to respond. Students might be invited to discuss their thinking about a question in small groups. Several possible answers could be provided and students allowed to vote on them. Or students could be asked to write down an answer, with the teacher then reading a selected few out loud.

## Rubric

A rubric is a set of assessment criteria that specifies characteristics, knowledge, and competencies that indicate a student's level of achievement. It is basically a list of characteristics that are used to assess a learning product's quality. Rubrics identify traits and components that indicate the extent to which a learning outcome has been achieved. Rubrics are often used to attach authentic meaning to both letter and number grades. Rubrics also offer advantages such as:

- Rubrics allow students to document the grade they earned rather than the grade given or assigned.
- Tests and research papers may not offer a valid reflection of learning outcomes while rubrics are tied to learning outcomes.
- Grades alone offer limited reflections of a student's learning.

## Informal assessment

Although there are no uniformly accepted definitions for formal and informal assessments, informal can mean techniques that are easily put into classroom routines, and learning activities to measure a student's learning outcome. Informal assessment can be used without interfering with instructional time. The results can be an indicator of the skills or subjects that interest a student, but they do not provide comparison to a broader group like standardized tests. Informal tests require clear understanding of the levels of a student's abilities. Informal assessments seek identification of a student's strengths and weaknesses without a regard to norms or grades. Such assessments may be done in structured or unstructured manners. Structured ones include checklists or observations. Unstructured assessments are those such as student work samples or journals.

## Questioning techniques

Key questions should be planned to give direction and structure to the lesson. Spontaneous questions that come up are fine, but the overall direction of the discussion should have been mostly planned. Here are some simple guidelines to asking questions that will help teacher's questioning skills:

- Be sure the question is clear. Think about what it is required from the student before asking the question.
- Frame the question without calling on a particular student. Other students are free to ignore the question when a student is called upon before the question is asked.
- After framing the question, pause to give the students a chance to think of an answer before calling on a student to respond. This pause, called wait time, is an important questioning skill. The wait time between a question and asking for response should be 2-4 seconds.

## Use of performance assessments

Performance assessments can be used to document and evaluate the work done by students during a fixed time period. These assessments tend to take the form of lengthy, multidisciplinary problem-solving activities. Teaching and learning with performance assessments should be documented and assessed with tools based on performance of real tasks. Students should have the opportunity to exhibit their expertise before family and community. Performance assessments may be short-answer or extended response. They include oral questions, traditional quizzes, open-ended prompts, and tests.

## Authentic assessment

Authentic assessment asks students to apply their skills and knowledge the same way that they would be used in real-world situations. It is a performance-based assessment that requires each student to exhibit his or her in-depth knowledge and understanding through a mastery demonstration. It is an assessment of authentic learning, which is the type of learning in which activities and materials are framed in real-life contexts. The underlying assumption of such an approach is that the material is meaningful to students, and thus more motivating and deeply processed. Some of the terms or concepts that are related to authentic learning include contextual learning and theme-based curriculum.

## Multiple assessment methods

Multiple assessment methods give a comprehensive view of how well students are achieving the learning outcomes that a program identifies. A quantitative assessment lets educators provide numerical evidence of student learning, while qualitative measures show descriptive evidence of what the student has learned. Selection of the appropriate assessment method is dependent upon the desired outcomes of student learning. For instance, if students completing a program should have knowledge of the discipline, the knowledge would be best measured by a carefully constructed quantitative assessment. But if students are expected to use multiple perspectives when solving a problem, the evidence might be better provided in some written form, and examined in a qualitative manner by using scoring rubrics.

## Constructed-response tests

Constructed-response tests are a type of non-multiple choice exam that requires some type of written or oral response. Selected-response tests consist of questions to be answered from a predetermined list of answers, with formats that include multiple choice, true/false, matching, or fill in the blanks. Each type of test has its benefits. Selected-response formats allow more questions to be asked in shorter time periods. Scoring is faster and it is easy to create comparable test forms. Since selected-response tests can normally be answered quickly, more items that covers several content areas can be administered in a short period of time. They can also be machine-scorable tests that allow quicker and more objective scoring. Constructed-response tests have the potential for gathering deeper information about a student's knowledge and understanding of a content area. Constructed-response items are more time consuming and allow fewer items to be covered.

## Portfolio assessments

A portfolio can be thought of as a scrapbook or photo album that records the progress and activities of the program and those who participate in it. It showcases them to interested parties both inside and outside of the program. Portfolios can be used to examine and measure progress by documenting the learning as it takes place. They extend beyond test scores to include a substantive picture of what a student is doing and experiencing. Portfolios are useful in documenting progress in higher-order goals such as applying skills and synthesizing experience beyond what standardized or norm-based tests can do. The portfolio contents are sometimes known as "evidence" or "artifacts." They can include drawings, writing, photos, video, audio tapes, computer discs, and copies of program-specific or standardized tests.

## Using portfolio assessment s

Portfolio assessment is best used for the following:
- Evaluating programs with flexible or individualized outcomes or goals.
- Allowing individuals and programs in the community to be involved in their own change and decisions to change.
- Giving information that provides a meaningful insight into behavioral change.
- Providing tools to ensure communications and accountability to a wide range of audiences. These participants, such as families or community members, may not be sophisticated in interpreting statistical data and can better appreciate more visual or experiential evidence of success being achieved.
- Assessing some of the more important and complex aspects of many constructs.

## Advantages of portfolio assessments

The advantages of using portfolio assessments include:
- Allows evaluators to see the student or group individually, with unique characteristics, needs, and strengths.
- Provides for future analysis and planning by showing a total pattern of an individual's strengths, weaknesses, or barriers to success.
- Serves as a concrete communication vehicle and provides ongoing communication or information exchange for those involved.

- Promotes ownership. Participants and groups can take an active role in where they have been and where they would like to go.
- Offers the possibility of addressing the limitations of traditional assessments. It offers the possibility of assessing more complex and important facets of a topic or area.
- Covers a broad scope of information and knowledge, from different people who know the program or person in different contexts.

## Process and product portfolios

Many portfolio assessments exist, but most fall into two types: process and product portfolios. Process portfolios document growth over time toward a goal. This documentation includes statements of end goals, criteria, and future plans. Also included should be baseline information or items used to describe a participant's performance or mastery at the beginning of the program. Other items may be selected at different interim points to demonstrate the steps toward mastery. Product portfolios include examples of the best efforts of a group or participant. These include final evidence, or items which demonstrate that end goals are achieved. They can encourage reflection about learning or change. They can help to show a sense of strength and ownership and to showcase or communicate a person's accomplishments.

## Characteristics of developing portfolios

Portfolios used for assessment have certain essential characteristics including:
- Having multiple data sources including both people and artifacts. People can be teachers, participants, or community members. Artifacts can be test scores, drawings, writings, videotapes, or audiotapes.
- Having authentic evidence that is related to program activities.
- Being dynamic and capturing change and growth. Portfolios should include different stages of mastery which will allow a much deeper understanding of the change process.
- Being explicit in that participants should know what is expected of them.
- Being integrated, meaning having the evidence to establish a connection between program activities and life experiences.
- Being based on ownership, or having the participant help to determine what evidence to include to show that the goals are being met.
- Being multipurposed, or allowing for assessment of the effectiveness of the program while also assessing the performance of the participant.

## Miscue analysis

A miscue analysis is an assessment in which a child reads a story aloud and the teacher checks for errors in the recognition and comprehension of words. Such an analysis might be performed in the following manner:
- The teacher instructs the student that they will read a passage aloud without the teacher's help.
- A videotape or audiotape should be made for analysis after the session.
- After reading the teacher marks all miscues, including insertions, mispronunciations, omissions, and corrections by the student.
- The teacher records the miscues by writing what the text said in one column and what the reader said in another.
- The miscues are analyzed using criteria, including whether the miscue went with the preceding context and whether it was corrected.
- Percentages are calculated based on the total number of miscues.

## Self-evaluations

Self-evaluations let students synthesize their past work over a given time period and do reflective writing. Self-evaluations are occasions for reflection and feedback. The goal is not right or wrong answers but thoughtful, tentative responses to questions. There are different types of self-evaluations, including those which ask students to look back and assess their own work, those which ask students to make connections over the entire term, and those which ask students to look ahead to future tasks. Self-evaluations can be a series of final entries in their journals as well as short or more extensive assignments that are both in and out of class.

## Samples of student work for assessment

Teachers can construct an assessment rubric by collecting a range of student work samples that all respond to the same skill and performance assessment. The teacher begins constructing the rubric by collecting a small range of work samples that do not necessarily respond to the same performance and skill assessment. The teacher then decides the assessment criteria for the rubric. The teacher will then group together related words or phrases to define each stack of work samples. The teacher clearly defines the terms and goals of the assessment in the rubric. The students are actively involved in developing the assessment measurements for the rubric with the teacher. The teacher makes known the expectations for the rubric. The teacher considers the forms of assessment used to evaluate student work.

## Journals and reflective thought

Journals let students write an ongoing record of thoughts, ideas, experiences, and reflections on a given topic. They go beyond the demands of usual written assignments as they promote integration of personal thoughts and expression with materials for a class. Journals provide a systematic means of collecting evidence and documenting learning for self-evaluation and reflections. Journals can be structured or free-form. Structured journals are when students are given specific questions, a set of guidelines, or a target on which to base their writing. Free-form lets students record thoughts and feelings with little direction. Whatever the form, journals are valuable in assessing a student's ability to observe, challenge, doubt, question, explore, and solve problems.

## Journals in assessments

Using journals for assessments require setting certain guidelines. Such guidelines that are helpful include:
- Designing journals to reflect specific learning objectives or goals of the course.
- Providing adequate instructions to students so they are aware of expectations. To promote effective writing, students should be given specific exercises or guiding questions.
- Explicitly discussing policies about privacy and confidentiality of the information. If journals are to be read or shared with others this should be highlighted. A teacher must disclose and report information that indicates a potential danger or harm.
- Periodically reviewing journals and providing feedback. Feedback would include constructive remarks, suggestions, questions, or encouragement.

## Types of journals

Journals can take on many forms. This all depends on the course, class objectives, topic, and instructor. The following are ideas that might stimulate instructors in developing their journal assignments based on class needs:

- 44 -

- Observational journal. An observational journal is used to increase a student's awareness of the relationship between events in the real world and class material. A teacher might want to assign students a specific location for a certain amount of time and have them record their observations.
- Personal experience journal. A personal experience journal lets students reflect upon their experiences in the context of a specific theory or idea. These journals promote active critical processing of course material and active encoding.
- Reading journal. A reading journal is to encourage reading assignment processing. The journals may target relationships between what students read and what they experience.

Journals for classes may take on many different forms. Some types of journals that might help stimulate a teacher's own journal assignment include:
- Minute reflection journal. These journals can be used in class to promote critical thinking that is related to particular presentations, activities, or discussions. Teachers may pose questions, then require students to take two or three minutes and record initial thoughts and reactions.
- Listening journals. These journals reflect on a presentation to clarify misconceptions or confusion. Listening journals are best suited for more difficult subjects. After information is presented, the teacher requires the student to paraphrase and explain what they heard. This can be used to monitor understanding and to clarify any confusion over concepts.
- Expansion journals. These are used to encourage a deep analysis of a particular concept or topic. After instruction, students select a single topic and expand on the information.

There are different forms of journals for classes. Here are some that might give teachers ideas for their class use:
- Daily reflection journals. These are used to encourage expression of thoughts, insights, and ideas in writing on a habitual basis. These can include emotional and personal thoughts. This can enhance personal insight as well as showing a grasp of writing strategies.
- Learning log journal. These journals promote reflection on the learning process and aid in self-assessment of strengths and weaknesses.
- Exchange journal. These journals are used in interactions between two or more peers, utilizing questions and answers.
- Academic journals. These are curriculum-oriented writings that promote reflection on material, both before and after instruction. These journals can help teachers focus on issues relevant to student concerns.

**Test validity and reliability**

A test is valid when it measures what it is supposed to measure. The validity of a test depends on the purpose for which it is to be used. For instance, a thermometer might measure temperature, but it cannot measure barometric pressure. A test is reliable when it yields results that are consistent. A test may be reliable and valid, valid and unreliable, reliable and invalid, or neither valid nor reliable. A test must be reliable for it to measure validity and the validity of a test is constrained by its reliability. If a test does not consistently measure a construct or domain, then it may not be expected to have a high degree of validity.

**Types of test validity**

Types of test validity include:
- Face validity. This asks the question: Does the test measure what should be measured?

- Content validity. This asks: Is the full content of the concept being defined included in the measure? It must include a broad sample of what is tested, emphasize material that is important and, require skills that are appropriate.
- Criterion validity. This asks: Is the measure consistent with what is already known and expected? There are two subcategories, which are predictive and concurrent.
- Predictive validity predicts a known association between the construct being measured and something else.
- Concurrent validity is associated with indicators that pre-exist or with something that already measures the same concept.
- Construct validity. This shows the measure that relates to a number of other measures that are specified.
- Discriminant validity. This type does not associate with unrelated constructs.

## Terms regarding consistency

Tests are reliable if they yield consistent results. The types of reliability include:
- Inter-observer. This requires consistent results among testers who are rating the same information.
- Test-retest. This requires the same results from testing at two different times with no treatment in between.
- Parallel-forms. This requires that two tests with different forms, supposedly testing the same material, yield the same results.
- Split-half reliability. This requires that items which are divided in half, such as odd versus even questions, provide the same results. For all forms of reliability, a quantitative measurement of reliability can be used.

## Threats to test internal validity

Factors affecting how valid a test is by itself include:
- History. Outside events that happen during the course of what is being studied may influence the results. It does not make the test less accurate.
- Maturation. Change due to aging or development between or within groups may affect validity.
- Instrumentation. The reliability is questioned because of a calibration change in a measuring device or changes in human ability to measure difference, such as fatigue or experience.
- Testing. Test-taking experience affects results. This refers to either physical or mental changes, such as changes in the attitude or physiological response of a participant after repeated measures.
- Statistical regression. This is the tendency to regress towards the mean, making some scores higher or lower.

If a measure is not reliable, some variation will occur between repeated measures.

## Additional threats totest  internal validity

A test may have the following threats to its internal validity:
- Selection. Participants in a group may be alike in certain ways, but will respond differently to the independent variable.
- Mortality. Participants drop out of a test, making the group unequal. Who drops out and why can be a factor.

- Interaction. Two or more threats can interact, such as selection-maturation when there is a difference between age groups causing groups to change at different ages.
- Contamination. This is when a comparison group in some way impacts another group, causing an increase of efforts. This is also called "compensatory rivalry."

## Test reliability

Views in recent decades on test reliability include:
- Temporal stability. This refers to implementing the same form of testing on two or more separate occasions to the same group of students. This is not practical as repeated measurements are likely to result in higher scores on later tests after students become familiar with the format.
- Form equivalence. This is relative to two different test forms based on the same content, administered once to the same group of students.
- Internal consistency. This relates to the coefficient of test scores obtained from a single test. When no pattern is found in the student responses, the test is probably too difficult and the students resorted to randomly guessing at the answers.
- Reliability is a necessary but insufficient condition for a test to be valid. The test might reflect consistent measurement but it may not be especially valid.

## Additional views of test validity

Some conventional views on test validity in recent years include:
- Face validity. This means that a test is valid at face value. As a check on face validity, psychometricians traditionally sent test items to teachers for modification. This was abandoned for a long time because of its vagueness and subjectivity. But face validity returned in the 1990s in another form, with validity defined as making common sense, being persuasive, and appearing right to the reader.
- Content validity. This draws inferences from test scores to a large domain of items that are similar to those on a test. The concern with content validity is a sample-population representation, meaning that the knowledge and skills covered by the test should be representative of the larger knowledge and skill domain.

## Regression analysis

Regression analysis can be used to establish validity of the criteria of a test. An independent variable may be used as a predictor of the dependent variable, which is the criterion variable. The correlation coefficient between them is known as the validity coefficient. For instance, test scores are the criterion variable. It is hypothesized that if the student passes the test, he or she would meet the criteria of knowing all the specific subject matter. Criterion validity values prediction over explanation. Prediction is concerned with mathematical or non-casual dependence, whereas explanation pertains to casual or logical dependence. For instance, one can predict the weather based on the mercury height in a thermometer. The mercury could satisfy the criterion validity as a predictor. Yet one cannot say why the weather changes because of the mercury's height.

## Sources of test invalidity

Two particular threats to test validity are known as "construct underrepresentation" and "construct-irrelevant variance." The first term indicates that the task being measured in the assessment fails to include important discussions or facets of the construct. So the test results will indicate a student's abilities within only a portion of the construct intended to be measured by the test. The second term means that a test measures too many variables. Many of these variables are irrelevant to the interpreted construct. This can take two forms. "Construct-irrelevant easiness" occurs when outside clues in format permit some individuals to respond correctly or appropriately in ways which are irrelevant to the assessed construct. "Construct-irrelevant difficulty" occurs when outside aspects make it more difficult for individuals to respond correctly.

## Assessing student reading strengths

A number of tests are available on the Internet for assessing comprehension levels, as well as paper and pencil charts for assessing fluency orally. Likewise, there are tests that determine the understanding of affixes, prefixes, suffixes, compounds, and contractions to name a few. The biggest problem is deciding which test to use in obtaining a snapshot of the child's ability to read and comprehend. The reading specialist and classroom teacher can work together to administer these tests and develop a plan of action to help at-risk students. These tests may be formal or standardized. They may either be norm-referenced or criterion-referenced. Good classroom teachers and reading specialists will blend the results of these tests to come up with an instructional model for the student.

## Communicating reading evaluation with parents

Parents of children who have been assessed as having problems with reading should be told the various steps that are necessary for an accurate and fair determination. The first step is using what is already known. A group of people, most often the reading specialist and teacher, evaluates the child with information that is already available. If more information is needed, the second step is collecting more information. The school will ask the parent for permission to evaluate the child. The school then collects more information. The third step is deciding whether the child is eligible for special education or related services. Those who are doing the evaluation then come to the parents to decide. The fourth step is developing the child's educational program. If the child is eligible for special education, a program to meet the child's needs will be developed.

## Evaluation necessities

Parents whose children are being tested for reading problems should be assured by teachers or reading specialists that the evaluation:
- Uses the native language such as Spanish or sign language unless it is clearly impossible to do so.
- Does not discriminate against the child because he or she has some type of disability or comes from a background that is racially or culturally different.
- Is administered by evaluators who know how to give the tests they decide to use.
- Will be used to determine if the child has a disability and to select the educational program that fits the child's needs. These decisions cannot be based solely on one evaluation.

## Culturally diverse parents

Communicating with a family about their child's reading development can be a challenge, especially if it is an exceptional child with culturally-diverse parents. Those who provides services to students and families of different cultural backgrounds should be aware of unique perspectives or communications styles that are common to those cultures. It is not always easy to tell how parents are reacting when they are told that their child has a disability, since people deal with feelings such as anxiety, anger, disappointment, and embarrassment in different ways. It is especially important for parents who have been educated outside of the mainstream of education in the United States to be informed of the educational choices that are available to their child. To do this, professionals should be sensitive to different values and experiences as well as beliefs that may be held by various ethnic and cultural groups toward special education.

In explaining the reading development of a child from a culturally diverse background, educators should use sensitivity by sending messages home to the parents in their native language, using an appropriate reading level, and listening to the messages that are returned. Courtesy, sincerity, and ample opportunity and time show concerns that can promote communications with and participation by parents who come from backgrounds that are culturally different. It is important during meetings that parents are given ample opportunity to respond without interruption. If a parent is formulating a response but does not express it quickly, this should not be viewed as a lack of interest on the part of the parent. Educators should listen with empathy and realize that parents can only develop trust as their understanding of programs and policies increases.

When communicating with families of different cultural backgrounds regarding their children's reading progress, educators should carefully consider these observations:

- Sharing space. People from different cultures use, value, and share space differently. It is considered appropriate for people to stand very close to each other while talking in some cultures, whereas others like to remain farther apart. For instance, Hispanics often view Americans as distant because they prefer more space.
- Touching. Rules for touching differ from culture to culture. In Hispanic and other Latin cultures there is often more touching seen when talking and individuals usually embrace when greeting each other. It is not customary in Vietnamese or other Asian cultures to shake hands with those of the opposite sex.
- Eye contact. It is customary among African-Americans to avert eyes when speaking, while Anglo Americans prefer to make direct eye contact.

## Conjoint behavioral consultation

Conjoint behavioral consultation (CBC) is a partnership model of service delivery in which parents, educators, other primary caregivers, and service providers all work in collaboration to meet the developmental needs of children, address their concerns, and achieve success by promoting the competencies of all parties concerned. CBC creates an opportunity for families and schools to work together for a common interest and to build upon and promote the capabilities and strengths of the family members and school personnel. Individual needs are identified and acted upon using an organized approach that is data-based and that has mutual and collaborative interactions between parents and children, along with the guidance and assistance of consultants such as school psychologists.

Conjoint behavioral consultant partnerships (CBC) can be implemented through four stages: needs identification, needs analysis, plan development, and plan evaluation. Three of these stages use interviews to structure the decisions to be made. Overall, the goal is to effectively address needs and desires of parents and teachers for the children. Specific objectives include:

- Addressing concerns as they happen across, rather than only within, individual settings.
- Enhancing home-school partnerships to benefit student learning and performance.
- Establishing joint responsibility for solving problems.
- Improving communications between children, families, and school personnel.
- Assessing needs in a comprehensive and functional way.
- Promoting continuity and consistency among agents of change and across various settings.
- Providing opportunities for parents to become empowered using strength-based orientation.

**"Reading First Program"**

The Reading First Program is a federal initiative adopted by the states and school districts with a goal of ensuring that all children in the United States learn to read by the end of the third grade. The program helps states and districts apply some of the scientific research on successful reading instruction, as well as instructional and assessment tools, to teach all children to read. These assessment tools include progress monitoring. The program will help provide necessary aid to states and districts by establishing research-based reading programs for children in kindergarten through the third grade. Funds for the program also focus on providing increased teacher professional development to ensure that all teachers have the skills they need to effectively teach this program.

**Reading First professional development programs**

Training in the five essential components of reading instruction is one of the most important elements of a quality professional development plan under the Reading First initiative. Teachers should learn effective strategies for providing explicit and systematic instruction for each component. Those components are:

- Phonemic awareness. Teachers should understand the difference between phonemic awareness and phonics. Phonemic awareness focuses on hearing sounds and learning how those sounds are put together.
- Phonics. Teachers should be trained in explicit and systematic phonics instruction based on scientifically based reading research.
- Fluency. Teachers will learn the various techniques for reading fluency, such as teacher modeling, repeating reading aloud, and choral reading.
- Reading vocabulary. Teachers can learn several effective techniques for teaching vocabulary.
- Reading comprehension. Professional development can give teachers certain comprehension strategies to help students understand what they read.

**Reading First guidelines for implementing plans**

There are certain requirements for implementing federal Reading First professional development plans. They include:

- The plans must be closely aligned with the principles of scientifically-based reading research and the five essential components of reading instruction. The programs must provide instruction in scientifically-based reading instructional materials, programs, strategies, and approaches. Also, the programs must train teachers in the appropriate use of assessment tools and in the analysis and interpretation of gathered data.
- An eligible professional development provider must deliver the professional development program. To be eligible, the provider must be able to train teachers, including special education teachers, in reading instruction that is grounded in scientifically-based reading research.
- Teachers must be instructed in teaching all components of reading instruction and must understand how the components are related, the progression in which they should be taught, and the underlying structure of the English language.

**Implementing Reading First programs**

Certain leadership guidelines are needed for educators implementing Reading First programs. Included in such guidelines are:

- Provide a vision. Implementing such a program requires a clear vision of how students and teacher will benefit from a new approach to reading. Teachers should understand that they can make a greater impact on many students' reading skills because they are better able to diagnose reading problems.
- Set priorities. The name Reading First Initiative is so named because reading is critical to the future success of students in a number of content areas.
- Create ownership. Programs will run more efficiently when teachers help in decision-making.
- Foster peer support. Teachers should have the time to meet with reading specialists and other colleagues for formal professional development as well as informal opportunities to talk.

## Reading First summer programs

Since Reading First is a federal initiative, many states may have similar state guidelines for carrying out the initiative, such as summer reading programs. Some guideline examples might include:
- The use of Reading First-approved core, supplemental, and intervention programs.
- Daily 90-minute uninterrupted reading instructional blocks. This would include systematic delivery of explicit instruction using approved core reading program material.
- Intervention services provided for students who are below the mastery of reading skills.
- Evidence of teacher's use of data to drive instruction. Reports on the program developed by the state will include information on the number of students served, the summer school teacher credentials, student achievement gain, and percentage of students meeting end of grade benchmarks at the beginning and end of the summer program.

## Literary research across grade levels

Just as students must perform research at the university level, reading specialists also do research— about research. Finding literary research and disseminating it across grade levels may be crucial to the success of a reading program. Some tips for finding such research include:
- Focus the topic. State the topic as a question and ask other questions that might also address the topic.
- Find overviews or background information. Abstracts of research can give the major aspects of the topic being researched without going into a lot of detail. Abstracts can also be used to find out important facts such as names of people and concepts that can be used as keywords in a search.
- Prepare the search. Circle the main words in the topic statement. Brainstorm for related words that might be used to describe the topic.
- Find books. Books can provide detailed information on a topic.

## School district reading programs

A school district might implement reading program guidelines that include the following:
- Each student in the district has the right to learn to read, regardless of race, creed, color, gender, or social or economic status.
- Reading is not just a curriculum subject. Reading is a developmental process which involves language, emotions, thinking, interaction, and judgments. Reading permeates the entire curriculum at every grade level.
- Reading requires skills which can and should be taught at appropriate times in appropriate ways.
- The district will provide educational programs and developmental reading instruction for grades K-12 that will ensure that every student at every grade level has the opportunity to acquire reading skills.

## Peer helpers

The peer helper and adult resource connection is not often understood by educators who are unfamiliar with the concept, but that linkage is a bedrock of the program. Young people with serious worries can be helped by their peers and by adults. Help can come early and can take place where there is trust. Students can build a circle of support around them with such programs. It is a challenge, however, because students often feel rejected or neglected by their peers. Research shows that the best way to keep stress away is being part of a stable, tight-knit group. Peer helpers can be trained to help with continued needs that help foster more well-rounded communities within schools.

## Intended outcomes for peer helpers

Intended outcomes for peer helpers include:
- The helpers being more likely to refer their friends to adults for help when there is a need.
- The helpers will know when, where, and how to make referrals to the right resource people.
- An increased understanding of the seriousness of depression can be gained by the peer helpers, and they can help identify the mixed behavior types that can be warning signs of depression.
- The helpers can identify and respond to warning signs of suicide.
- Peer helpers can develop an increased opportunity to improve the quality of a school's circle of support.
- Peer helpers show an increased level of personal development such as the sense of personal efficacy, self-esteem, social responsibility, and locus of control.

## Conveying high expectations

Researchers have found certain ways that a school may let students know that the school's expectations of them are high:
- Establish policies that emphasize how important it is to achieve academically. This can be done by notifying parents if students are not meeting the academic expectations or setting minimally acceptable achievement levels for students to participate in sports or extracurricular activities.
- Use slogans that communicate high expectations for the students such as "Yes we can."
- Protect instructional time and discourage tardiness, absenteeism, and interruptions.
- Provide insistent coaching to students who experience difficulty with learning tasks. Researchers say that excusing children from trying hard to succeed in academics because it is not fair or because it is hopeless to expect any more does not really help students in learning. It detracts from academic skills and can also lower motivation and self-esteem.

## Curriculum-based assessment

Instructional strategies are not fail-proof when it comes to teaching students new skills. But a number of data-based strategies have been identified that, when used with an objective and systematic assessment, can lead to a curriculum that will help improve student performance. Such an assessment is curriculum-based. These are models of assessment that emphasize a direct relationship to the student's curriculum. These assessments use measures from the curriculum to evaluate the effectiveness of instruction and determine what changes to the instruction can lead to more effective teaching methods and improved student achievement. The assessment provides information on how the student's behavior changes on a generic task of constant difficulty. Increases in the behavior being measured on equivalent forms of the task would represent growth academically.

## Problem-solving process

A problem-solving process can be used with methods to assess or measure how well the curriculum is meeting students' needs so that changes in the curriculum can be made. The process includes:

- Identify the problem to be solved. For instance, a marked underachievement in reading.
- Identify alternative solutions to the problem, such as a new reading method.
- Implement new programs and test alternative solutions. Revise unsuccessful solutions.
- Terminate the problem. This includes revising unsuccessful instructional programs. When making changes in a student's instructional program, teachers should be aware of various alterable characteristics of instruction that are under the direct control of the teacher.

## Evolutionary changes vs. revolutionary changes

Instructional changes can be viewed as either revolutionary or evolutionary. Revolutionary changes are those with major modifications in an instructional program. Evolutionary changes are minor ones. Evolutionary changes may be made in certain parts of the instructional plan such as time, activity, materials, or motivation. A revolutionary change could include the method of instruction from a language experience approach to direct instruction. Technically sound achievement indicators for such decisions include the number of words read correctly for reading, and the number of correct letter sequences in two minutes or the number of words spelled in two minutes for spelling. For written expression, the indicators could be the number of words written, the number of correctly spelled words, or the number of correct word sequences in two minutes.

## Culturally responsive curricula

Effective curricula that are culturally responsive share certain characteristics. These include:

- The curriculum is integrated and interdisciplinary. It does not rely on one-time activities or "sprinkling" the traditional curriculum with a few minority individuals.
- It is authentic, connected to the child's real life, and child-centered. It uses materials from the child's culture and history to illustrate concepts and principles.
- It develops critical thinking skills.
- It often incorporates strategies that use cooperative learning, whole language instruction, and self-esteem building, and recognizes diverse styles of learning.
- It is supported by appropriate staff development and pre-service preparation.
- It is part of a coordinated strategy. Successful implementation requires a school climate that is receptive and the recognition that the hidden curriculum in any school can be a powerful ally or a powerful enemy.

## Curriculum materials for cultural relevance

A number of criteria should be evaluated when looking for curriculum materials that are culturally relevant. Teachers should look for invisibility, stereotyping, selectivity, imbalance, unreality, isolation, language bias, and fragmentation. Also to be looked for in books is the inappropriate treatment of African Americans, Native Americans, Asian Americans, and Hispanic Americans, especially when the "one size fits all view" is expressed. This is where instructional material reflects through generalization that there is a single Hispanic, African, Asian, or Native culture. The sidebar approach also should be avoided. This is where a few isolated events relevant to ethnic experiences are relegated to a box or sidebar that is set apart from the rest of the text.

## Adjusting teaching styles for different cultures

There are commonly differences found among cultures in how one prefers to learn some type of information and how that knowledge is displayed. A lack of understanding of different learning styles and the influence of one's cultural background can bring conflict, lack of achievement, and confusion. It is common for a culturally different student's preferred ways of learning to be in contrast with those ways that are used in American schools and are suggested for teacher training programs. It is important to discern the learning preferences for a recently arrived immigrant student, and then teach to those preferences. Evaluation of the learning and teaching styles and process for acquiring a second culture and language may change how students are taught in America. Some studies suggest that teachers understanding preferred learning styles of students allows them to adjust their teaching style to maximize teaching effectiveness.

## Facilitating culturally-relevant approaches

A teacher can become a facilitator in transferring school knowledge to that of real life by involving a student's home culture in learning. Ways to do this include:
- Have students share artifacts from home that are reflective of their culture.
- Have students write about traditions that their families share.
- Have students research different aspects of their culture.
- Have members of the community who share a culture with your students speak to the class on various subjects.
- Involve the class in making something relevant to other cultures (such as a piñata for studying the Hispanic culture.)

## School wide reading programs

When critically looking at goals and needs, schools should recognize that the ultimate goal is better results. Measuring progress, being accountable for results, and making changes based on reliable data are vital aspects of school wide improvement. Many school leaders look upon this process as a work in progress. Continuous data-driven accountability involves teams of teachers and reading specialists engaging in the following activities:
- Combine information from multiple measurements on all groups of students.
- Organize data to clarify strengths and needs of the school as a whole.
- Disaggregate information on students to determine whether some subgroups are experiencing common problems.
- Keep alert to the implications of the quality of education supported by the school as a whole.

## Continuously-monitored school literacy program

Monitoring a school literacy program involves systematically examining students' reading progress and teachers' instructional strategies. Monitoring is a continuous process. Any monitoring has three basic components: collecting information regularly, analyzing and evaluating that information, and taking action to improve student performance. Other activities may precede these components such as articulating questions on which to focus the monitoring and determining gaps in practice. When teachers monitor the school's literacy program, they keep tabs on student achievement and success in reading and writing. They collect literacy-focused assessment data including standardized tests and alternative assessments. They also look beyond assessment data to children's attitudes toward reading, comments from families, and other pertinent information.

## Concerns in monitoring literacy programs

Before the monitoring of literacy programs can begin, teachers and administrators should be aware of some concerns about monitoring. Attempts to evaluate reading programs and student reading achievement often confuses the issue instead of making it clearer. Reasons for the confusion include the fact that the evaluation is often initiated as an afterthought. A plan is not in place to answer initial evaluation questions before the process of teaching reading starts in classrooms. Secondly, the evaluation may be hampered by unclear objectives. If little attention has been given to why the evaluation is taking place, it may not be clear what is being evaluated. There is also confusion about the term evaluation. Evaluation determines the worth of something. Evaluation systems are based on data and assessment information.

## Continuous progress monitoring

Continuous progress monitoring in order to critically analyze school programs such as reading is an ongoing strategy with multiple measurements. Useful information requires assessments often, at least four times a year. Measurement strategies include qualitative methods such as personal interviews and focus groups, along with standardized tests and surveys. These provide in-depth information about the results of reforms. No single survey or all-purpose data collection tool will meet all of a school's information needs. Multiple measurements are vital in tracking the process of change. Data systems should not be relied upon for monitoring everything. When making a change, teachers rely on both hard data and their intuition, but those perspectives should be validated by assessments from the outside.

## Data sources

Data sources can be used to critically analyze school wide programs such as reading so that any appropriate changes can be made to meet students' goals and needs. Many schools have linked aligned instructional benchmarks to broader objectives that are periodically measured by their state's assessment programs. Schools, through aligned assessments, can examine results for several purposes to track absolute progress, compare progress to benchmark goals, and to find patterns that reveal progress or weaknesses over time. An ongoing analysis of data can determine timely adjustments. Aligned information can allow educators to examine instructional variations that might make a difference in academic achievements. This lets educators ask: What should be done at various levels within the classroom or school wide to prevent the problems identified by the data?

## Sense of ownership

Continuous monitoring that allows analysis of school wide programs such as reading gives the faculty and staff a sense of ownership by putting accountability in their hands. Few surprises exist in continuous monitoring because the school is in control of its own assessment. Teachers and school leaders score many of their own tests so they learn the results immediately. As teams of reading specialists and classroom teachers examine the data, they look for information about different aspects of the subject within the school. With data analysis, questions may be asked such as: Are there grades with an especially strong or weak showing in the subject? Are non-English or limited-English speakers improving their use of test materials?

## Reading specialist

Reading specialists help staff develop knowledge of literacy theory and instructions. They are consultants and collaborating teachers for classroom teachers, aides, parents, and other teachers such as special education, speech, music, and art. Some schools have chosen to replace reading specialists with teaching assistants who lack specialized literacy training. When this happens, a grave injustice is done to students, teachers, and the literacy program. Reading specialists provide expert instruction to learners who differ in language, learning style, culture, and ability. They share effective learning strategies and practices with school staff and parents, and they serve as experts for the school and district on information about reading and literacy instruction.

## Professional development

Classroom teachers often feel pressured to meet student achievement goals and may even worry about job security because of the high-stakes involved in testing. Educators think of themselves as professionals, but a professional attitude is not always fostered by school leaders. These leaders should create and advance a climate that gives teachers access to cutting-edge, research-based professional development in reading programs to encourage them to share instructional methods and strategies. Districts interested in starting professional development must initiate or find programs that:
- Provide a strong correlation to district and school goals.
- Are based on scientific reading research.
- Include a format that provides ongoing training.
- Offer frequent opportunities for teacher dialogue and sharing as part of the process.

## Accelerating reading achievement

There are times when student performance on state standardized tests is subpar. When this is the case, taking a focused look at what areas need assistance is the first step. Even if achievement is lagging overall, reading may be the best place to start since it is the prime academic skill. Armed with a starting point, reading teachers and reading specialists can join forces with the core academic content area teachers of selected students. Establishing regular lines of communication between the reading teacher and specialist and the content area teachers can be a significant factor in improving problem areas. The content teachers can communicate how students are doing on specific assignments, as well as their overall progress, effort, attitude, and achievement. Actions can then be focused on the individual students and improvement can occur.

## Home-school connections

Schools are now opening their doors more as community resources to serve students and families. So-called "full-service" schools show that they are paying attention to the students' holistic needs as well as their academic needs. These schools offer health, counseling, social service, and other programs to support learning and growth. Some community-initiated activities are also transforming schools. These communities are taking responsibility to use information about schools to offer new ways to improve schools. They are working with schools on recurring problems. The schools are beginning to change in ways that bring more voices to the table when it comes to decision-making.

## Community involvement

Schools that actively develop students' critical thinking skills and real-world knowledge applications, as well as provide services and enrichment activities, should forge new relationships with communities in order to improve learning for the school's students. This allows community member to become more familiar with the school and its staff. It also structures the school to meet some of the broader needs that the families of students might have. The school can also become a resource for families and community members. The school can serve as a center for community meetings, local theatrical productions, candidate nights, health screening, or other activities that help the community. Forging these good relationships can help the school in a number of ways, such as developing support for school bond initiatives that require the community to vote.

## Home and school socialization

Student success appears to be related to congruence between home and school socialization. Studies show that high achievers have a home environment that is congruent with a school environment. High achievers learned how to independently and obediently complete tasks at home. Such behaviors are important to school success as well. A dissonance between home and school may be caused by cultural differences in some cases. Some studies have indicated that black children prefer and tend to perform better in communal learning settings while white students tend toward more competitive settings. Cultural dissonance may also lead to wrong interpretations of parent behaviors, creating misunderstandings between school and home.

## Predictions

Predictions of students' academic achievement can be made by looking at the congruence between their home and school cultures. Students have the tendency to be more successful when their home and school cultures have similarities. There also tends to be less success when there is a disconnection between the home and the school cultures. Moving from the familiar environment of the home to a more unfamiliar environment at the school can be especially detrimental for many minority and low-income students. This effect can be minimized or eliminated when the schools work with the students and their families in helping both adapt to the school environment.

## Community and family partnerships

Literacy programs that involve parent and community components can be created in a number of ways. Some will focus on the school aspect, while others focus on the parents or community as the most active part of the program. Both approaches have the same goal, which is to engage all the members of a community in ensuring that children are literate. A formal school, family, and community partnership is one way to meet such goals. This is a comprehensive program that consists of activities that are chosen by each school to enable students to reach their literacy goals. Well-organized partnerships can create goal-oriented activities that allow students to reach high levels of achievement in literacy.

Nearly everyone in education agrees that parents and local communities should be involved in education. Studies show that children perform better when parents are involved in their children's schools. Community members can become involved in schools, acting as role models and mentors, and giving an extra measure of support for both students and teachers. There is no one approach for getting schools, parents, and communities together for literacy programs, but there are different types of activities that will help them work together in supporting literacy. This includes assistance with parenting, communicating, volunteering, reading at home, decision-making, and collaborating with the community. Schools should consider a community's unique character and needs in starting a community and family involvement program.

## Community members making a home-school connection

There are a number of concrete steps that community members can take to help schools improve and especially to help more children to read. Community members can:
- Become a learning partner or tutor. The citizen can tutor a child in the child's own neighborhood or in a local elementary school. Volunteers might read with or to a child for 30 minutes a week for at least eight weeks, and could also take the child to the library to get him or her a library card.
- Volunteer to serve as a community coordinator for a community reading program. A number of organizations can work to recruit tutors. This person can also work with local schools to match community members and children.
- Ask organizations to help support community reading programs. Local businesses can be encouraged to donate supplies or allow employees time off to volunteer in school.

## Parental education and socioeconomic status

The exact nature of the impact parental education and social economic status has on student achievement although it does have an impact. Studies have found that parental education and family socioeconomic status alone are not necessarily predictors of how students will achieve academically. Studies have found that parental education accounts for about a quarter of the variance in student test scores while socioeconomic status accounts for slightly more than a quarter. Other research indicates that dysfunctional home environments, low expectations from parents, parenting that is ineffective, differences in language and high mobility levels may account for the low achievement levels among those students that come from lower socioeconomic levels.

## Negative peer influences

Students, teenagers specifically, look to each other to learn and this sometimes brings about problems. Teenagers are growing and learning and through this development the students look toward each other to acquire what their peers deem to be acceptable. In many instances this may lead to inaccurate understandings. Teenagers purposely acquire knowledge sometimes that is unmistakably wrong and continue to use it in everyday situations. Some students are so influenced by their culture that, even though they are capable of speaking properly, they will not do so for fear they will not fit in with their peers. These students who are properly taught will acknowledge to adults they are speaking in slang yet still do so because their culture has shaped them to do so.

## Hispanic culture reading lesson

Children can be find places on the map of the United States with names that come from the Spanish language such as San Francisco, Los Angeles, and Pueblo. An activity can be done that invites students to use the library, class or Internet to find Hispanic Americans in history. Students can be invited to design a postage stamp of the Hispanic Heritage stamp series that might show a famous Hispanic American or some aspect of the Hispanic-American culture or history. Students can be given a list of Spanish words and be invited to find the English equivalent such as "ensalada" -- "salad." Invite students to create books to help them learn the Spanish words for the numbers one to 10 and for the common colors. For example, 1 -- uno, yellow -- amarillo.

## Text structure knowledge

A reader's knowledge about the text patterns and structures of different genres and their ability to use those understandings effectively help them to formulate meaning. For example, poems may rhyme or have repeating patterns, expository passages develop logically, short stories or novels have elements such as characters and setting, headings indicate the major text sections, and summaries sum up the main points of a text. When students become aware of the text structure, they will better understand what is being read and will remember it for longer periods. Readers use text knowledge to differentiate between narrative and expository reading and will accordingly adapt their reading strategies.

## Prior knowledge

Prior knowledge is a combination of one's attitudes, experiences and knowledge which already exist. Attitudes can range from beliefs about ourselves as learners or being aware of our own strengths and weaknesses. It can also be our level of motivation and responsibility for our own learning. The experiences from our daily activities, especially ones with our friends and families, give us a background from which we derive most of our understanding. Individual events in our lives provide us experiences from which to draw from; both bad and good and influence how we deal with future situations. This knowledge is drawn from a wide variety of things, from knowledge of specific content areas and the concepts within, to the goals that we have for ourselves academically.

## Dialect

A dialect is a regionally or socially distinctive variety of a language which is characterized by particular accents, phrases, vocabulary and grammar. While it may be easy to distinguish between a dialect and a language, the difference is often a matter of degree. For instance, two individuals are said to speak different languages when they are unable to understand one another's speech. Comparatively, they are said to speak differing dialects if they can understand one other, albeit not perfectly.

There are exceptions, however. An example would be when a single dialect, most often that spoken by the majority of the population, comes to predominance as the official, standard form of the language, even so far as becoming the accepted, written form of that language. Hence, the English dialect spoken by a majority of those who speak English becomes standard English, not because it has unique linguistic features but because of its predominance among those who speak English.

## Interrelatedness of reading, writing and speaking

Language is developed as it is used, in response to the demands placed upon it. A number of factors shape language, including the nature of the speaker or writer, that of the audience, the relationship between the two, one's purpose for speaking or writing, the nature of the subject at hand and the medium through which one communicates.

A language may be enhanced in its development by a wide variety of tasks in which it is used. For instance, students acquire most of their knowledge through language, and as such, education would be a means through which language itself is developed. This development is enhanced by the various opportunities to use language in many different situations, in order to attend to diverse tasks.

## Distinctions between writing and speaking

Distinctions between writing and speech are fundamental to discussions that surround language. Speech is that form of communication expressed orally which can be perceived audially, while writing is that form of communication which is expressed through a shared set of symbols, known to both the author and the reader, representing speech.

Other aspects of this relationship between writing and speech are less tangible. Both writing and speech are forms of communication, which in itself is an abstract concept. A common difference between the two is the structure of written language. The symbols which express speech in writing may not correspond directly to sound, and sounds may not always be expressed phonetically in the written language. For instance, as writing is a means of reproducing the spoken word, and the spoken word is a means of reproducing an abstract thought, it may be difficult to pronounce contrasts between words that look and sound alike but have different meanings.

## Difficulty of phonemic awareness

Phonemic awareness is difficult because:
- There are about 40 phonemes or sound units in the English language despite there being only 26 letters in the alphabet.
- There are 250 different spellings representing distinct sounds such as "f," which may be represented as "ph" or "gh."
- Phonemes, or sound units, are not necessarily obvious. They must be learned. The sounds that make up words are not distinctly separate from one other, a state referred to as being "coarticulated." Additionally, words such as "fat" and "hat" are said to have different phonemes "f" and "h" in English despite little difference in sound to distinguish the words. These are called a "minimal pair." If no minimal pair can be found to demonstrate two distinct sounds, these sounds may be termed "allophones," which are variant sounds not recognized by a speaker as distinct and as such are not significantly different in language. They are therefore looked upon as being the same.

## Guided oral reading

Guided oral reading is an instruction strategy that may help students improve various reading skills, including fluency in reading. In general, a teacher, parent or peer will read a passage aloud and model for the student an example of fluent reading. Students then reread the text quietly, sometimes several times, on their own. The text should be at the student's level of independent reading. Students then read aloud and reread the same passage. Usually reading the text four times is sufficient. Another technique is to have an adult or peer read with the student by modeling fluent reading and then ask the student if he or she will read the same passage aloud while being encouraged by the adult or peer.

## Phonological system

Language is defined as a system of expressing and receiving information in a meaningful way.  Speech is the verbal expression of language.  Four language systems have been identified:  Phonological (sound) system, Syntactic (structural) system, Semantic (meaning) system, and Pragmatic (social & cultural) system.

The Phonological, or sound, system of language refers to the meaningful sounds of a language and their corresponding letters.  These meaningful sounds are called phonemes.  There are approximately 40 phonemes in the English language, and by the time a child is four or five years of age, he should be pronouncing most of these correctly.

A grapheme is a letter or combination of letters in the written language which represents a phoneme in the spoken language.  In the English language, a phoneme is often represented by more than one grapheme.  For example, the word "thin" has four graphemes (t-h-i-n) but only three phonemes (th-i-n). The phoneme "th" is considered a digraph, a term referring to two letters representing one sound.

- 60 -

## Syntactic system

Language is defined as a system of expressing and receiving information in a meaningful way. Speech is the verbal expression of language. Four language systems have been identified: Phonological (sound) system, Syntactic (structural) system, Semantic (meaning) system, and Pragmatic (social & cultural) system.

The Syntactic, or structural, system of language refers to the structural organization (grammar) of a language which dictates how words are combined into sentences. Components of syntax include word order, capitalization and punctuation. Children apply these rules when creating sentences varying from simple sentences to compound ones and eventually complex sentences. By the time a child is four or five years of age, he should be able to utilize the same grammar as other family members.

Another component of the Syntactic system is the concept of morphemes, which are the smallest units of meaning. The individual parts of a morpheme mean nothing on their own. For example, the word "thin" is a single morpheme made up of four graphemes (t-h-i-n) and three phonemes (th-i-n).

## Terms

Semantic property
Contains the components of a word's meaning. For example, female is a semantic property of girl, woman, waitress, etc.

Semantic class
Contains words sharing a semantic property. Semantic classes can intersect. For instance, the words female and young can be components of the semantic class for girl.

Semantic feature
A notational method that may be used to express whether semantic properties exist or do not exist by using a plus or minus sign.
Semantic change

The change in one meaning of a word. Each word has a varieties of connotations and senses which can be removed, added, or altered over time. Sometimes such change is to the extent that words of a particular time period mean something very different than the same words from a previous time.

Semantic progression
Refers to the evolution of word usage, normally to where the original meaning is very different from its original usage.

## Progress monitoring

Progress monitoring is a classroom-based assessment for reading instruction that evaluates how well a child is learning based upon a systematic review by teachers of children who perform academic tasks equivalent to those which are a part of the student's daily classroom instruction. Unlike a one-time test for proficiency, this type of ongoing assessment helps to determine whether students are making sufficient progress or require more help in achieving grade-level reading objectives. Progress monitoring should have certain benchmarks to ensure reliability and validity. Progress monitoring can assess the efficacy of various components of a student's instruction in reading such as in phonemic awareness, phonics, fluency, vocabulary and reading comprehension.

## Socratic questioning

Socratic questioning is at the heart of critical thinking skills. It is more than just having a one-word answer or an agreement and disagreement from students. Socratic questions force students to make assumptions, sort through both relevant and irrelevant points and, additionally, explain those points. This instruction can take many different forms including:
- Raising basic issues.
- Probing beneath the surface of matters.
- Pursing areas of thought fraught with problems.
- Helping students find the structure of their own thinking.
- Helping students develop clarity, accuracy and relevance.
- Helping students make judgments by reasoning on their own.
- Helping students to think about evidence, conclusions, assumptions, implications, points of view, concepts and interpretations.

## Metadiscursive

Research shows that teaching in content areas should include teaching students to be metadiscursive, meaning that they should not only be able to be part of many different discourse communities but that they should also know why and how it is that they are taking part as well as what those engagements mean for them and others in the realm of larger power relationships and social position.

This does not mean that the historical limitations in integrating content literacy should be ignored. Teaching content literacy should still focus on the knowledge and beliefs of students and teachers, which requires considering questions such as how teachers balance the notion of subject-matter literacy as a metadiscursive practice while encountering probable resistance from students who have become comfortable with the notion that content area learning is a matter of rote memory and information reproduction.

## Trade books

Trade books are instructional materials written specifically for students but are not textbooks, per se. They may be used to help improve reading skills, develop knowledge of content areas and further understand the world. Trade books can be a valued complement to teaching and curriculum. They may also affect the appreciation which a student has for content-related literature. These books should not replace thorough instruction in reading skills, however. Trade books also are not an alternative to teaching concepts of content areas, but rather, these texts can help students understand concepts by putting them into an appropriate context. Teachers can use strategies such as this to help develop better reading skills and help students comprehend the text.

## Organizing stories

Writers create and then search through their drafts to find narrative elements which might improve their work. Throughout this process they must consider the points which they are trying to make and ask themselves what messages and themes exist in their work, and how they might be expressed in final form. Additionally, a rough draft can serve as an outline that lists statements central to a story. Sentences and paragraphs need to be carefully analyzed, whether one is writing fiction or non-fiction, and during this process, labeling paragraphs helps to organize the story through the linkage of similar blocks of text. In news writing, reporters use the "inverted pyramid" model to organize a story from the most to least important pieces of information. This theoretically makes it easier in the editing process because editors know where to find the least important text. That is not always the case, however. Writers who are comparing or contrasting items may find that a point-by-point or block-by-block approach to story organization is more beneficial for their purposes.

## Writing developmental process

Writing is a developmental process. It requires teachers to give students a greater degree of responsibility in making decisions about topics, genre and collaboration whenever they are writing. Teachers who recognize writing as a process understand that:

- Writing is recursive. The writer moves within the components. Some writers might produce drafts during revision while others may naturally combine revision and editing.
- Both process and writing product should be evaluated and assessed to allow both student and teacher to focus on the learning taking place during writing rather than merely on the finished work.
- The basic components of writing are similar from person to person yet each writer is unique and develops their own writing process.
- Writing abilities are mostly acquired through practice and frequent writing.
- Many writers attribute their skill to reading frequently.

## Publishing student writing

Publishing a student's writing is a means of helping students look positively on literature. Publication rewards a student's interest in writing and also boosts his confidence level. Publishing is a means by which an instructor can help and encourage a student who is reluctant to write. This also helps children practice their writing and as such develop their writing skills. Schools have traditionally had limited means of publishing student work, oftentimes merely a student newspaper or an occasional literary journal. The feedback one gets writing in class may not bring about the feelings that one would have when seeing their work in print and read by others. But the Internet provides opportunities for publishing student work. There now exist a number of websites which specifically publish student work, while using a class web page or a weblog (blog) is another alternative available to instructors.

## Use of weblogs (blogs)

Weblogs, usually called "blogs," are an easy way for students to publish their work. This can be done in various ways: students can manage their own individual blogs or the class can have one together to which a group of students contribute. There are a number of considerations which the student should take into account before producing a blog, as it is on the Internet. The students should consider which topics are appropriate about which to write. Their teachers, parents and classmates can see their blogs, as can total strangers. Students should consider topics with which they are comfortable, and whether they will be interesting. They need consider their audience, and as such the types of details that they should include as well as any background information which the audience might require in order to comprehend the work.

## Word consciousness

When teachers foster word consciousness, students are able to better develop their vocabularies. Word consciousness is an awareness and an interest in words, the meanings of those words and the power of the word. Word-conscious students possess a larger vocabulary and are able to use that vocabulary correctly. Students can enjoy words and can be eager to learn new ones. They also know how to learn them. Teachers can help students develop word consciousness in several ways. For instance, a teacher might call the students' attention to the ways authors choose words in order to express meanings. Another means is to encourage students to engage in word play, such as using puns. Teachers may help them research the origin or history of a word, or encourage the students to look for examples of a word's usage in their daily lives.

## Dramatic activities as scaffolding

Elementary and English as a Second Language classes can receive scaffolding for effective literacy from dramatic activities. Researchers have found that scaffolded play with students of elementary age allow them to participate in language learning in an active way. Students may also be more motivated to discuss, organize, rewrite and perform in the dramatic presentation.

Students have also become more engaged in which there were interwoven activities involving literature, drama, music and movement, even for at-risk students in grades K-3. Activities involving bilingual children in which their own cultural experiences are called upon and valued also helps motivate and support literacy and meaningful learning environments.

## Combined grade classes

Combined classes are those which include more than one grade level in a classroom. These classes are sometimes referred to as split classes, blended classes or double-year classes. These classes will usually include the required curriculum for each of the two grades that are represented, yet some class activities may take place with children who are from both of the combined grades. This type of grouping takes place more frequently in smaller schools, yet on occasion in larger schools when the number of children in different age groups tends to have fluctuated. The main purpose of such classes appears to be maximizing resource use with regard to personnel and space instead of capitalizing on the diversity of ability and experience within the groups of mixed ages.

## Reducing student disruption

Little data exists demonstrating that punitive "zero tolerance" policies have significantly improved school safety or student behavior. Researchers have begun to discover that which is and is not efficacious in preventing school violence. The programs that seem to be most effective are proactive rather than reactive, involving families, students, teachers and communities. They include a number of components that help address the complexity of school violence and disruption. There is far more data available supporting the effectiveness of bullying prevention programs, anger management or peer mediation programs than there is to support how well violence and disruption is stemmed by technological means such as surveillance cameras or metal detectors.

## Eye coordination problems

Four general types of eye coordination problems can affect a young reader -- astigmatism, eye-hand coordination, visual motor problems and other conditions, and esophoria. Children will get into postures that are distorted while trying to get one eye to function. They will often put their head down on their arms, covering an eye with their hand or rotating their head so that their nose bridge interferes with one eye's vision. Esophoria is another eye coordination problem that tends to turn eyes inward. A child will see objects smaller than they really are. The only way that a child can view the object as larger is to move it closer to him or her.

## Discrepancy criteria

Most state and federal guidelines for identifying those with reading disabilities have as a foundation an ability-achievement discrepancy. It is usually operationalized as an IQ-achievement discrepancy. An assumption behind such guidelines has been that poor readers with discrepancies or the reading disabled, have a unique type of poor reading, different from other poor reading types. Such criteria have been attacked by reading disability researchers, who argue that there are many similarities between those who read poorly and have discrepancies and poor readers who have no discrepancies such as children whose IQs are on level with their reading ability but are not low enough for them to be termed intellectually disabled. Both groups seem to have problems with word decoding and phonological functions and little evidence is present to support the notion that poor readers with discrepancies can eventually perform better than those with none.

## Intrinsic processing disorder and processing tests

An educational diagnosis of reading disorders normally employs processing tests, which test memory, language ability, and visual and auditory processing. Poor readers do have certain difficulties in certain processing measures such as decoding words and phonological processing. These tests can provide early identification of reading problems and also help plan an educational program for the student. The problem is that word decoding and phonological processing measures are not always emphasized in identification of reading disabilities in schools. Many such measures lack validity and reliability and interpretations of these tests also present problems. A poor performance on these tests is most often interpreted as evidence of a processing disorder intrinsic to the reader, but researchers emphasize that processing is shaped not only by innate characteristics such as genetics but also experiences such as reading in class.

## Warning behaviors of dyslexia

Some "red flag" behaviors that may indicate dyslexia include:
1. Avoiding difficult tasks, especially those that involve reading, writing or spelling.
2. Spending entirely too much time on tasks or not completing work.
3. Propping up their head when writing.
4. Guessing when he or she does not know a word.
5. Knowing a word one day but not remembering it the next day.
6. Mixing manuscript with cursive letters.
7. Having a vocabulary that exceeds their reading ability.
8. Conceptually understanding math but having difficulty with reading and writing problems.
9. Having a wide spread between verbal and mathematics scores on standardized tests.
10. Demanding excessive attention or acting inappropriately.

## Scoring an informal reading inventory

Once written comprehension questions are chosen, a teacher will want to determine the number of errors that are permissible for the students. Students are often graded and grouped into three categories: independent (the student can read on their own), instructional (the student could read if classroom help is available) and frustration (the student will most likely find this piece too difficult even in a classroom setting). Where the child falls on that scale depends upon the amount of errors per 100 words that the student commits. For example, an "independent" reader might commit one or two errors per 100 words and score 90 percent or higher on comprehension questions.

## Portfolio assessments

Portfolio assessments are not as useful for the following situations:
- Evaluating programs that have very concrete, uniform purposes or goals. For instance, it would not be necessary to compile a portfolio for a programs such as immunizing children by the age of five because the immunizations are the same and the evidence is usually straightforward and clear.
- Allowing a teacher to rank participants or a program in a quantitative or standardized way, even though evaluators or staff members of the program might be able to make subjective judgments on that which is relative.
- Comparing participants or programs to standardized norms. Portfolios can and often do include some kinds of standardized test scores along with other types of evidence. However, this is not the main purpose in using portfolio assessments.

## Portfolio development

The main factors that guide the design and development of a portfolio are:
- Purpose. The primary concern is understanding the purpose that is to be served by the portfolio. This will define guidelines for collecting materials. For instance, is the goal to report progress? To identify special needs? For program accountability? For all such reasons?
- Assessment criteria. The next decision to make is about what are the criteria standards, such as what will be considered a success, and what strategies are needed to meet the goals. Items are then selected to provide evidence of meeting said criteria or making progress with respect to the goals which have been set.
- Evidence. A number of considerations in collecting data are needed. What are the sources of evidence? How often should evidence be collected? How can sense be made of the evidence?

## Running records

Running records give teachers an important tool for making decisions on appropriate grouping, materials and support when taken over time in early literacy training. They are based on structured observations of children's reading and writing behaviors and exemplify authentic assessment which is critical with emergent readers as they come across new reading material.

The student reads from a text and the teacher watches closely, coding behaviors on a sheet of paper. Words that are accurately read are given a check. Errors receive a line with reader behaviors recorded above the line and teacher actions recorded below. A goal of the running records for this level would be to help students develop a "self-extending" system, which indicates that children learn to apply strategies of self-monitoring and self-correction on more difficult texts for extended amounts of text.

## Scoring running records

Certain points should be remembered when taking and scoring running records. These include:
- Running records must be analyzed to offer data for instructional use in addition to being scored.
- Consider what text the student read, up to and including the error when analyzing a substitution.

- Do not make professional judgments base on the results of one running record. Reviewing the analysis and accuracy of scores of a number of running records is the only way to understand a student's reading process.
- Individual errors are studied for gaining insight into the reader's process.
- When analyzing a record, circle the cues that the reader used and not the ones that were neglected.

## Observation

Observation is one of the most powerful techniques that a teacher has. The purpose is to build a picture of a student's personal, social and cognitive development and how they are making progress in their learning. Only when a number of cameos, vignettes, snapshots, notes or indicators exist can teachers start looking for patterns in student behavior and make judgments about their performance. Dating such records will help record the contexts along with observed achievement characteristics in order to build a historical profile that is useful. Supporting and acknowledging students working at different levels requires flexibility and tailoring to the individual student. The formats should suit the particular activities, reflect the activities' goals and support the recording of different levels and rates of students' work.

## Anecdotal records

Anecdotal records are written records kept in a positive tone of a child's progress that are based on milestones particular to the child's emotional, physical, aesthetic and cognitive development. They include specific dates, times and events of incidents throughout the school day. Some teachers use notebooks for such tasks while others use sticky pads. The notes will either become part of the child's file at the end of the year, stay with the teacher's records or be disposed of. Anecdotal records are useful in parent conferences when a teacher explains how a child is performing. They also help keep track of a student's behavior. Keeping such records is useful in supporting why and how a teacher makes decisions.

## Grading journals

Grading student journals can be very subjective due to their personal natures. For fair and consistent grading which reflects assignments, a teacher should have established a set of criteria for evaluation. These criteria should help assist students in preparing journals that are effective in addition to helping with grading. The grading system should be reflective of the learning objectives and assignment goals. Rubrics for grading may be either analytical or holistic systems of scoring. In holistic rubrics, students are given overall criteria for assigning a grade based on the complete journal. For instance the criteria for an "A" might include that students have complete entries in the journals which are insightful, well-developed, of appropriate length, focus on proper objectives and use proper grammar, punctuation and spelling.

## Reliability of evaluations

Some scholars and testing experts argue that performance, portfolio and responsive evaluations -- where tasks vary greatly from student to student and where multiple tasks may be simultaneously evaluated -- are not reliable. A difficulty cited is that there are more than one source of errors in measuring performance assessment. For instance, a writing skill test score might have its reliability affected by graders, or other such factors. There may also be confusion about diversity of reliability indices. Nonetheless, different reliability measures share a common thread. One such commonality is constituted in measurement procedures in situations such as internal consistency. Oftentimes for convenience in computing, the reliability index is based upon a single data collection. The ultimate reference, however, should go beyond just one testing occasion to other such occasions.

## Modifying reading instruction

Reading specialists know that a viable reading program takes into consideration the needs and learning styles of all students, but in reality there are a number of obstacles to making this happen. For instance, there may be deficiencies in finances or personnel. Education also operates under a system of mandates, theories, strategies and trends that are fragmented. In this case, reading series or manuals may attempt to bring some degree of consistency to a district or building, yet they are not always used.

In an ideal district, the need for reading specialists is substantially reduced. The financially less privileged districts, however, need more reading specialists than can generally be afforded.

Classroom teachers have long recognized that there is a problem in ensuring that those who need a reading specialist indeed obtain the help of one. Those children in need of help may have failed in the mainstream environment and thus need ways to match their strengths and needs. It should be recognized that children may not always seem enthusiastic about reading, yet despite their attempts to mask their enthusiasm, they do in actuality want to learn how to read. The specialist can work with the classroom teacher so that he or she will take ownership of these children who need help. Working with the classroom teacher will bring extra benefits to the student and the classroom. Both the classroom teacher and reading specialist can work together to provide what the student needs, find out the student's achievements or lack thereof and then, if necessary, work to modify the instruction in order to benefit the child's progress in learning to read.

## Performance factors and modified course

Teachers may look for specific performance factors that can be passed along to the reading specialist or others for assessment in order to decide if a child needs modified reading instruction. These factors are:
- Continuous improvement. Are the student's grades improving, stagnating or declining?
- Comparative performance. Do the results show that the student is doing well in comparison to other children in comparable settings?
- Absolute performance. Do the results show the student is reaching the school's desired level of performance?
- Small-group performance. Do the results show that children of a similar group as the student (limited English, Title I students) are making better progress that that of the student in question?

## Collaboration among colleagues

The reading specialist in a school setting provides a wide variety of services, many of which are in a collaborative effort with colleagues. The specialist works with teachers to promote and develop the literacy program as well as developing thinking strategies in the classroom. As a diagnostician, the specialist administers both group and individual evaluations of reading achievement and recommends activities to build comprehension. For intervention, the specialist works with teachers as well as students and small groups for providing instruction and for building competencies in literacy. In addition, the reading specialist works with the staff and parents in order to promote various events in order to gather support for the literacy program and which support literacy as a whole.

## Parental expectations

Various research has found that parental expectations have a significant impact upon school performance as well as being critical to achievement in academics. High expectations from parents are usually found in association with higher levels of educational attainment. Parenting practices that are effective and associated with high levels of academic achievement include expectations that children receive high numerical grades of their schoolwork. Additionally, research indicates that child rearing beliefs, ways to academically enrich home environments and standards of behavior that are acceptable both in and out of school are likewise important to achieving academically. Insofar as behavior is concerned, the children who succeed have greater adaptability to conforming with behavioral standards at school; something many have already learned through parental expectations.

## Phonics approach

The Phonics approach teaches reading and spelling in a methodical fashion by emphasizing the basic relationships between symbols and sounds. These relationships are then applied to words as a way of discerning their meaning. Phonics is an approach often used with beginning readers or with people who are new to a language. The Phonics approach relies heavily on repetitive drills to teach students consonants, vowels, and how some letters blend together. Students then take the next step of combining individual sounds into words. Phonics teaches students to recognize unfamiliar words by breaking them down into smaller, more recognizable letter-sound groupings. As students advance, however, research shows they often depend more on word order than on phonics to figure out the meaning of unfamiliar words. One problem with the Phonics approach is the complexity of the English language. The same letter or letter combination does not always represent the same sound.

## Contextual cues

A reader's knowledge of how the language works is a factor in how successfully that reader will comprehend a text. For example, readers may comprehend more thoroughly if they know the position of words in a sentence, punctuation marks, and word relationships within sentences. This is all done through the contextual cue systems—graphophonic, syntactic, semantic, and pragmatic—in order to make sense out of what they have read. Proficient readers are most concerned with meaning. They use a continuous formulation of meaning in order to figure out how much attention should be paid to the text in confirming or correcting predictions, as well as in making other predictions. Middle-level students must continue to balance the use of interacting language cue systems in order to extract meaning from texts.

## Fluency

The amount of practice that is required for fluency and automaticity in reading by children varies. Some children can read a word once and then recall it again with more speed. Other youngsters may need exposures numbering 20 or more. On average, children need between four and 14 exposures to have automaticity in the recognition of new words. Thus, it is vital that children who are learning reading read a large amount of text at their independent reading level and that the format of the text provide practice that is specific to the skills being learned. Fluency and automaticity in reading words—along with phonemic awareness and phonics skills—are necessary, but not sufficient, for constructing meaning from text. Children must understand what is being read.

**Terms**

Syntactic hierarchy
Syntactic hierarchy from smaller to larger units is morpheme, word, phrase, sentence and text.

Syntactic processing
Involves the ability to identify clauses, noun phrases, verb phrases, propositional phrases, adjectives, articles, nouns and verbs and assemble them in sentence that are syntactically acceptable.

Syntactic development
Measured by the mean length of utterance which is based on the average length of a child's sentences, scored on transcripts of spontaneous speech. Each unit of meaning, including root words and inflections, is recorded. Sometime after the second year following a child's attainment of a 50 word vocabulary, multiple word utterances begin to appear. These are usually telegraphic and normally without articles, propositions, or other grammatical modifications.

**Laptop computers**

Students may use laptops in the classroom, take them on field trips or go home with them. If they are used appropriately, laptops can help develop project-based learning and multimedia activities as students work to collect data, brainstorm or produce projects. Among the advantages of having class laptops are that:
- They are portable within the school and outside of class.
- They may be taken on field trips and used for investigations.
- They can provide immediate data processing and graphic feedback.
- Feedback and analysis that is immediate prompts next-step decision-making in the field.
- It allows files to be shared.
- The computers generate reports and projects.
- They can provide access to experts through e-mail or the Internet.

**Surveys**

Surveys help gather information of any type, regardless of whether or not specific names need to be attached. Surveys are useful in determining how a student feels about the instruction. They may be used to determine the level of knowledge on various issues related to the content that is being studied. This could help provide a baseline of where the students are. Surveys that are similar can then be given at a later time to determine what the students have learned. Surveys are useful in determining how the student feels about what he or she has learned in the class from their point of view. Unlike a standardized test score that shows academic outcomes, a survey can provide a more personal level of knowledge that the student may have gained from the class.

**Black-white achievement gap**

The black-white achievement gap refers to a general difficulty African-American students experience with academic achievement. They consistently perform below non-minority peers in reading, science, and mathematics. The gap has had negative economic and social effects. Some studies have suggested the difference may be caused by cultural linguistic or cultural differences. Good language skills are necessary for reading. Vocabulary skills support reading development in both younger and older readers. African-American children have been shown to have receptive and expressive vocabulary skills that are below those of their age level. But vocabulary breadth can be increased by direct teaching methods. Such teaching methods may act as a start in improving reading for young African-American children and may narrow the so-called gap.

## Mixed-age or multi-age grouping

Mixed-age or multi-age grouping refers to grouping children so that the age span of the class is greater than one year, as in the nongraded approach. Mixed-age and multi-age grouping emphasize teaching and curriculum practices that realize the greatest benefits from the cooperation and interaction of children of various ages. In multi-age classes, teachers encourage the children with different levels of development and experience to help each other with all classroom activities, including application and mastery of basic literacy and mathematical skills. But teachers should use small temporary subgroupings in mixed-age classes for groups of children who require the same types of instruction to help them acquire basic skills.

## Family history

Research on reading problems suggests that children whose parents or older siblings have shown reading problems are at greater risk for reading difficulties than those children of otherwise similar backgrounds. Factors identified as family risk factors include family history of reading problems, home literacy environment, verbal interaction, language other than English, nonstandard dialect, and family-based socioeconomic status. Family patterns of reading problems can be attributed to factors that are shared either genetically or environmentally. Most studies of familial incidence diagnose a child with a reading disability using a severity criterion that would identify between 5 to 10 percent of children who have normal intelligence and have had a commonly effective education.

## Literary genres

Literary genres refer to the basic generic types of poetry, drama, fiction, and nonfiction. Literary genre is a method of classifying and analyzing literature. There are numerous subdivisions within genre, including such categories as novels, novellas, and short stories in fiction. Drama may also be subdivided into comedy, tragedy, and many other categories. Poetry and nonfiction have their own distinct divisions.

Genres often overlap, and the distinctions among them are blurred, such as that between the nonfiction novel and docudrama, as well as many others. However, the use of genres is helpful to the reader as a set of understandings that guide our responses to a work. The generic norm sets expectations and forms the framework within which we read and evaluate a work. This framework will guide both our understanding and interpretation of the work. It is a useful tool for both literary criticism and analysis.

## Varieties of fiction

Fiction is a general term for any form of literary narrative that is invented or imagined rather than being factual. For those individuals who equate fact with truth, the imagined or invented character of fiction tends to render it relatively unimportant or trivial among the genres. Defenders of fiction are quick to point out that the fictional mode is an essential part of being. The ability to imagine or discuss what-if plots, characters, and events is clearly part of the human experience.

Fiction is much wider than simply prose fiction. Songs, ballads, epics, and narrative poems are examples of non-prose fiction. A full definition of fiction must include not only the work itself but also the framework in which it is read. Literary fiction can also be defined as not true rather than nonexistent, as many works of historical fiction refer to real people, places, and events that are treated imaginatively as if they were true. These imaginary elements enrich and broaden literary expression.

## Drama

Drama is any work in which actors or actresses assume roles before an audience in a theatre, motion pictures, television, or radio. Drama is a major literary genre that may be subdivided into three major groups:

Tragedy: a drama in which the leading character has a disastrous end. The character usually represents something significant, whether good or bad. Tragedy may be seen as an attempt to extract a value from human mortality, giving the subgenre a positive view of human life, despite its inevitable end.

Tragicomedy: a drama that includes both comic and tragic elements. Tragicomedy thus results in a bittersweet mix of literary value. As George Bernard Shaw once commented, tragicomedy is a much deeper and grimmer entertainment than tragedy.

Comedy: a type of drama that satirizes the misadventures of its characters. Comedy often emphasizes society and its mores rather than the individual (more common in tragedies). Its origins may be traced to the primitive celebrations of spring.

## Prose

*Prose* is derived from the Latin and means "straightforward discourse." Prose fiction, although having many categories, may be divided into three main groups:

Short stories: a fictional narrative, the length of which varies, usually under 20,000 words. Short stories usually have only a few characters and generally describe one major event or insight. The short story began in magazines in the late 1800s and has flourished ever since.

Novels: a longer work of fiction, often containing a large cast of characters and extensive plotting. The emphasis may be on an event, action, social problems, or any experience. There is now a genre of nonfiction novels pioneered by Truman Capote's *In Cold Blood* in the 1960s. Novels may also be written in verse.

Novellas: a work of narrative fiction longer than a short story but shorter than a novel. Novellas may also be called short novels or novelettes. They originated from the German tradition and have become common forms in all of the world's literature.

## Narrative technique and tone of a novel

The following are important questions to address to better understand the voice and role of the narrator and incorporate that voice into an overall understanding of the novel:

Who is the narrator of the novel? What is the narrator's perspective, first person or third person? What is the role of the narrator in the plot? Are there changes in narrators or the perspective of narrators?

Does the narrator explain things in the novel, or does meaning emerge from the plot and events? The personality of the narrator is important. She may have a vested interest in a character or event described.

Some narratives follow the time sequence of the plot, whereas others do not. A narrator may express approval or disapproval about a character or events in the work.

Tone is an important aspect of the narration. Who is actually being addressed by the narrator? Is the tone familiar or formal, intimate or impersonal? Does the vocabulary suggest clues about the narrator?

## Figurative language

Poetry is a genre in which language is used in all its variations and embellishments to convey a sense, mood, or feeling the poet deems important. Poetry uses elaborate linguistic constructions to explain the world in creative ways.

Poetry manipulates language itself to convey impressions in new and innovative constructions. It makes extensive use of figurative devices—such as conceits, similes, metaphors, and many more—to express things in fresh ways.

Poets use figurative language to suggest rather than give direct meanings. This language provides a creative experience for the reader, who is asked to understand meaning in unconventional terms. Poets relish opportunities to express themselves in creative and unusual words. Figurative language provides both poet and reader an opportunity for unique expression and understanding. Emotions, feelings, and moods are evoked by the skillful use of figurative language.

## Elegy

An elegy is a mournful or sorrowful poem, usually lamenting the dead. It typically expresses the poet's sorrow for the loss of a friend or lover, or more generally for the sadness of the human condition. Consolation is a recurring theme in an elegy, in some way consoling the audience for the brevity of human existence.

The first elegy was "The Idylls of Theocritus," in early Greek literature. More modern examples include Milton's "Lycidas," Thomas Gray's "Elegy Written in a Country Church Yard," Shelley's "Adonais," and W. H. Auden's "In Memory of W. B. Yeats."

In formal poetic convention, an elegy refers to any poem, regardless of subject, written in elegiac distiches (alternating lines of dactylic hexameter and pentameter).

The usual understanding of the term in poetry is the sorrowful or mournful mood that is the signature of the elegy. This type of work is much less common in modern poetry although it still occurs.

## Epic

Originally, epics were long narrative poems that focused on a hero's adventures and triumphs. The hero generally undergoes a series of trials that test his courage, character, and intellect. Epic poems have certain conventions, such as the use of a muse and exhaustive lists of armies, ships, and catalogues. These written and oral epics transmitted folk culture from generation to generation.

The best known of the original epics were written by Homer and Virgil. Milton's "Paradise Lost" is an example of a more recent epic as is Cervantes's *Don Quixote*.

Epic theatre, pioneered by Bertolt Brecht, is a further refinement of the form.

Epics have come to mean any dramatic work of poetry, prose, drama, film, or music that depends on spectacles and lavish productions sometimes based on historical events.

## Essays

Essays are usually defined as prose compositions dealing with one or two topics. The word *essay* is from the French *essayer*, meaning to try or attempt. The term was coined by Michel de Montaigne (1533–92), who is still regarded as a master of the form. Essays tend to be informal in style and are usually personal in approach and opinion.

Francis Bacon (1561–1626) pioneered essays that were dogmatic and impersonal, leading to a division of essays called formal and familiar, respectively. Some essays have been adapted to verse, whereas others are a hybrid of essay and fiction.

Essays usually begin with an observation or musing on a subject. Formal essays tend to present an argument, whereas familiar essays are less dogmatic and reflect the personal views of the author. They do not try to convince but proffer opinions and observations on a subject.
Essays have been written about countless subjects, from public policy to existential anxiety. Literary essays are popular, and some of the best were written by notable authors, such as Henry James, Virginia Woolf, and T. S. Eliot.

## Analogy, simile, and metaphors

An analogy is a literary device that compares two things. It functions as an extended metaphor. In a broader sense, analogies refer to the process of reasoning from parallel examples.

Similes are figures of speech that use a grammatical connection, such as *like, as if*, or *as* to explain comparisons.

Metaphors, in a narrow sense, are figures of speech that highlight the similarities between two elements, conventionally called tenor and vehicle. Metaphors may be direct or indirect. A direct metaphor states the comparison directly, whereas an indirect metaphor only implies the comparison. Metaphors have always been a major device in poetry and are now seen in every aspect of language.

All these literary devices are used to enrich and emphasize observed qualities. They are present in all genres.

## Hyperbole, personification, and foreshadowing

Hyperbole is a figure of speech that uses extreme exaggeration for dramatic effect. It usually functions to compare and is used quite often in romantic works. Love poetry is an example of a subgenre that fosters the use of hyperbole. Hyperbole may also be used farcically for comic effect.

Personification is another figure of speech, which attributes human qualities to an inanimate object or abstract entity. Personification helps us to use our self-knowledge and extrapolate it to understand abstract concepts, forces of nature, and common events. Personification is sometimes achieved by similes or analogies to strengthen the imagery.

Foreshadowing uses hints in a narrative to let the audience anticipate future events in the plot. Foreshadowing can be indicated by a number of literary devices and figures of speech, as well as through dialogue between characters. In Ibsen's play *Hedda Gabler*, Hedda plays with a gun early in the play, which foreshadows her eventual suicide. In Shakespeare's *Macbeth*, the three witches in the opening scene foreshadow horrific events to come. Examples abound in all forms of literature but are perhaps most evident in drama.

## Protagonists, antagonists, heroes, and villains

A protagonist is the central character in a play or story. The character opposing the protagonist is called the antagonist. Either may be the hero or villain of a drama or work of fiction. In modern literature, the protagonist–antagonist struggle is often represented as an internal conflict in one individual. Freudian thought has had a great influence on this inward battle of psychological forces in a person.

The hero or heroine is also the major figure in a literary work. The term may be used instead of protagonist. Finally, the villain is the major evil character in a literary work. Usually the villain opposes the protagonist but sometimes is the protagonist of a work. The roles of heroes and villains are exaggerated in melodrama and often seen in early films. The conflict in these cases usually involves a fair damsel. Modern literature usually reflects a more mixed character, with both qualities present in a character.

## Climax, anticlimax, and closure

A climax occurs when a state of tension in a literary work reaches its peak, usually with a resolution of some kind. There may be many or only one climax in a work, depending on the plotting and length of the story. A climax is usually preceded by an increasing level of tension, usually between the protagonist and antagonist. The climax may take the form of action, speech, or symbolism.

An anticlimax occurs in fiction or drama when a critical point in the work is resolved and the dramatic tension recedes. The term can be used negatively if it refers to a weakness in a drama or story. Sometimes an anticlimax is used to enhance a scene or serve as a respite from a period of action.

Closure is the modification of the structure of a work that makes absence of further development unlikely. It creates the expectation of nothing and leaves the reader or audience satisfied that the plot development is over. Closure often has a dramatic force of its own and sometimes is the final climax.

## Ballads

The original meaning of ballad was song closely associated with dance. Over time, the ballad formed a branch of narrative using verse. Folk ballads, the most common form, typically deal with love affairs, tragic endings, and occasionally historical and military subjects. The narration is often told in dialogue form, arranged in quatrains with the second and fourth lines rhyming. Ballads are derived from folk tales and oral traditions and use direct, descriptive language. Ballads have been popular for centuries, and folk music is an extension of the ballad form. The term *ballad* is still used extensively to note songs that tell a story, usually with a romantic or tragic theme. Ballads are sometimes derived from historical sources, lending them a sense of stories told in verse. Minstrels were the early performers of ballads and were important in preserving the cultural and historical records of many peoples. Ballads have also been adopted by poets, as in Wilde's "The Ballad of Reading Gaol."

## Emily Dickinson

Emily Dickinson is ranked as one of America's greatest poets. Dickinson's poetry is highly formal, her language both subtle and creative, and it reflects the quiet life she led. Dickinson's topics include death, art, love, pain, and betrayal, all couched in her wonderful poetic language. She wrote more than 1,800 poems, yet only ten are known to have been published in her lifetime. Her fame has grown through the generations, and she is at last recognized as a poetic genius.

Born in Amherst, Massachusetts, in 1830, she was educated at Mt. Holyoke seminary. She returned to Amherst and went into virtual seclusion in her parents' home. She saw very few people socially and rarely left the house. Despite this isolation, Dickinson's work is vibrant and alive, reflecting her keen observation of the world. Dickinson is a true American literary voice, rivaling Walt Whitman. She died in Amherst in 1886.

## Robert Louis Stevenson

Robert Louis Stevenson was a Scottish essayist, novelist, poet, and short-story writer. After writing for weeklies for a few years, his *Treasure Island* (1883) brought him acclaim and wealth. Stevenson followed this success with *Kidnapped* (1886), *The Strange Case of Dr. Jekyll and Mr. Hyde* (1886), and *The Master of Ballantrae* (1889), all critical and financial successes. Stevenson also wrote a book of verse for children, *A Child's Garden of Verses* (1885). His swashbuckling tales and colorful language engaged the fancy of the public, and he retired a wealthy man.

Stevenson was born in Edinburgh in 1850 and educated in law. His life was tainted by chronic tuberculosis, and he sought cures and more healthy climates all over the world. Stevenson finally found the relief he sought in Samoa, where he settled and lived the last years of his life. He died there in 1894, at the young age of 44.

## Rudyard Kipling

Kipling, the favorite writer of the British Empire, was a novelist, poet, and short-fiction writer of great skill. His novels of British imperialism, such as *Kim* (1901), carved a unique literary niche for Kipling. His poetry was much beloved; outstanding examples are "Gunga Din," "Mandalay," and "Danny Deever." Kipling's story collections for children include *The Jungle Book* (1894) and *Just So Stories* (1902). Kipling's descriptions of British colonial life became a window for the world to understand the glory and excesses of the empire.

Kipling was born in Bombay in 1865 and educated in England. He returned to India for several years, working as a journalist and fledgling poet. Returning to England, his prose collection captured the fancy of the nation. Kipling lived for four productive years in Vermont and then went home for good. The first English writer to win a Nobel Prize for Literature, he died in England in 1936.

## Robert Frost

Robert Frost, American poet, is remembered as a master of the technical aspects of poetry while remaining true to his New England heritage. Frost will always be remembered for his masterful simplicity in such poems as "Stopping By the Woods on a Snowy Evening" (1923) and "The Road Not Taken" (1916). While living in England before World War I, Frost published two collections of poetry. Returning to New England, he published a number of anthologies, including *Complete Poems* (1945), *West Running Brook* (1928), *A Witness Tree* (1942), and *In the Clearing* (1962).

Frost was born in California in 1874 and was educated at Dartmouth College and Harvard. He received the Pulitzer Prize four times and capped his career by reading "The Gift Outright" at the inaugural of John Kennedy in 1961. Frost died in 1963.

## Children's literature

Children's literature is designed to be read and enjoyed primarily by young readers. Early children's literature was written exclusively for educational purposes. Beginning in the middle of the 18th century, children's books were written to entertain as well as edify. Adventure stories for boys became popular in the 19th century, as did fiction designed for girls, such as Louisa May Alcott's *Little Women* (1868) and Johanna Spyri's *Heidi* (1880). Mark Twain and Robert Louis Stevenson became important writers of children's fiction during this time.

Recent years have emphasized more realism in children's literature. Opposed to the traditional view of shielding children from the realities of life, many now advocate books that are not only realistic but also tragic, providing an opportunity for catharsis for young readers. An example of this type of fiction is William Armstrong's *Sounder* (1969), a novel of the evils of a segregated society written for young readers.

## Instrumental phonetics

Phonetics seeks to provide a descriptive terminology for the sounds of spoken language. This includes the physiology for the production of speech sounds; the classification of speech sounds, including vowels and consonants; the dynamic features of speech production; and the study of instrumental phonetics, the investigation of human speech by laboratory techniques. The dynamic aspects of phonetics include voice quality, stress, rhythm, and speech melody.

Instrumental phonetics underlines both the complexity of speech production and the subtlety of the human brain in interpreting a constantly changing flow of acoustic data as recognizable speech sounds. The correlation between acoustic quality, auditory perception, and articulatory position is a complex and not yet fully understood process. It represents a fertile area of research for phoneticians, psychologists, and perhaps philosophers.

## Nouns and pronouns

Nouns name persons, places, things, animals, objects, time, feelings, concepts, and actions, and are usually signaled by an article (*a, an, the*). Nouns sometimes function as adjectives modifying other nouns. Nouns used in this manner are called noun/adjectives. Nouns are classified for a number of purposes: capitalization, word choice, count/no count nouns, and collective nouns are examples.

A pronoun is a word used in place of a noun. Usually the pronoun substitutes for the specific noun, called the antecedent. Although most pronouns function as substitutes for nouns, some can function as adjectives modifying nouns. Pronouns may be classed as personal, possessive, intensive, relative, interrogative, demonstrative, indefinite, and reciprocal. Pronouns can cause a number of problems for writers, including pronoun-antecedent agreement, distinguishing between *who* and *whom*, and differentiating pronouns, such as *I* and *me*.

# Verbs

The verb of a sentence usually expresses action or being. It is composed of a main verb and sometimes supporting verbs. These helping verbs are forms of *have, do*, and *be,* and nine modals. The modals are *can, could, may, might, shall, should, will, would*, and *ought.* Some verbs are followed by words that look like prepositions but are so closely associated with the verb as to be part of its meaning. These words are known as particles, and examples include *call off, look up*, and *drop off.*

The main verb of a sentence is always one that would change form from base form to past tense, past participle, present participle, and *–s* forms. When both the past-tense and past-participle forms of a verb end in *–ed,* the verb is regular. In all other cases, the verb is irregular. The verb *to be* is highly irregular, having eight forms instead of the usual five.

## Types of verbs

Linking verbs link the subject to a subject complement, a word, or word group that completes the meaning of the subject by renaming or describing it.

A transitive verb takes a direct object, a word, or word group that names a receiver of the action. The direct object of a transitive verb is sometimes preceded by an indirect object. Transitive verbs usually appear in the active voice, with a subject doing the action and a direct object receiving the action. The direct object of a transitive verb is sometimes followed by an object complement, a word or word group that completes the direct object's meaning by renaming or describing it.

Intransitive verbs take no objects or complements. Their pattern is subject + verb.

A dictionary will disclose whether a verb is transitive or intransitive. Some verbs have both transitive and intransitive functions.

## Adjectives, articles, and adverbs

An adjective is a word used to modify or describe a noun or pronoun. An adjective usually answers one of these questions: Which one? What kind? How many? Adjectives usually precede the words they modify although they sometimes follow linking verbs, in which case they describe the subject.

Articles, sometimes classed as adjectives, are used to mark nouns. There are only three: the definite article *the* and the indefinite articles *a* and *an.*

An adverb is a word used to modify or qualify a verb, adjective, or another adverb. It usually answers one of these questions: When? Where? How? Why? Adverbs modifying adjectives or other adverbs usually intensify or limit the intensity of words they modify. The negators *not* and *never* are classified as adverbs.

Writers sometimes misuse adverbs, and multilingual speakers have trouble placing them correctly.

## Prepositions and conjunctions

A preposition is a word placed before a noun or pronoun to form a phrase modifying another word in the sentence. The prepositional phrase usually functions as an adjective or adverb. There are a limited number of prepositions in English, perhaps around 80. Some prepositions are more than one word long. *Along with, listen to*, and *next to* are some examples.

Conjunctions join words, phrases, or clauses, and they indicate the relationship between the elements that are joined. There are coordinating conjunctions that connect grammatically equal elements, correlative conjunctions that connect pairs, subordinating conjunctions that introduce a subordinate clause, and conjunctive adverbs, which may be used with a semicolon to connect independent clauses. The most common conjunctive adverbs include *then, thus,* and *however.* Using conjunctions correctly helps avoid sentence fragments and run-on sentences.

## Sentence subject

The subject of a sentence names who or what the sentence is about. The complete subject is composed of the simple subject and all of its modifiers.

To find the complete subject, ask, who? Or, what? Insert the verb to complete the question. The answer is the complete subject. To find the simple subject, strip away all the modifiers in the complete subject.

In imperative sentences, the verb's subject is understood, but not actually present in the sentence. Although the subject ordinarily comes before the verb, in sentences that begin with *There are* or *There was*, the subject follows the verb.

The ability to recognize the subject of a sentence helps in editing a variety of problems, such as sentence fragments and subject-verb agreement, as well as the choice of pronouns.

## Sentence patterns

Sentence patterns fall into five common modes with some exceptions. They are:

Subject + linking verb + subject complement
Subject + transitive verb + direct object
Subject + transitive verb + indirect object + direct object

Subject + transitive verb + direct object + object complement

Subject + intransitive verb

Common exceptions to these patterns are questions and commands, sentences with delayed subjects, and passive transformations. Writers sometimes use the passive voice when the active voice would be more appropriate.

## Subordinate word groups

Subordinate word groups cannot stand alone. They function only within sentences, as adjectives, adverbs, or nouns.

Prepositional phrases begin with a preposition and end with a noun or noun equivalent, called its object. Prepositional phrases function as adjectives or adverbs.

Subordinate clauses are patterned like sentences, having subjects, verbs, and objects or complements. They function within sentences as adverbs, adjectives, or nouns.

Adjective clauses modify nouns or pronouns and begin with a relative pronoun or relative adverb.

Adverb clauses modify verbs, adjectives, and other adverbs.

Noun clauses function as subjects, objects, or complements. In both adjective and noun clauses words may appear out of their normal order. The parts of a noun clause may also appear in their normal order.

## Verbal phrases

A verbal phrase is a verb form that does not function as the verb of a clause. There are three major types of verbal phrases:

Participial phrases: These always function as adjectives. Their verbals are always present participles, always ending in –*ing*, or past participles frequently ending in –*d,–ed,–n,–en*, or –*t*. Participial phrases frequently appear immediately following the noun or pronoun they modify.

Gerund phrases: Gerund phrases are built around present participles, and they always function as nouns, usually as subjects, subject complements, direct objects, or objects of a preposition.

Infinitive phrases are usually structured around *to* plus the base form of the verb. They can function as nouns, as adjectives, or as adverbs. When functioning as a noun, an infinitive phrase may appear in almost any noun slot in a sentence, usually as a subject, subject complement, or direct object. Infinitive phrases functioning as adjectives usually appear immediately following the noun or pronoun they modify. Adverbial phrases usually qualify the meaning of the verb.

## Appositive and absolute phrases

Strictly speaking, appositive phrases are not subordinate word groups. Appositive phrases function somewhat as adjectives do, to describe nouns or pronouns. Instead of modifying nouns or pronouns, however, appositive phrases rename them. In form, they are nouns or noun equivalents. Appositives are said to be in apposition to the nouns or pronouns they rename. For example, in the sentence "Terriers, hunters at heart, have been dandied up to look like lap dogs," *hunters at heart* is in apposition to the noun *terriers*.

An absolute phrase modifies a whole clause or sentence, not just one word, and it may appear nearly anywhere in the sentence. It consists of a noun or noun equivalent usually followed by a participial phrase. Both appositive and absolute phrases can cause confusion in their usage in grammatical structures. They are particularly difficult for a person whose first language is not English.

## Sentence classification

Sentences are classified in two ways: according to their structure or to their purpose.

Writers use declarative sentences to make statements, imperative sentences to issue requests or commands, interrogative sentences to ask questions, and exclamatory sentences to make exclamations.

Depending on the number and types of clauses they contain, sentences may be classified as simple, compound, complex, or compound-complex.

Clauses come in two varieties: independent and subordinate. An independent clause is a full sentence pattern that does not function within another sentence pattern; it contains a subject and modifiers plus a verb and any objects, complements, and modifiers of that verb, and it either stands alone or could stand alone. A subordinate clause is a full sentence pattern that functions within a sentence as an adjective, an adverb, or a noun but cannot stand alone as a complete sentence.

## Sentence structure

The four major types of sentence structure are:

Simple sentences: Simple sentences have one independent clause with no subordinate clauses. A simple sentence may contain compound elements—a compound subject, verb, or object, for example—but does not contain more than one full sentence pattern.

Compound sentences: Compound sentences are composed of two or more independent clauses with no subordinate clauses. The independent clauses are usually joined with a comma and a coordinating conjunction or with a semicolon.
Complex sentences: A complex sentence is composed of one independent clause with one or more dependent clauses.

Compound-complex sentences: A compound-complex sentence contains at least two independent clauses and at least one subordinate clause. Sometimes they contain two full sentence patterns that can stand alone. When each independent clause contains a subordinate clause, this makes the sentence both compound and complex.

## Subject-verb agreement

In the present tense, verbs agree with their subjects in number, (singular or plural) and in person (first, second, or third). The present tense ending –s is used with a verb if its subject is third person singular; otherwise, the verb takes no ending. The verb to be varies from this pattern, and, alone among verbs, it has special forms in both the present and past tense.Problems with subject-verb agreement tend to arise in certain contexts:

- Words between subject and verbs
- Subjects joined by and
- Subjects joined by or or nor
- Indefinite pronouns, such as someone
- Collective nouns
- Subject after the verb
- Pronouns who, which, and that
- Plural form, singular meaning
- Titles, company names, and words mentioned as words

## Problems with verbs

The verb is the heart of the sentence. Verbs have several potential problems, including the following:

Irregular verbs: These are verbs that do not follow usual grammatical rules.

Tense: Tenses indicate the time of an action in relation to the time of speaking or writing about the action.

Mood: There are three moods in English: the indicative, used for facts, opinions, and questions; the imperative, used for orders or advice; and the subjunctive, used for wishes. The subjunctive mood is the most likely to cause problems. The subjunctive mood is used for wishes and in *if* clauses expressing conditions contrary to facts. The subjunctive, in such cases, is the past tense form of the verb; in the case of *be*, it is always *were*, even if the subject is singular. The subjunctive mood is also used in *that* clauses following verbs such as *ask, insist, recommend*, and *request*. The subjunctive, in such cases, is the base, or dictionary, form of the verb.

## Pronouns

Pronouns are words that substitute for nouns: *he, it, them, her, me,* and so on. Four frequently encountered problems with pronouns include the following:
Pronoun-antecedent agreement: The antecedent of a pronoun is the word the pronoun refers to. A pronoun and its antecedent agree when they are both singular or plural, or of the same gender.

Pronoun reference: A pronoun should refer clearly to its antecedent. A pronoun's reference will be unclear if it is ambiguous, implied, vague, or indefinite.

Personal pronouns: Some pronouns change their case form according to their grammatical structure in a sentence. Pronouns functioning as subjects appear in the subjective case, those functioning as objects appear in the objective case, and those functioning as possessives appear in the possessive case.

Who or whom: *Who*, a subjective-case pronoun, can be used only as subjects and subject complements. *Whom*, an objective-case pronoun, can be used only for objects. The words *who* and *whom* appear primarily in subordinate clauses or in questions.

## Repairing sentence fragments

As a rule, a part of a sentence should not be treated as a complete sentence. A sentence must be composed of at least one full independent clause. An independent clause has a subject and a verb and can stand alone as a sentence. Some fragments are clauses that contain a subject and a verb but begin with a subordinating word. Other fragments lack a subject, verb, or both.

A sentence fragment can be repaired by combining the fragment with a nearby sentence, punctuating the new sentence correctly, or turning the fragment into a sentence by adding the missing elements. Some sentence fragments are used by writers for emphasis. Although sentence fragments are sometimes acceptable, readers and writers do not always agree on when they are appropriate. A conservative approach is to write in complete sentences only unless a special circumstance dictates otherwise.

## Run-ons

Run-on sentences are independent clauses that have not been joined correctly. An independent clause is a word group that does or could stand alone in a sentence. When two or more independent clauses appear in one sentence, they must be joined in one of these ways:
1. Revision with a comma and a coordinating conjunction
2. Revision with a semicolon, a colon, or a dash, used when independent clauses are closely related and their relationship is clear without a coordinating conjunction

3. Revision by separating sentences, used when both independent clauses are long or if one is a question and one is not: Separate sentences may be the best option in this case.
4. Revision by restructuring the sentence: For sentence variety, consider restructuring the sentence, perhaps by turning one of the independent clauses into a subordinate phrase or clause.

Usually one of these choices will be an obvious solution to the run-on sentence. The fourth technique above is often the most effective solution but requires the most revision.

## Double negative and superlative

Standard English allows two negatives only if a positive meaning is intended. "The team was not displeased with its performance" is an example. Double negatives used to emphasize negation are nonstandard.
Negative modifiers—such as *never, no*, and *not*—should not be paired with other negative modifiers or negative words, such as *none, nobody, nothing*, and *neither*. The modifiers *hardly, barely,* and *scarcely* are also considered negatives in Standard English, so they should not be used with other negatives, such as *not, no one,* or *never.*

Do not use double superlatives or comparatives. When *–er* or *–est* has been added to an adjective or adverb, avoid using *more* or *most*. Avoid expressions such as *more perfect* and *very round.* Either something is or is not. It is not logical to suggest that absolute concepts come in degrees. Use the comparative to compare two things and the superlative to compare three or more things.

## Comma

The comma was invented to help readers. Without it, sentence parts can run together, making meanings unclear. Various rules for comma use include the following:
- Use a comma between a coordinating conjunction joining independent clauses.
- Use a comma after an introductory clause or phrase.
- Use a comma between items in a series.
- Use a comma between coordinate adjectives not joined with *and*. Do not use a comma between cumulative adjectives.
- Use commas to set off nonrestrictive elements. Do not use commas to set off restrictive elements.
- Use commas to set off transitional and parenthetical expressions, absolute phrases, and elements expressing contrast.
- Use commas to set off nouns of direct address, the words *yes* and *no*, interrogative tags, and interjections.
- Use commas with dates, addresses, titles, and numbers.
- Use commas to prevent confusion.
- Use commas to set off direct quotations.

## Unnecessary commas

- Do not use a comma between compound elements that are not independent clauses.
- Do not use a comma after a phrase that begins with an inverted sentence.
- Do not use a comma between the first or after the last item in a series or before the word *although*.
- Do not use a comma between cumulative adjectives, between an adjective and a noun, or between an adverb and an adjective.

- Do not use commas to set off restrictive or mildly parenthetical elements or to set off an indirect quotation.
- Do not use a comma to set off a concluding adverb clause that is essential to the meaning of the sentence or after the word *although*.
- Do not use a comma to separate a verb from its subject or object. 8. Do not use a comma after a coordinating conjunction or before a parenthesis.
- Do not use a comma with a question mark or an exclamation point.

## Semicolon

The semicolon is used to connect major sentence elements of equal grammatical rank. Some rules regarding semicolons include the following:

- Use a semicolon between closely related independent clauses not joined with a coordinating conjunction.
- Use a semicolon between independent clauses linked with a transitional expression.
- Use a semicolon between items in a series containing internal punctuation.
- Avoid using a semicolon between a subordinate clause and the rest of the sentence.
- Avoid using a semicolon between an appositive word and the word it refers to.
- Avoid using a semicolon to introduce a list.
- Avoid using a semicolon between independent clauses joined by *and, but, or, nor, for, so,* or *yet.*

## Colon

The colon is used primarily to call attention to the words that follow it. In addition, the colon has some other conventional uses:
- Use a colon after an independent clause to direct attention to a list, an appositive, or a quotation.
- Use a colon between independent clauses if the second summarizes or explains the first.
- Use a colon after the salutation in a formal letter, to indicate hours and minutes, to show proportions, between a title and subtitle, and between city and publisher in bibliographic entries.

A colon must be preceded by a full independent clause. Avoid using colons in the following situations:
- Between a verb and its object or complement
- Between a preposition and its object
- After *such as, including,* or f*or example*

## Apostrophe

An apostrophe is used to indicate that a noun is possessive. Possessive nouns usually indicate ownership, as in *Bill's coat* or *the dog's biscuit.* Sometimes ownership is only loosely implied, as in *the dog's coat* or *the forest's trees.* If it is unclear whether a noun is possessive, turning into phrase may clarify it.
If the noun is plural and ends in–*s*, add only an apostrophe. To show joint possession, use –*'s* with the last noun only. To show individual possession, make all nouns possessive.

An apostrophe is often optional in plural numbers, letters, abbreviations, and words mentioned as words. Common errors in using apostrophes include the following:
- Using an apostrophe with nouns that are not possessive
- Using an apostrophe in the possessive pronouns *its, whose, his, hers, ours, yours,* and *theirs*

## Quotation marks

Use quotation marks to enclose direct quotations of a person's words, spoken or written. Do not use quotation marks around indirect quotations. An indirect quotation reports someone's ideas without using that person's exact words.

Set off long quotations of prose or poetry by indenting. Use single quotation marks to enclose a quotation within a quotation. Quotation marks should be used around the titles of short works: newspaper and magazine articles, poems, short stories, songs, episodes of television and radio programs, and subdivisions of books or web sites.

Punctuation is used with quotation marks according to convention. Periods and commas are placed inside quotation marks, whereas colons and semicolons are placed outside quotation marks. Question marks and exclamation points are placed either inside or outside quotation marks, depending on the rest of the material in the sentence.

Do not use quotation marks around the title of your own essay.

## Dash, parentheses, and brackets

Dashes are used for the following purposes:
- To set off parenthetical material that deserves emphasis
- To set off appositives that contain commas
- To prepare for a list, a restatement, an amplification, or a dramatic shift in tone or thought

Unless there is a specific reason for using the dash, omit it. It can give text a choppy effect.

Parentheses are used to enclose supplemental material, minor digressions, and afterthoughts. They are also used to enclose letters or numbers, labeling them items in a series. Parentheses should be used sparingly, as they break up text in a distracting manner when overused.

Brackets are used to enclose any words or phrases that have been inserted into an otherwise word-for-word quotation.

## End punctuations

Use a period to end all sentences except direct questions or genuine exclamations. Periods should be used in abbreviations according to convention. Problems can arise when there is a choice between a period and a question mark or exclamation point. If a sentence reports a question rather than asking it directly, it should end with a period, not a question mark.

Question marks should be used following a direct question. If a polite request is written in the form of a question, it may be followed by a period. Questions in a series may be followed by question marks even when they are not in complete sentences.

Exclamation marks are used after a word group or sentence that expresses exceptional feeling or deserves special emphasis. Exclamation marks should not be overused, being reserved for appropriate exclamatory interjections.

## Ellipsis mark and slash

The ellipsis mark consists of three spaced periods (...) and is used to indicate when certain words have been deleted from an otherwise word-for-word quotation. If a full sentence or more is deleted in the middle of a quoted passage, a period should be inserted before the ellipsis dots. The ellipsis mark should not be used at the beginning of a quotation. It should also not be used at the end of a quotation unless some words have been deleted from the end of the final sentence.

The slash (/) may be used to separate two or three lines of poetry that have been run into a text. If there are more than three lines of poetry they should be handled as an indented quotation. The slash may occasionally be used to separate paired terms such as passed/failed or either/or. In this case, a space is not placed before or after the slash. The slash should be used sparingly, only when it is clearly appropriate.

## Brainstorming

Brainstorming is a technique used frequently in business, industry, science, and engineering. It is accomplished by tossing out ideas, usually with several other people, to find a fresh approach or a creative way to approach a subject. This can be accomplished by an individual by simply free associating about a topic. Sitting with paper and pen, every thought about the subject is written down in a word or phrase. This is done without analytical thinking, just recording what arises in the mind about the topic. The list is then read over carefully several times. The writer looks for patterns, repetitions, clusters of ideas, or a recurring theme. Although brainstorming can be done individually, it works best when several people are involved. Three to five people are ideal. This allows an exchange of ideas and points of view and often results in fresh ideas or approaches.

## Investigating a subject

Asking and answering questions provides a more structured approach to investigating a subject. Several types of questions may be used to illuminate an issue.
- Questions to describe a topic: Questions—such as what is it? What caused it? What is it like or unlike? What is it a part of? What do people say about it?—help explore a topic systematically.
- Questions to explain a topic: Examples include who, how, and what is it? Where does it end and begin? What is at issue? How is it done?
- Questions to persuade involve the claims that can be made about it. What evidence supports the claims? Can the claims be refuted?  What assumptions support the claims?
- Questioning can be a very effective device, as it leads the writer through a systematic process to gain more information about a subject.

## Working thesis

A thesis states the main idea of the essay. A working or tentative thesis should be established early on in the writing process. This working thesis is subject to change and modification as writing progresses. It will serve to keep the writer focused as ideas develop.

The working thesis has two parts: a topic and a comment. The comment makes an important point about the topic. A working thesis should be interesting to an anticipated audience; it should be specific and limit the topic to a manageable scope. Three criteria are useful tools to measure the effectiveness of any working thesis. The writer applies these tools to ascertain the following:
- Is the topic of sufficient interest to hold an audience?

- Is the topic specific enough to generate interest?
- Is the topic manageable? Too broad? Too narrow? Can it be adequately researched?

## Research

Many writing assignments require research. Research is the process of gathering information for the writer's use. There are two broad categories of research:

1. Library research should be started after a research plan is outlined. Topics that require research should be listed and catalogues, bibliographies, periodical indexes checked for references. Librarians are usually an excellent source of ideas and information on researching a topic.
2. Field research is based on observations, interviews, and questionnaires. This can be done by an individual or a team, depending on the scope of the field research.

The specific type and amount of research will vary widely with the topic and the writing assignment. A simple essay or story may require only a few hours of research, whereas a major project can consume weeks or months.

## Rough plan

After information gathering has been completed and the fruits of the research organized effectively, the writer now has a rough or initial plan for the work. A rough plan may be informal, consisting of a few elements such as introduction, body, and conclusions, or a more formal outline. The rough plan may include multiple organizational strategies within the overall piece, or it may isolate one or two that can be used exclusively. At this stage, the plan is just that, a rough plan subject to change as new ideas appear, and the organization takes a new approach. In these cases, the need for more research sometimes becomes apparent, or existing information should be considered in a new way. A more formal outline leads to an easier transition to a draft, but it can also limit the new possibilities that may arise as the plan unfolds. Until the parameters of the piece become clear, it is usually best to remain open to possible shifts in approaching the subject.

## Title, introduction, and conclusion

A good title can identify the subject, describe it in a colorful manner, and give clues to the approach and sometimes the conclusion of the writing. It usually defines the work in the mind of the reader.

A strong introduction follows the lead of the title; it draws the readers into the work and clearly states the topic with a clarifying comment. A common style is to state the topic, and then provide additional details, finally leading to a statement of the thesis at the end. An introduction can also begin with an arresting quote, question, or strong opinion, which grabs the reader's attention.

A good conclusion should leave readers satisfied and provide a sense of closure. Many conclusions restate the thesis and formulate general statements that grow out of it. Writers often find ways to conclude in a dramatic fashion through a vivid image, quotation, or a warning. This in an effort to give the ending the punch to tie up any existing points.

## Examining paragraphs and sentences

Paragraphs are a key structural unit of prose used to break up long stretches of words into more manageable subsets and to indicate a shift in topics or focus. Each paragraph may be examined by identifying the main point of the section and ensuring that every sentence supports or relates to the main theme. Paragraphs may be checked to make sure the organization used in each is appropriate and that the number of sentences is adequate to develop the topic.

Sentences are the building blocks of the written word, and they can be varied by paying attention to sentence length, sentence structure, and sentence openings. These elements should be varied so that writing does not seem boring, repetitive, or choppy. A careful analysis of a piece of writing will expose these stylistic problems, and they can be corrected before the final draft is written. Varying sentence structure and length can make writing more inviting and appealing to a reader.

## Evaluating student writing

The evaluation of student writing should be structured to include three basic goals:
1. To provide students a description of what they are doing when they respond
2. To provide a pathway for potential improvement
3. To help students learn to evaluate themselves

To fulfill these goals, it is necessary for the concept of evaluation to be broadened beyond correcting or judging students. Any teacher response to a student's response should be considered part of the evaluation. In responding to student's responses, a teacher may use written or taped comments, dialogue with students, or conferencing between teacher and students to discuss classroom performance. Students may be asked to evaluate themselves and a teacher, and students can review past progress and plan directions for potential improvement.

## Literary tests

Literary tests are measures of a student's individual performance. Literary assessments are measures of performance of a group of students without reference to individuals. Tests take into consideration what the teacher has taught the students, whereas assessments do not.

For either tests or assessments, the teacher needs a clear purpose on which to base questions or activities. Students should be told of the purpose of the tests or assessments so they will know what to expect. Tests should be used sparingly as one tool among many that can be used to evaluate students. Tests should encourage students on formulation of responses rather than rote answers. They should evaluate students on the basis of their responses rather than correct answers. Improvement over time may be noted and the students praised for specific responses.

## Standardized achievement tests

These multiple-choice tests measure students' ability to understand text passages or apply literary concepts to texts. Although these tests are widely used, they have many limitations. They tend to be based on a simplistic model that ignores the complex nature of a reader's engagement with a text. These tests also do not measure students' articulation of responses. The purpose of these tests is to rank students in group norms so that half the students are below the norm.

To accurately measure a student's abilities, teachers should employ open-ended written or oral-response activities. In developing such tests, teachers must know what specific response patterns they wish to measure. The steps involved in measuring these response patterns must be clearly outlined. Teachers may wish to design questions that encourage personal expressions of responses. This would obviate the pitfall of testing primarily facts about literature rather than how students relate and use this information to engage texts.

## Primary and secondary sources

Primary sources are the raw material of research. This can include results of experiments, notes, and surveys or interviews done by the researcher. Other primary sources are books, letters, diaries, eyewitness accounts, and performances attended by the researcher.

Secondary sources consist of oral and written accounts prepared by others. This includes reports, summaries, critical reviews, and other sources not developed by the researcher.

Most research writing uses both primary and secondary sources: primary sources from first-hand accounts and secondary sources for background and supporting documentation. The research process calls for active reading and writing throughout. As research yields information, it often calls for more reading and research, and the cycle continues.

## Research question and hypothesis

The result of a focusing process is a research question, which is a question or problem that can be solved through research data. A hypothesis is a tentative answer to the research question that must be supported by the research. A research question must be manageable, specific, and interesting. Additionally, it must be argumentative, capable of being proved or disproved by research.

It is helpful to explore a topic with background reading and notes before formulating a research question and a hypothesis. Create a database containing the knowledge to be used in approaching the task of identifying the research question. This background work will allow the writer to formulate a specific question and a tentative answer, the hypothesis. The process of exploring a topic can include brainstorming, free-writing, and scanning your memory and experience for information.

## Library

After reviewing personal resources for information, the library is the next stop. Use index cards or notepads for documentation. Create a system for reviewing data. It is helpful to create key words to trigger responses from sources. Some valuable guidelines for conducting library research include the following:

- Consult the reference librarian for sources and ideas.
- Select appropriate general and specific reference books for examination. Encyclopedias are a good place to start. There are numerous specialized encyclopedias to assist in research.
- Survey biographical dictionaries and indexes for information.
- Review almanacs, yearbooks, and statistical data.
- Scan periodical indexes for articles on the research topic.
- Determine if there are specialized indexes and abstracts that may be helpful.
- Review the computer or card catalog for relevant references.

## Drafting research essay

Before beginning the research essay, revisit the purpose, audience, and scope of the essay. An explicit thesis statement should summarize major arguments and approaches to the subject. After determining the special format of the essay, a survey of the literature on the subject is helpful. If original or first-hand research is involved, prepare a summary of the methods and conclusions.

A clustering strategy assembles all pertinent information on a topic in one physical place. The preparation of an outline may be based on the clusters, or a first draft may be developed without an outline. Formal outlines use a format of thesis statement, main topic, and supporting ideas to shape the information. Drafting the essay can vary considerably among researchers, but it is useful to use an outline or information clusters to get started. Drafts are usually done on a point-to-point basis.

The introduction to a research essay is particularly important, as it sets the context for the essay. It needs to draw the reader into the subject and provide necessary background to understand the subject. It is sometimes helpful to open with the research question and explain how the question will be answered. The major points of the essay may be forecast or previewed to prepare readers for the coming arguments.

In a research essay, it is a good idea to establish the writer's credibility by reviewing credentials and experience with the subject. Another useful opening involves quoting several sources that support the points of the essay, again to establish credibility. The tone should be appropriate to the audience and subject, maintaining a sense of careful authority while building the arguments. Jargon should be kept to a minimum, and language should be carefully chosen to reflect the appropriate tone.

## Drafting the conclusion

The conclusion to a research essay helps readers summarize what they have learned. Conclusions are not meant to convince, as this has been done in the body of the essay. It can be useful to leave the reader with a memorable phrase or example that supports the argument. Conclusions should be both memorable and logical restatements of the arguments in the body of the essay.

A specific-to-general pattern can be helpful, opening with the thesis statement and expanding to more general observations. A good idea is to restate the main points in the body of the essay, leading to the conclusion. An ending that evokes a vivid image or asks a provocative question makes the essay memorable. The same effect can be achieved by a call for action, or a warning. Conclusions may be tailored to the audience's background, in terms of language, tone, and style.

## Reviewing research essay draft

Checklist for Reviewing a Draft of a Research Essay
- Introduction: Is the reader's attention gained and held by the introduction?
- Thesis: Does the essay fulfill the promise of the thesis? Is it strong enough?
- Main points: Are the main points listed and ranked in order of importance?
- Organization: What is the organizing principle of the essay? Does it work?
- Supporting information: Is the thesis adequately supported? Is the thesis convincing?
- Source material: Are there adequate sources and are they smoothly integrated into the essay?
- Conclusion: Does the conclusion have sufficient power? Does it summarize the essay well?
- Paragraphs, sentences, words: Are these elements effective in promoting the thesis?
- Overall review: Evaluate the essay's strengths and weaknesses. What revisions are needed?

## Early assessment of a writing assignment

An early assessment of the writing assignment is very helpful. Understanding the subject, and your relationship to it, is important. Determine if this subject is broad enough for the assignment, or perhaps it must be narrowed to be effectively addressed. If a choice of topics is offered, it is wise to select one of which you have significant prior knowledge or one that can be reasonably investigated in the time given for the work. An important part of assessing the topic will be to decide how much detail to use in writing.

Where will the information for the project come from? Will field research be necessary or will secondary sources suffice? Is there a need to use personal interviews, questionnaires, or surveys to accumulate information? How much reading will need to be done? What kind of documentation will be used? Answering these questions will help estimate the time needed for research.

## Formal outlines

A formal outline may be useful if the subject is complex and includes many elements. Following is a guide to preparing formal outlines:
- Always put the thesis at the top so it may be referred to as often as necessary during the outlining.
- Make subjects similar in generality as parallel as possible in the formal outline.
- Use complete sentences rather than phrases or sentence fragments in the outline.
- Use the conventional system of letters and numbers to designate levels of generality.
- Assign at least two subdivisions for each category in the formal outline.
- Limit the number of major sections in the outline. If there are too many major sections, combine some of them and supplement with additional subcategories.
- Remember the formal outline is still subject to change; remain flexible throughout the process.

## Introduction

An introduction announces the main point of the work. It will usually be a paragraph of 50 to 150 words, opening with a few sentences to engage the reader, and concluding with the essay's main point. The sentence stating the main point is called the thesis sentence. If possible, the sentences leading to the thesis should attract the reader's attention with a provocative question, vivid image, description, paradoxical statement, quotation, or anecdote. The thesis sentence could also appear at the beginning of the introduction. Some types of writing do not lend themselves to stating a thesis in one sentence. Personal narratives and some types of business writing may be better served by conveying an overriding purpose of the text, which may or may not be stated directly. The important point is to impress the audience with the rationale for the writing.

## Effective thesis

Creating an effective thesis is an art. The thesis should be a generalization rather than a fact and should be neither too broad nor too narrow in scope. A thesis prepares readers for facts and details, so it may not be a fact itself. It is a generalization that requires further proof or supporting points. Any thesis too broad may be an unwieldy topic and must be narrowed. The thesis should have a sharp focus and avoid vague, ambivalent language. The process of bringing the thesis into sharp focus may help in outlining major sections of the work. This process is known as blueprinting, and it helps the writer control the shape and sequence of the paper. Blueprinting outlines major points and supporting arguments that are used in elaborating on the thesis. A completed blueprint often leads to a development of an accurate first draft of a work. Once the thesis and opening are complete, it is time to address the body of the work.

## Body and conclusion

The body of the essay should fulfill the promise of the introduction and thesis. If an informal outline has not been done, now is the time for a more formal one. Constructing the formal outline will create a skeleton of the paper. Using this skeleton, the writer finds it much easier to fill out the body of an essay. It is useful to block out paragraphs based on the outline to ensure they contain all the supporting points and are in the appropriate sequence.

The conclusion of the essay should remind readers of the main point, without belaboring it. It may be relatively short, as the body of the text has already made the case for the thesis. A conclusion can summarize the main points and offer advice or ask a question. Never introduce new ideas in a conclusion. Avoid vague and desultory endings, instead close with a crisp, often positive, note. A dramatic or rhetorical flourish can end a piece colorfully.

## Revision and editing

Revising sentences is done to make writing more effective. Editing sentences is done to correct any errors. Revising sentences is usually best done on a computer, on which it is possible to try several versions easily. Some writers prefer to print out a hard copy and work with this for revisions. Each works equally well and depends on the individual preference.

Spelling and grammar checks on software are a great aid to a writer, but not a panacea. Many grammatical problems—such as faulty parallelism, mixed constructions, and misplaced modifiers—can slip past the programs. Even if errors are caught, the writing still must be evaluated for effectiveness. A combination of software programs and writer awareness is necessary to ensure an error-free manuscript.

## Main point of a paragraph

A paragraph should be unified around a main point. A good topic sentence summarizes the paragraph's main point. A topic sentence is more general than subsequent supporting sentences are. Sometime the topic sentence will be used to close the paragraph if earlier sentences give a clear indication of the direction of the paragraph. Sticking to the main point means deleting or omitting unnecessary sentences that do not advance the main point.

The main point of a paragraph deserves adequate development, which usually means a substantial paragraph. A paragraph of two or three sentences often does not develop a point well enough, particularly if the point is a strong supporting argument of the thesis. An occasional short paragraph is fine, particularly if it is used as a transitional device. A choppy appearance should be avoided.

## Illustrations

Examples are a common method of development and may be effectively used when a reader may ask, "For example?" Examples are selected instances, not an inclusive catalog. They may be used to suggest the validity of topic sentences.

Illustrations are extended examples, sometimes presented in story form for interest. They usually require several sentences each, so they are used sparingly. Well-selected illustrations can be a colorful and vivid way of developing a point. Stories that command reader interest, developed in a story form, can be powerful methods of emphasizing key points in an essay. Stories and illustrations should be specific and relate directly to a point or points being made in the text. They allow more colorful language and instill a sense of human interest in a subject. Used judiciously, illustrations and stories are excellent devices.

## Analogies

Analogies draw comparisons between items that appear to have nothing in common. Analogies are employed by writers to attempt to provoke fresh thoughts and changed feelings about a subject. They may be used to make the unfamiliar more familiar, to clarify an abstract point, or to argue a point. Although analogies are effective literary devices, they should be used thoughtfully in arguments. Two things may be alike in some respects but completely different in others.

Cause and effect is an excellent device best used when the cause and effect are generally accepted as true. As a matter of argument, cause and effect is usually too complex and subject to other interpretations to be used successfully. A valid way of using cause and effect is to state the effect in the topic sentence of a paragraph and add the causes in the body of the paragraph. This adds logic and form to a paragraph and usually makes it more effective.

## Point of view

Point of view is the perspective from which writing occurs. There are several possibilities:
- First person is written so that the *I* of the story is a participant or observer.

- Second person is a device to draw the reader in more closely. It is really a variation or refinement of the first-person narrative.
- Third person, the most traditional form of point of view, is the omniscient narrator, in which the narrative voice, presumed to be the writer's, is presumed to know everything about the characters, plot, and action. Most novels use this point of view.
- A multiple point of view is narration delivered from the perspective of several characters.

In modern writing, the stream-of-consciousness technique is often used. Developed fully by James Joyce, this technique uses an interior monologue that provides the narration through the thoughts, impressions, and fantasies of the narrator.

## Dramatic plot

When studying dramatic works, significant events in the story should be recognized.  Major shifts or reversals in the plot, and subsequent action should be followed carefully.  Aristotle's "Poetics" described a typical progression pattern of a plot as follows:
- Exposition
- Complication
- Reversal
- Recognition
- Resolution

This progression is still valid today as we study and analyze plots.  The plot may follow the pattern of comedy (ending with a celebration), or tragedy (ending with death).  The plot may be explained through dialogue, stage action, and off-stage events or by a chorus. While plots of well known plays are easily understood and analyzed, more esoteric drama requires more careful attention to the plot's complexities.

## Discourse theory

Discourse theory includes the views that language is either an abstract system of linguistic forms or an individual form of activity, and that language is a continuous generative process that is used in a social and verbal interaction of speakers. Such views espouse more focused and increased interaction leading to higher forms of learning. It is an intense social interaction where creative energies are found through the partial or total restructuring of ideological systems. Such interactions are seen by some as most beneficial when crossing cultural boundaries. Other discourse theorists have posited that it is not the isolated words that learners assimilate through dialogic interaction but rather the discourses and genres.

## Paradigms and morphosyntax

The concept of a paradigm is closely related to inflection. The paradigm of a lexeme is the set of all of its word forms and is organized by their grammatical categories. Examples of paradigms include verb conjugation or declensions of nouns. Word forms of lexemes can normally be arranged into tables and classified by shared features that include tense, aspect, number, case, gender, or mood. Categories that are used to group word forms into paradigms cannot be chosen arbitrarily and must be categorized with regard to syntactic rules. The main difference between word formation and inflection is that inflectional forms are organized into paradigms which are defined by requirements of syntactic rules. The area of morphology dealing with that relationship is called morphosyntax and is related to inflection and paradigms, but not compounding or word formation.

## Prose and poetry

Prose is language as it is ordinarily spoken as opposed to verse or language with metric patterns. Prose is used for everyday communication, and is found in textbooks, memos, reports, articles, short stories, and novels. Distinguishing characteristics of prose include:
- It may have some sort of rhythm, but there is no formal arrangement.
- The common unit of organization is the sentence.
- It may include literary devices of repetition and balance.
- It must have more coherent relationships among sentences than a list would.

Poetry, or verse, is the manipulation of language with respect to meaning, meter, sound, and rhythm. A line of poetry can be any length and may or may not rhyme. Related groups of lines are called stanzas, and may also be any length. Some poems are as short as a few lines, and some are as long as a book. Poetry is a more ancient form of literature than prose.

## Fiction and nonfiction

Fiction is a literary work usually presented in prose form that is not true. It is the product of the writer's imagination. Examples of fiction are novels, short stories, television scripts, and screenplays.

Nonfiction is a literary work that is based on facts. In other words, the material is true. The purposeful inclusion of false information is considered dishonest, but the expression of opinions or suppositions is acceptable. Libraries divide their collections into works of fiction and nonfiction. Examples of nonfiction include historical materials, scientific reports, memoirs, biographies, most essays, journals, textbooks, documentaries, user manuals, and news reports.

## Style, tone, and point of view

Style is the manner in which a writer uses language in prose or poetry. Style is affected by:
- Diction or word choices
- Sentence structure and syntax
- Types and extent of use of figurative language
- Patterns of rhythm or sound
- Conventional or creative use of punctuation

Tone is the attitude of the writer or narrator towards the theme of, subject of, or characters in a work. Sometimes the attitude is stated, but it is most often implied through word choices. Examples of tone are serious, humorous, satiric, stoic, cynical, flippant, and surprised.

Point of view is the angle from which a story is told. It is the perspective of the narrator, which is established by the author. Common points of view are:
- Third person – Third person points of view include omniscient (knows everything) and limited (confined to what is known by a single character or a limited number of characters). When the third person is used, characters are referred to as he, she, or they.
- First person – When this point of view is used, the narrator refers to himself or herself as "I."

## Alliteration, assonance, and onomatopoeia

Alliteration is the repetition of the first sounds or stressed syllables (usually consonants) in words in close proximity. An example is: "Chirp, chirp," said the chickadee.

Assonance is the repetition of identical or similar vowel sounds, particularly in stressed syllables, in words in close proximity. Assonance is considered to be a form of near rhyme. An example is: the quiet bride cried.

Onomatopoeia refers to words that imitate sounds. It is sometimes called echoism. Examples are hiss, buzz, burp, rattle, and pop. It may also refer to words that correspond symbolically to what they describe, with high tones suggesting light and low tones suggesting darkness. An example is the *gloom* of night versus the *gleam* of the stars.

## Meter

A recurring pattern of stressed and unstressed syllables in language creates a rhythm when spoken. When the pattern is regular, it is called meter. When meter is used in a composition, it is called verse. The most common types of meter are:
- Iambic – An unstressed syllable followed by a stressed syllable
- Anapestic – Two unstressed syllables followed by a stressed syllable
- Trochaic – One stressed syllable followed by an unstressed syllable
- Dactylic – A stressed syllable followed by two unstressed syllables
- Spondaic – Two consecutive syllables that are stressed almost equally
- Pyrrhic – Two consecutive syllables that are equally unstressed

## Blank and free verse

Blank verse is unrhymed verse that consists of lines of iambic pentameter, which is five feet (sets) of unstressed and stressed syllables. The rhythm that results is the closest to natural human speech. It is the most commonly used type of verse because of its versatility. Well-known examples of blank verse are Shakespearean plays, Milton's epic poems, and T. S. Eliot's *The Waste Land*.

Free verse lacks regular patterns of poetic feet, but has more controlled rhythm than prose in terms of pace and pauses. Free verse has no rhyme and is usually written in short lines of irregular length. Well-known examples of free verse are the King James translation of the Psalms, Walt Whitman's *Leaves of Grass*, and the poetry of Ezra Pound and William Carlos Williams.

## Short story

A short story is prose fiction that has the same elements as a novel, such as plot, characters, and point of view. Edgar Allan Poe defined the short story as a narrative that can be read in one sitting (one-half to two hours), and is limited to a single effect. In a short story, there is no time for extensive character development, large numbers of characters, in-depth analysis, complicated plot lines, or detailed backgrounds. Historically, the short story is related to the fable, the exemplum, and the folktale. Short stories have become mainly an American art form. Famous short story writers include William Faulkner, Katherine Anne Porter, Eudora Welty, Flannery O'Connor, O. Henry, and J. D. Salinger.

## Primary and secondary research information

Primary research material is material that comes from the "horse's mouth." It is a document or object that was created by the person under study or during the time period under study. Examples of primary sources are original documents such as manuscripts, diaries, interviews, autobiographies, government records, letters, news videos, and artifacts (such as Native American pottery or wall writings in Egyptian tombs).

Secondary research material is anything that is not primary. Secondary sources are those things that are written or otherwise recorded about the main subject. Examples include a critical analysis of a literary work (a poem by William Blake is primary, but the analysis of the poem by T. S. Eliot is secondary), a magazine article about a person (a direct quote would be primary, but the report is secondary), histories, commentaries, and encyclopedias.

## Emotions

Poetry is designed to appeal to the physical and emotional senses. Using appeals to the physical senses through words that evoke sight, sound, taste, smell, and touch also causes the imagination to respond emotionally. Poetry appeals to the soul and memories with language that can be intriguingly novel and profoundly emotional in connotation. Poetry can focus on any topic, but the feelings associated with the topic are magnified by the ordered presentation found in poetry. Verse, however, is merely a matter of structure. The thing that turns words into poetry is the feeling packed into those words. People write poetry to express their feelings and people read poetry to try to experience those same feelings. Poetry interprets the human condition with understanding and insight. Children respond well to poetry because it has an inviting, entertaining sound that they are eager to mimic.

## Line structure

A line of poetry can be any length and can have any metrical pattern. A line is determined by the physical position of words on a page. A line is simply a group of words on a single line. Consider the following example:

> "When I consider how my light is spent,
>  E're half my days, in this dark world and wide,"

These are two lines of poetry written by John Milton. Lines may or may not have punctuation at the end, depending, of course, on the need for punctuation. If these two lines were written out in a paragraph, they would be written with a slash line and a space in between the lines: "When I consider how my light is spent, / E're half my days, in this dark world and wide."

## Stanza

A stanza is a group of lines. The grouping denotes a relationship among the lines. A stanza can be any length, but the separation of lines into different stanzas indicates an intentional pattern created by the poet. The breaks between stanzas indicate a change of subject or thought. As a group of lines, the stanza is a melodic unit that can be analyzed for metrical and rhyme patterns. Various common rhyme patterns have been named. The Spenserian stanza, which has a rhyme pattern of a b a b b c b c c, is an example. Stanzas of a certain length also have names. Examples include the couplet, which has two lines; the tercet, which has three lines; and the quatrain, which has four lines.

## Literacy

Literacy is commonly understood to refer to the ability to read and write. UNESCO has further defined literacy as the "ability to identify, understand, interpret, create, communicate, compute, and use printed and written materials associated with varying contexts." Under the UNESCO definition, understanding cultural, political, and historical contexts of communities falls under the definition of literacy.

While reading literacy may be gauged simply by the ability to read a newspaper, writing literacy includes spelling, grammar, and sentence structure. To be literate in a foreign language, one would also need to have the ability to understand a language by listening and to speak the language. Some argue that visual representation and numeracy should be included in the requirements one must meet to be considered literate. Computer literacy refers to one's ability to utilize the basic functions of computers and other technologies.

Subsets of reading literacy include phonological awareness, decoding, comprehension, and vocabulary.

## Phonological awareness

A subskill of literacy, phonological awareness is the ability to perceive sound structures in a spoken word, such as syllables and the individual phonemes within syllables. Phonemes are the sounds represented by the letters in the alphabet. The ability to separate, blend, and manipulate sounds is critical to developing reading and spelling skills.

Phonological awareness is concerned with not only syllables, but also onset sounds (the sounds at the beginning of words) and rime (the same thing as rhyme, but spelled differently to distinguish syllable rime from poetic rhyme). Phonological awareness is an auditory skill that does not necessarily involve print. It should be developed before the student has learned letter to sound correspondences. A student's phonological awareness is an indicator of future reading success.

## Teaching phonological awareness

Classroom activities that teach phonological awareness include language play and exposure to a variety of sounds and contexts of sounds. Activities that teach phonological awareness include:
- Clapping to the sounds of individual words, names, or all words in a sentence
- Practicing saying blended phonemes
- Singing songs that involve phoneme replacement (e.g., The Name Game)
- Reading poems, songs, and nursery rhymes out loud
- Reading patterned and predictable texts out loud
- Listening to environmental sounds or following verbal directions
- Playing games with rhyming chants or fingerplays
- Reading alliterative texts out loud
- Grouping objects by beginning sounds
- Reordering words in a well-known sentence or making silly phrases by deleting words from a well-known sentence (perhaps from a favorite storybook)

## Alphabetic principle

The alphabetic principle refers to the use of letters and combinations of letters to represent speech sounds. The way letters are combined and pronounced is guided by a system of rules that establishes relationships between written and spoken words and their letter symbols. Alphabet writing systems are common around the world. Some are phonological in that each letter stands for an individual sound and words are spelled just as they sound. However, there are other writing systems as well, such as the Chinese logographic system and the Japanese syllabic system.

## Language skill development

Children learn language through interacting with others, by experiencing language in daily and relevant context, and through understanding that speaking and listening are necessary for effective communication. Teachers can promote language development by intensifying the opportunities a child has to experience and understand language.
Teachers can assist language development by:
- Modeling enriched vocabulary and teaching new words
- Using questions and examples to extend a child's descriptive language skills
- Providing ample response time to encourage children to practice speech
- Asking for clarification to provide students with the opportunity to develop communication skills
- Promoting conversations among children
- Providing feedback to let children know they have been heard and understood, and providing further explanation when needed

## Oral and written language development

Oral and written language develops simultaneously. The acquisition of skills in one area supports the acquisition of skills in the other. However, oral language is not a prerequisite to written language. An immature form of oral language development is babbling, and an immature form of written language development is scribbling.

Oral language development does not occur naturally, but does occur in a social context. This means it is best to include children in conversations rather than simply talk at them. Written language development can occur without direct instruction. In fact, reading and writing do not necessarily need to be taught through formal lessons if the child is exposed to a print-rich environment. A teacher can assist a child's language development by building on what the child already knows, discussing relevant and meaningful events and experiences, teaching vocabulary and literacy skills, and providing opportunities to acquire more complex language.

**Print-rich classroom environment**

A teacher can provide a print-rich environment in the classroom in a number of ways. These include:

A. Displaying the following in the classroom:
- Children's names in print or cursive
- Children's written work
- Newspapers and magazines
- Instructional charts
- Written schedules
- Signs and labels
- Printed songs, poems, and rhymes

B. Using graphic organizers such as KWL charts or story road maps to:
- Remind students about what was read and discussed
- Expand on the lesson topic or theme
- Show the relationships among books, ideas, and words

C. Using big books to:
- Point out features of print, such as specific letters and punctuation
- Track print from right to left
- Emphasize the concept of words and the fact that they are used to communicate

**Print and book awareness**

Print and book awareness helps a child understand:
- That there is a connection between print and messages contained on signs, labels, and other print forms in the child's environment
- That reading and writing are ways to obtain information and communicate ideas
- That print runs from left to right and from top to bottom
- That a book has parts, such as a title, a cover, a title page, and a table of contents
- That a book has an author and contains a story
- That illustrations can carry meaning
- That letters and words are different
- That words and sentences are separated by spaces and punctuation
- That different text forms are used for different functions
- That print represents spoken language
- How to hold a book.

To be appropriately prepared to learn to read and write, a child should learn:
- That each letter is distinct in appearance
- What direction and shape must be used to make each letter
- That each letter has a name, which can be associated with the shape of a letter
- That there are 26 letters in the English alphabet, and letters are grouped in a certain order
- That letters represent sounds of speech
- That words are composed of letters and have meaning
- That one must be able to correspond letters and sounds to read

## Decoding

Decoding is the method or strategy used to make sense of printed words and figure out how to correctly pronounce them. In order to decode, a student needs to know the relationships between letters and sounds, including letter patterns; that words are constructed from phonemes and phoneme blends; and that a printed word represents a word that can be spoken. This knowledge will help the student recognize familiar words and make informed guesses about the pronunciation of unfamiliar words. Decoding is not the same as comprehension. It does not require an understanding of the meaning of a word, only a knowledge of how to recognize and pronounce it. Decoding can also refer to the skills a student uses to determine the meaning of a sentence. These skills include applying knowledge of vocabulary, sentence structure, and context.

## Reading through phonics

Phonics is the process of learning to read by learning how spoken language is represented by letters. Students learn to read phonetically by sounding out the phonemes in words and then blending them together to produce the correct sounds in words. In other words, the student connects speech sounds with letters or groups of letters and blends the sounds together to determine the pronunciation of an unknown word.

Phonics is a commonly used method to teach decoding and reading, but has been challenged by other methods, such as the whole language approach. Despite the complexity of pronunciation and combined sounds in the English language, research shows that phonics is a highly effective way to teach reading. Being able to read or pronounce a word does not mean the student comprehends the meaning of the word, but context aids comprehension. When phonics is used as a foundation for decoding, children eventually learn to recognize words automatically and advance to decoding multisyllable words with practice.

## Fluency

Fluency is the goal of literacy development. It is the ability to read accurately and quickly. Evidence of fluency includes the ability to recognize words automatically and group words for comprehension. At this point, the student no longer needs to decode words except for complex, unfamiliar ones. He or she is able to move to the next level and understand the meaning of a text. The student should be able to self-check for comprehension and should feel comfortable expressing ideas in writing.
Teachers can help students build fluency by continuing to provide: reading experiences and discussions about text, gradually increasing the level of difficulty; reading practice, both silently and out loud; word

analysis practice; instruction on reading comprehension strategies; and opportunities to express responses to readings through writing.

## Vocabulary

When students do not know the meaning of words in a text, their comprehension is limited. As a result, the text becomes boring or confusing. The larger a student's vocabulary is, the better their reading comprehension will be. A larger vocabulary is also associated with an enhanced ability to communicate in speech and writing. It is the teacher's role to help students develop a good working vocabulary. Students learn most of the words they use and understand from listening to the world around them (adults, other students, media, etc.) They also learn from their reading experiences, which include being read to and reading independently.

Carefully designed activities can also stimulate vocabulary growth, and should emphasize useful words that students see frequently, important words necessary for understanding text, and difficult words such as idioms or words with more than one meaning.

## Promoting vocabulary development

A student's vocabulary can be developed by:
- Calling upon a student's prior knowledge and making comparisons to that knowledge
- Defining a word and providing multiple examples of the use of the word in context
- Showing a student how to use context clues to discover the meaning of a word
- Providing instruction on prefixes, roots, and suffixes to help students break a word into its parts and decipher its meaning
- Showing students how to use a dictionary and a thesaurus
- Asking students to practice new vocabulary by using the words in their own writing
- Providing a print-rich environment with a word wall
- Studying a group of words related to a single subject, such as farm words, transportation words, etc. so that concept development is enhanced.

## Affixes, prefixes, and root words

Affixes are syllables attached to the beginning or end of a word to make a derivative or inflectional form of a word. Both prefixes and suffixes are affixes.

A prefix is a syllable that appears at the beginning of a word that, in combination with the root or base word, creates a specific meaning. For example, the prefix "mis" means "wrong." When combined with the root word "spelling," the word "misspelling" is created, which means the "wrong spelling."
A root word is the base of a word to which affixes can be added. For example, the prefix "in" or "pre" can be added to the root word "vent" to create "invent" or "prevent," respectively. The suffix "er" can be added to the root word "work" to create "worker," which means "one who works." The suffix "able," meaning "capable of," can be added to "work" to create "workable," which means "capable of working."

## Suffix

A suffix is a syllable that appears at the end of a word that, in combination with the root or base word, creates a specific meaning. There are three types of suffixes:

- Noun suffixes – There are two types of noun suffixes. One denotes the act of, state of, or quality of. For example, "ment" added to "argue" becomes "argument," which is defined as "the act of arguing." The other denotes the doer, or one who acts. For example "eer" added to "auction" becomes "auctioneer," meaning "one who auctions." Other examples include "hood," "ness," "tion," "ship," and "ism."
- Verb suffixes – These denote "to make" or "to perform the act of." For example, "en" added to "soft" makes "soften," which means "to make soft." Other verb suffixes are "ate" (perpetuate), "fy" (dignify), and "ize" (sterilize).
- Adjectival suffixes – These include suffixes such as "ful," which means "full of." When added to "care," the word "careful" is formed, which means "full of care." Other examples are "ish," "less," and "able."

## Context clues

Context clues are words or phrases that help the reader figure out the meaning of an unknown word. They are built into a sentence or paragraph by the writer to help the reader develop a clear understanding of the writer's message. Context clues can be used to make intelligent guesses about the meaning of a word instead of relying on a dictionary. Context clues are the reason most vocabulary is learned through reading.

There are four types of commonly used context clues:
- Synonyms – A word with the same meaning as the unknown word is placed close by for comparison.
- Antonyms – A word with the opposite meaning as the unknown word is placed close by for contrast.
- Explanations – An obvious explanation is given close to the unknown word.
- Examples – Examples of what the word means are given to help the reader define the term.

## Comprehension

The whole point of reading is to comprehend what someone else is trying to say through writing. Without comprehension, a student is just reading the words without understanding them or increasing knowledge of a topic. Comprehension results when the student has the vocabulary and reading skills necessary to make sense of the whole picture, not just individual words. Students can self-monitor because they know when they are comprehending the material and when they are not. Teachers can help students solve problems with comprehension by teaching them strategies such as pre-reading titles, sidebars, and follow-up questions; looking at illustrations; predicting what's going to happen in the story; asking questions to check understanding while reading; connecting to background knowledge; and relating to the experiences or feelings of the characters.

## Improving comprehension

Teachers can model in a read-aloud the strategies students can use on their own to better comprehend a text. First, the teacher should do a walk-through of the story illustrations and ask, "What's happening here?" Based on what they have seen, the teacher should then ask students to predict what the story will be about. As the book is read, the teacher should ask open-ended questions such as, "Why do you think the character did this?" and "How do you think the character feels?" The teacher should also ask students if they can relate to the story or have background knowledge of something similar. After the reading, the teacher should ask the students to retell the story in their own words to check for comprehension. This retelling can take the form of a puppet show or summarizing the story to a partner.

## Prior knowledge

Even preschool children have some literacy skills, and the extent and type of these skills have implications for instructional approaches. Comprehension results from relating two or more pieces of information. One piece comes from the text, and another piece might come from prior knowledge (something from a student's long-term memory). For a child, that prior knowledge comes from being read to at home; taking part in other literacy experiences, such as playing computer or word games; being exposed to a print-rich environment at home; and observing examples of parents' reading habits. Children who have had extensive literacy experience are better prepared to further develop their literacy skills in school than children who have not been read to, have few books or magazines in their homes, are seldom exposed to high-level oral or written language activities, and seldom witness adults engaged in reading and writing. Children with a scant literacy background are at a disadvantage. The teacher must not make any assumptions about their prior knowledge, and should use intense, targeted instruction. Otherwise, reading comprehension will be limited.

## Literal vs. critical comprehension

Literal comprehension refers to the skills a reader uses to deal with the actual words in a text. It involves skills such as identifying the topic sentence, main idea, important facts, and supporting details; using context clues to determine the meaning of a word; and sequencing events.

Critical comprehension involves prior knowledge and an understanding that written material, especially in nonfiction, is the author's version of the subject and not necessarily anybody else's. Critical comprehension involves analysis of meaning, evaluation, validation, questioning, and the reasoning skills a reader uses to recognize:
- Inferences and conclusions
- Purpose, tone, point of view, and themes
- The organizational pattern of a work
- Explicit and implicit relationships among words, phrases, and sentences
- Biased language, persuasive tactics, valid arguments, and the difference between fact and opinion

## Metacognition

Metacognition is thinking about thinking. For the student, this involves taking control of their own learning process, self-monitoring progress, evaluating the effectiveness of strategies, and making adjustments to strategies and learning behaviors as needed.

Students who develop good metacognitive skills become more independent and confident about learning. They develop a sense of ownership about their education and realize that information is readily available to them.

Metacognitive skills can be grouped into three categories:
- Awareness – This involves identifying prior knowledge; defining learning goals; inventorying resources such as textbooks, libraries, computers, and study time; identifying task requirements and evaluation standards; and recognizing motivation and anxiety levels.

- Planning – This involves doing time estimates for tasks, prioritizing, scheduling study time, making checklists of tasks, gathering needed materials, and choosing strategies for problem solving or task comprehension.
- Self-monitoring and reflection – This involves identifying which strategies or techniques work best, questioning throughout the process, considering feedback, and maintaining focus and motivation.

## Metacognitive skills

In terms of literacy development, metacognitive skills include taking an active role in reading, recognizing reading behaviors and changing them to employ the behaviors that are most effective, relating information to prior knowledge, and being aware of text structures.

For example, if there is a problem with comprehension, the student can try to form a mental image of what is described, read the text again, adjust the rate of reading, or employ other reading strategies such as identifying unknown vocabulary and predicting meaning.

Being aware of text structures is critical to being able to follow the author's ideas and relationships among ideas. Being aware of difficulties with text structure allows the student to employ strategies such as hierarchical summaries, thematic organizers, or concept maps to remedy the problem.

## Puppetry

Using puppets in the classroom puts students at ease and allows them to enjoy a learning experience as if it were play. The purpose of using puppetry is to generate ideas, encourage imagination, and foster language development. Using a puppet helps a child "become" the character and therefore experience a different outlook.

Language development is enhanced through the student interpreting a story that has been read in class and practicing new words from that story in the puppet show. Children will also have the opportunity to practice using descriptive adjectives for the characters and the scene, which will help them learn the function of adjectives.

Descriptive adjectives and verbs can also be learned by practicing facial expressions and movements with puppets. The teacher can model happy, sad, eating, sleeping, and similar words with a puppet, and then ask students to do the same with their puppets. This is an especially effective vocabulary activity for ESL children.

## Drama activities

Drama activities are fun learning experiences that capture a child's attention, engage the imagination, and motivate vocabulary expansion.

For example, after reading a story, the teacher could ask children to act it out as the teacher repeats the story. This activity, which works best with very young learners, will help children work on listening skills and their ability to pretend. The best stories to use for this passive improvisation are ones that have lots of simple actions that children will be able to understand and perform easily. Older children can create their own improvisational skits and possibly write scripts.

Visualization also calls upon the imagination and encourages concentration and bodily awareness. Children can be given a prompt for the visualization and then asked to draw what they see in their mind's eye.

Charades is another way to act out words and improve vocabulary skills. This activity can be especially helpful to encourage ESL students to express thoughts and ideas in English. These students should be given easier words to act out to promote confidence.

## Types of figurative language

A simile is a comparison between two unlike things using the words "like" or "as." Examples are Robert Burn's sentence "O my love's like a red, red, rose" or the common expression "as pretty as a picture."

A metaphor is a direct comparison between two unlike things without the use of "like" or "as." One thing is identified as the other instead of simply compared to it. An example is D. H. Lawrence's sentence "My soul is a dark forest."

Personification is the giving of human characteristics to a non-human thing or idea. An example is "The hurricane howled its frightful rage."

Synecdoche is the use of a part of something to signify the whole. For example, "boots on the ground" could be used to describe soldiers in a field.

Metonymy is the use of one term that is closely associated with another to mean the other. An example is referring to the "crown" to refer to the monarchy.

## Graphic organizers

The purpose of graphic organizers is to help students classify ideas and communicate more efficiently and effectively. Graphic organizers are visual outlines or templates that help students grasp key concepts and master subject matter by simplifying them down to basic points. They also help guide students through processes related to any subject area or task. Examples of processes include brainstorming, problem solving, decision making, research and project planning, and studying.
Examples of graphic organizers include:
- Reading – These can include beginning, middle, and end graphs or event maps.
- Science – These can include charts that show what animals need or how to classify living things.
- Math – These can include horizontal bar graphs or time lines.
- Language arts – These can include alphabet organizers or charts showing the components of the five-paragraph essay.
- General – These can include KWL charts or weekly planners.

## Second language acquisition

Since some students may have limited understanding of English, a teacher should employ the following practices to promote second language acquisition:
- Make all instruction as understandable as possible and use simple and repeated terms.
- Relate instruction to the cultures of ESL children.
- Increase interactive activities and use gestures or non-verbal actions when modeling.
- Provide language and literacy development instruction in all curriculum areas.

- Establish consistent routines that help children connect words and events.
- Use a schedule so children know what will happen next and will not feel lost.
- Integrate ESL children into group activities with non-ESL children.
- Appoint bilingual students to act as student translators.
- Explain actions as activities happen so that a word to action relationship is established.
- Initiate opportunities for ESL children to experiment with and practice new language.
- Employ multisensory learning.

## Summarization, question generation, and textual marking

It is important to teach students to use critical thinking skills when reading. Three of the critical thinking tools that engage the reader are:
- Summarization – The student reviews the main point(s) of the reading selection and identifies important details. For nonfiction, a good summary will briefly describe the main arguments and the examples that support those arguments. For fiction, a good summary will identify the main characters and events of the story.
- Question generation – A good reader will constantly ask questions while reading about comprehension, vocabulary, connections to personal knowledge or experience, predictions, etc.
- Textual marking – This skill engages the reader by having him or her interact with the text. The student should mark the text with questions or comments that are generated by the text using underlining, highlighting, or shorthand marks such as "?," "!," and "*" that indicate lack of understanding, importance, or key points, for example.

## Theories of language development

Four theories of language development are:
- Learning approach – This theory assumes that language is first learned by imitating the speech of adults. It is then solidified in school through drills about the rules of language structures.
- Linguistic approach – Championed by Noam Chomsky in the 1950s, this theory proposes that the ability to use a language is innate. This is a biological approach rather than one based on cognition or social patterning.
- Cognitive approach – Developed in the 1970s and based on the work of Piaget, this theory states that children must develop appropriate cognitive skills before they can acquire language.
- Sociocognitive approach – In the 1970s, some researchers proposed that language development is a complex interaction of linguistic, social, and cognitive influences

This theory best explains the lack of language skills among children who are neglected, have uneducated parents, or lives in poverty.

## Fairy tales, fables, and tall tales

A fairy tale is a fictional story involving humans, magical events, and usually animals. Characters such as fairies, elves, giants, and talking animals are taken from folklore. The plot often involves impossible events (as in "Jack and the Beanstalk") and/or an enchantment (as in "Sleeping Beauty"). Other examples of fairy tales include "Cinderella," "Little Red Riding Hood," and "Rumpelstiltskin."

A fable is a tale in which animals, plants, and forces of nature act like humans. A fable also teaches a moral lesson. Examples are "The Tortoise and the Hare," *The Lion King*, and *Animal Farm*.

A tall tale exaggerates human abilities or describes unbelievable events as if the story were true. Often, the narrator seems to have witnessed the event described. Examples are fish stories, Paul Bunyan and Pecos Bill stories, and hyperboles about real people such as Davy Crockett, Mike Fink, and Calamity Jane.

## Preadolescent and adolescent literature

Preadolescent literature is mostly concerned with the "tween" issues of changing lives, relationships, and bodies. Adolescents seeking escape from their sometimes difficult lives enjoy fantasy and science fiction. For both groups, books about modern, real people are more interesting than those about historical figures or legends. Boys especially enjoy nonfiction. Reading interests as well as reading levels for this group vary. Reading levels will usually range from 6.0 to 8.9. Examples of popular literature for this age group and reading level include:

- Series – Sweet Valley High, Bluford High, Nancy Drew, Hardy Boys, and Little House on the Prairie
- Juvenile fiction authors – Judy Blume and S. E. Hinton
- Fantasy and horror authors – Ursula LeGuin and Stephen King
- Science fiction authors – Isaac Asimov, Ray Bradbury, and H. G. Wells
- Classic books – *Lilies of the Field, Charlie and the Chocolate Factory, Pippi Longstocking, National Velvet, Call of the Wild, Anne of Green Gables, The Hobbit, The Member of the Wedding,* and *Tom Sawyer*

## Topic sentence

The topic sentence of a paragraph states the paragraph's subject. It presents the main idea. The rest of the paragraph should be related to the topic sentence, which should be explained and supported with facts, details, proofs, and examples.

The topic sentence is more general than the body sentences, and should cover all the ideas in the body of the paragraph. It may contain words such as "many," "most," or "several." The topic sentence is usually the first sentence in a paragraph, but it can appear after an introductory or background sentence, can be the last sentence in a paragraph, or may simply be implied, meaning a topic sentence is not present.

Supporting sentences can often be identified by their use of transition terms such as "for example" or "that is." Supporting sentences may also be presented in numbered sequence.

The topic sentence provides unity to a paragraph because it ties together the supporting details into a coherent whole.

## Cause and effect

Causes are reasons for actions or events. Effects are the results of a cause or causes. There may be multiple causes for one effect (evolutionary extinction, climate changes, and a massive comet caused the demise of the dinosaurs, for example) or multiple effects from one cause (the break-up of the Soviet Union has had multiple effects on the world stage, for instance). Sometimes, one thing leads to another and the effect of one action becomes the cause for another (breaking an arm leads to not driving, which leads to reading more while staying home, for example).

The ability to identify causes and effects is part of critical thinking, and enables the reader to follow the course of events, make connections among events, and identify the instigators and receivers of actions. This ability improves comprehension.

## Facts and opinions

Facts are statements that can be verified through research. Facts answer the questions of who, what, when, and where, and evidence can be provided to prove factual statements. For example, it is a fact that water turns into ice when the temperature drops below 32 degrees Fahrenheit. This fact has been proven repeatedly. Water never becomes ice at a higher temperature.

Opinions are personal views, but facts may be used to support opinions. For example, it may be one person's opinion that Jack is a great athlete, but the fact that he has made many achievements related to sports supports that opinion.

It is important for a reader to be able to distinguish between fact and opinion to determine the validity of an argument. Readers need to understand that some unethical writers will try to pass off an opinion as a fact. Readers with good critical thinking skills will not be deceived by this tactic.

## Invalid arguments

There are a number of invalid or false arguments that are used unethically to gain an advantage, such as:
- The "ad hominem" or "against the person" argument – This type attacks the character or behavior of a person taking a stand on an issue rather than the issue itself. The statement "That fat slob wants higher taxes" is an example of this type of argument.
- Hasty generalizations – These are condemnations of a group based on the behavior of one person or part. An example of this type of argument is someone saying that all McDonald's restaurants are lousy because he or she had a bad experience at one location.
- Faulty causation – This is assigning the wrong cause to an event. An example is blaming a flat tire on losing a lucky penny rather than on driving over a bunch of nails.
- Bandwagon effect – This is the argument that if everybody else is doing something, it must be a good thing to do. The absurdity of this type of argument is highlighted by the question: "If everybody else is jumping off a cliff, should you jump, too?"

It is important for a reader to be able to identify various types of invalid arguments to prevent being deceived and making faulty conclusions.

## Inductive reasoning and deductive reasoning

Inductive reasoning is using particulars to draw a general conclusion. The inductive reasoning process starts with data. For example, if every apple taken out of the top of a barrel is rotten, it can be inferred without investigating further that all the apples are probably rotten. Unless all data is examined, conclusions are based on probabilities. Inductive reasoning is also used to make inferences about the universe. The entire universe cannot be examined, but inferences can be made based on observations about what can be seen. These inferences may be proven false when more data is available, but they are valid at the time they are made if observable data is used.

Deductive reasoning is the opposite of inductive reasoning. It involves using general facts or premises to come to a specific conclusion. For example, if Susan is a sophomore in high school, and all sophomores take geometry, it can be inferred that Susan takes geometry. The word "all" does not allow for exceptions. If all sophomores take geometry, assuming Susan does too is a logical conclusion.

It is important for a reader to recognize inductive and deductive reasoning so he or she can follow the line of an argument and determine if the inference or conclusion is valid.

## Theme

Theme is the central idea of a work. It is the thread that ties all the elements of a story together and gives them purpose. The theme is not the subject of a work, but what a work says about a subject. A theme must be universal, which means it must apply to everyone, not just the characters in a story. Therefore, a theme is a comment about the nature of humanity, society, the relationship of humankind to the world, or moral responsibility. There may be more than one theme in a work, and the determination of the theme is affected by the viewpoint of the reader. Therefore, there is not always necessarily a definite, irrefutable theme. The theme can be implied or stated directly.

## Types of characters

Readers need to be able to differentiate between major and minor characters. The difference can usually be determined based on whether the characters are round, flat, dynamic, or static.

Round characters have complex personalities, just like real people. They are more commonly found in longer works such as novels or full-length plays.

Flat characters display only a few personality traits and are based on stereotypes. Examples include the bigoted redneck, the lazy bum, or the absent-minded professor.

Dynamic characters are those that change or grow during the course of the narrative. They may learn important lessons, fall in love, or take new paths.

Static characters remain the same throughout a story. Usually, round characters are dynamic and flat characters are static, but this is not always the case. Falstaff, the loyal and comical character in Shakespeare's plays about Henry IV, is a round character in terms of his complexity. However, he never changes, which makes him a reliable figure in the story.

## Adjective, adverb, and conjunction

The definitions for these grammatical terms are as follows:

Adjective – This is a word that modifies or describes a noun or pronoun. Examples are a *green* apple or *every* computer.

Adverb – This is a word that modifies a verb (*instantly* reviewed), an adjective (*relatively* odd), or another adverb (*rather* suspiciously).

Conjunctions: There are three types of conjunctions:
- Coordinating conjunctions are used to link words, phrases, and clauses. Examples are: and, or, nor, for, but, yet, and so.
- Correlative conjunctions are paired terms used to link clauses.
- Examples are: either/or, neither/nor, and if/then.
- Subordinating conjunctions relate subordinate or dependent clauses to independent ones. Examples are: although, because, if, since, before, after, when, even though, in order that, and while.

## Gerund, infinitive, noun, direct and indirect objects

The definitions for these grammatical terms are as follows:

Gerund – This is a verb form used as a noun. Most end in "ing." An example is: *Walking* is good exercise.
Infinitive – This is a verbal form comprised of the word "to" followed by the root form of a verb. An infinitive may be used as a noun, adjective, adverb, or absolute. Examples include:
- *To hold* a baby is a joy. (noun)
- Jenna had many files *to reorganize.* (adjective)
- Andrew tried *to remember* the dates. (adverb)
- *To be honest*, your hair looks awful. (absolute)

Noun – This is a word that names a person, place, thing, idea, or quality. A noun can be used as a subject, object, complement, appositive, or modifier.

Object – This is a word or phrase that receives the action of a verb.

A direct object states **to** whom/what an action was committed. It answers the question "to what?" An example is: Joan served *the meal.*
An indirect object states **for** whom/what an action was committed. An example is: Joan served *us* the meal.

## Preposition, prepositional phrase, pronoun, sentence, and verb

The definitions for these grammatical terms are as follows:

Preposition – This is a word that links a noun or pronoun to other parts of a sentence. Examples include above, by, for, in, out, through, and to.

Prepositional phrase – This is a combination of a preposition and a noun or pronoun. Examples include across the bridge, against the grain, below the horizon, and toward the sunset.

Pronoun – This is a word that represents a specific noun in a generic way. A pronoun functions like a noun in a sentence. Examples include I, she, he, it, myself, they, these, what, all, and anybody.
Sentence – This is a group of words that expresses a thought or conveys information as an independent unit of speech. A complete sentence must contain a noun and a verb (I ran). However, all the other parts of speech can also be represented in a sentence.

Verb – This is a word or phrase in a sentence that expresses action (Mary played) or a state of being (Mary is).

## Capitalization and punctuation

Capitalization refers to the use of capital letters. Capital letters should be placed at the beginning of:
- Proper names (Ralph Waldo Emerson, Australia)
- Places (Mount Rushmore, Chicago)
- Historical periods and holidays (Renaissance, Christmas)
- Religious terms (Bible, Koran)
- Titles (Empress Victoria, General Smith)

- All main words in literary, art, or music titles (Grapes of Wrath, Sonata in C Major)

Punctuation consists of:

Periods – A period is placed at the end of a sentence.

Commas – A comma is used to separate:
- Two adjectives modifying the same word (long, hot summer)
- Three or more words or phrases in a list (Winken, Blinken, and Nod; life, liberty, and the pursuit of happiness)

Phrases that are not needed to complete a sentence (The teacher, not the students, will distribute the supplies.)

## Colons and semicolons

Colons – A colon is used to:
- Set up a list (We will need these items: a pencil, paper, and    an eraser.)
- Direct readers to examples or explanations (We have one chore left: clean out the garage.)
- Introduce quotations or dialogue (The Labor Department reported on unemployment: "There was a 3.67% increase in unemployment in 2010."; Scarlett exclaimed: "What shall I do?")

Semicolons – A semicolon is used to:
- Join related independent clauses (There were five major hurricanes this year; two of them hit Florida.)
- Join independent clauses connected by conjunctive adverbs (Popular books are often made into movies; however, it is a rare screenplay that is as good as the book.)

Separate items in a series if commas would be confusing (The characters include: Robin Hood, who robs from the rich to give to the poor; Maid Marian, his true love; and Little John, Robin Hood's comrade-in-arms.)

## Subject-verb agreement

A verb must agree in number with its subject. Therefore, a verb changes form depending on whether the subject is singular or plural. Examples include "I do," "he does," "the ball is," and "the balls are."

If two subjects are joined by "and," the plural form of a verb is usually used. For example: *Jack and Jill want* to get some water (Jack wants, Jill wants, but together they want).

If the compound subjects are preceded by each or every, they take the singular form of a verb. For example: *Each man and each woman brings* a special talent to the world (each brings, not bring).

If one noun in a compound subject is plural and the other is singular, the verb takes the form of the subject nearest to it. For example: Neither the *students* nor their *teacher was* ready for the fire drill.

Collective nouns that name a group are considered singular if they refer to the group acting as a unit. For example: The *choir is going* on a concert tour.

## Syntax

Syntax refers to the rules related to how to properly structure sentences and phrases. Syntax is not the same as grammar. For example, "I does" is syntactically correct because the subject and verb are in proper order, but it is grammatically incorrect because the subject and verb don't agree.

There are three types of sentence structures:
- Simple – This type is composed of a single independent clause with one subject and one predicate (verb or verb form).
- Compound – This type is composed of two independent clauses joined by a conjunction (Amy flew, but Brenda took the train), a correlative conjunction (Either Tom goes with me or I stay here), or a semicolon (My grandfather stays in shape; he plays tennis nearly every day).
- Complex – This type is composed of one independent clause and one or more dependent clauses joined by a subordinating conjunction (Before we set the table, we should replace the tablecloth).

## Types of paragraphs

Illustrative – An illustrative paragraph or essay explains a general statement through the use of specific examples. The writer starts with a topic sentence that is followed by one or more examples that clearly relate to and support the topic.

Narrative – A narrative tells a story. Like a news report, it tells the who, what, when, where, why, and how of an event. A narrative is usually presented in chronological order.

Descriptive – This type of writing appeals to the five senses to describe a person, place, or thing so that the readers can see the subject in their imaginations. Space order is most often used in descriptive writing to indicate place or position.

Process – There are two kinds of process papers: the "how-to" that gives step-by-step directions on how to do something and the explanation paper that tells how an event occurred or how something works.

## Definition paragraph

A definition paragraph or essay describes what a word or term means. There are three ways the explanation can be presented:

Definition by synonym – The term is defined by comparing it to a more familiar term that the reader can more easily understand (A phantom is a ghost or spirit that appears and disappears mysteriously and creates dread).

Definition by class – Most commonly used in exams, papers, and reports, the class definition first puts the term in a larger category or class (The Hereford is a breed of cattle), and then describes the distinguishing characteristics or details of the term that differentiate it from other members of the class (The Hereford is a breed of cattle distinguished by a white face, reddish-brown hide, and short horns).

Definition by negation – The term is defined by stating what it is not and then saying what it is (Courage is not the absence of fear, but the willingness to act in spite of fear).

## Types of essays

A comparison and contrast essay examines the similarities and differences between two things. In a paragraph, the writer presents all the points about subject A and then all the points about subject B. In an essay, the writer might present one point at a time, comparing subject A and subject B side by side.

A classification paper sorts information. It opens with a topic sentence that identifies the group to be classified, and then breaks that group into categories. For example, a group might be baseball players, while a category might be positions they play.

A cause and effect paper discusses the causes or reasons for an event or the effects of a cause or causes. Topics discussed in this type of essay might include the causes of a war or the effects of global warming. A persuasive essay is one in which the writer tries to convince the audience to agree with a certain opinion or point of view. The argument must be supported with facts, examples, anecdotes, expert testimony, or statistics, and must anticipate and answer the questions of those who hold an opposing view. It may also predict consequences.

## Purpose and audience

Early in the writing process, the writer needs to definitively determine the purpose of the paper and then keep that purpose in mind throughout the writing process. The writer needs to ask: "Is the purpose to explain something, to tell a story, to entertain, to inform, to argue a point, or some combination of these purposes?"
Also at the beginning of the writing process, the writer needs to determine the audience of the paper by asking questions such as: "Who will read this paper?," "For whom is this paper intended?," "What does the audience already know about this topic?," "How much does the audience need to know?," and "Is the audience likely to agree or disagree with my point of view?" The answers to these questions will determine the content of the paper, the tone, and the style.

## Drafting, revising, editing, and proofreading

Drafting is creating an early version of a paper. A draft is a prototype or sketch of the finished product. A draft is a rough version of the final paper, and it is expected that there will be multiple drafts.

Revising is the process of making major changes to a draft in regards to clarity of purpose, focus (thesis), audience, organization, and content.

Editing is the process of making changes in style, word choice, tone, examples, and arrangement. These are more minor than the changes made during revision. Editing can be thought of as fine tuning. The writer makes the language more precise, checks for varying paragraph lengths, and makes sure that the title, introduction, and conclusion fit well with the body of the paper.

Proofreading is performing a final check and correcting errors in punctuation, spelling, grammar, and usage. It also involves looking for parts of the paper that may be omitted.

## Title and conclusion

The title is centered on the page and the main words are capitalized. The title is not surrounded by quotation marks, nor is it underlined or italicized. The title is rarely more than four or five words, and is very rarely a whole sentence. A good title suggests the subject of the paper and catches the reader's interest.

The conclusion should flow logically from the body of the essay, should tie back to the introduction, and may provide a summary or a final thought on the subject. New material should never be introduced in the conclusion. The conclusion is a wrap-up that may contain a call to action, something the writer wants the audience to do in response to the paper. The conclusion might end with a question to give the reader something to think about.

## Introduction

The introduction contains the thesis statement, which is usually the first or last sentence of the opening paragraph. It needs to be interesting enough to make the reader want to continue reading. Possible openings for an introduction include:
- The thesis statement
- A general idea that gives background or sets the scene
- An illustration that will make the thesis more concrete and easy to picture
- A surprising fact or idea to arouse curiosity
- A contradiction to popular belief that attracts interest
- A quotation that leads into the thesis

## Types of sentences

A declarative sentence makes a statement and is punctuated by a period at the end. An example is: The new school will be built at the south end of Main Street.

An interrogative sentence asks a question and is punctuated by a question mark at the end. An example is: Why will the new school be built so far out?

An exclamatory sentence shows strong emotion and is punctuated by an exclamation mark at the end. An example is: The new school has the most amazing state-of-the-art technology!

An imperative sentence gives a direction or command and may be punctuated by an exclamation mark or a period. Sometimes, the subject of an imperative sentence is you, which is understood instead of directly stated. An example is: Come to the open house at the new school next Sunday.

## Parallelism, euphemism, hyperbole, and climax

Parallelism – Subjects, objects, verbs, modifiers, phrases, and clauses can be structured in sentences to balance one with another through a similar grammatical pattern. Parallelism helps to highlight ideas while showing their relationship and giving style to writing.
Examples are:
- Parallel words – The killer behaved coldly, cruelly, and inexplicably.
- Parallel phrases – Praised by comrades, honored by commanders, the soldier came home
- a hero.
- Parallel clauses – "We shall fight on the beaches, we shall fight on the landing grounds, we shall fight in the hills." (Winston Churchill)

Euphemism – This is a "cover-up" word that avoids the explicit meaning of an offensive or unpleasant term by substituting a vaguer image. An example is using "expired" instead of "dead."

Hyperbole – This is an example or phrase that exaggerates for effect. An example is the extravagant overstatement "I thought I would die!" Hyperbole is also used in tall tales, such as those describing Paul Bunyan's feats.

Climax – This refers to the process of building up to a dramatic highpoint through a series of phrases or sentences. It can also refer to the highpoint or most intense event in a story.

## Bathos, oxymoron, irony, and malapropism

Bathos – This is an attempt to evoke pity, sorrow, or nobility that goes overboard and becomes ridiculous. It is an insincere pathos and a letdown. It is also sometimes called an anticlimax, although an anticlimax might be intentionally included for comic or satiric effect.

Oxymoron – This refers to two terms that are used together for contradictory effect, usually in the form of an adjective that doesn't fit the noun. An example is: a "new classic."

Irony – This refers to a difference between what is and what ought to be, or between what is said and what is meant. Irony can be an unexpected result in literature, such as a twist of fate. For example, it is ironic that the tortoise beat the hare.

Malapropism – This is confusing one word with another, similar-sounding word. For example, saying a movie was a cliff dweller instead of a cliffhanger is a malapropism.

## Transitional words and phrases

Transitional words are used to signal a relationship. They are used to link thoughts and sentences. Some types of transitional words and phrases are:
- Addition – Also, in addition, furthermore, moreover, and then, another
- Admitting a point – Granted, although, while it is true that
- Cause and effect – Since, so, consequently, as a result, therefore, thus
- Comparison – Similarly, just as, in like manner, likewise, in the same way
- Contrast – On the other hand, yet, nevertheless, despite, but, still
- Emphasis – Indeed, in fact, without a doubt, certainly, to be sure
- Illustration – For example, for instance, in particular, specifically
- Purpose – In order to, for this purpose, for this to occur
- Spatial arrangement – Beside, above, below, around, across, inside, near, far, to the left
- Summary or clarification – In summary, in conclusion, that is, in other words
- Time sequence – Before, after, later, soon, next, meanwhile, suddenly, finally

## Pre-writing techniques

Pre-writing techniques that help a writer find, explore, and organize a topic include:
- Brainstorming – This involves letting thoughts make every connection to the topic possible, and then spinning off ideas and making notes of them as they are generated. This is a process of using imagination, uninhibited creativity, and instincts to discover a variety of possibilities.

- Freewriting – This involves choosing items from the brainstorming list and writing about them nonstop for a short period. This unedited, uncensored process allows one thing to lead to another and permits the writer to think of additional concepts and themes.

Clustering/mapping – This involves writing a general word or phrase related to the topic in the middle of a paper and circling it, and then quickly jotting down related words or phrases. These are circled and lines are drawn to link words and phrases to others on the page. Clustering is a visual representation of brainstorming that reveals patterns and connections.

## Listing and charting

Prewriting techniques that help a writer find, explore, and organize a topic include:

Listing – Similar to brainstorming, listing is writing down as many descriptive words and phrases (not whole sentences) as possible that relate to the subject. Correct spelling and grouping of these descriptive terms can come later if needed. This list is merely intended to stimulate creativity and provide a vibrant vocabulary for the description of the subject once the actual writing process begins.

Charting – This prewriting technique works well for comparison/contrast purposes or for the examination of advantages and disadvantages (pros and cons). Any kind of chart will work, even a simple two-column list. The purpose is to draw out points and examples that can be used in the paper.

## Purpose of writing

Writing always has a purpose. Two of the five reasons to write are:

To tell a story – The story does not necessarily need to be fictional. The purposes are to explain what happened, to narrate events, and to explain how things were accomplished. The story will need to make a point, and plenty of details will need to be provided to help the reader imagine the event or process.

To express oneself – This type of writing is commonly found in journals, diaries, or blogs. This kind of writing is an exercise in reflection that allows writers to learn something about themselves and what they have observed, and to work out their thoughts and feelings on paper.

Three of the five reasons to write are:

To convey information – Reports are written for this purpose. Information needs to be as clearly organized and accurate as possible. Charts, graphs, tables, and other illustrations can help make the information more understandable.

To make an argument – This type of writing also makes a point, but adds opinion to the facts presented. Argumentative, or persuasive, writing is one of the most common and important types of writing. It should follow rules of logic and ethics.

To explore ideas – This is speculative writing that is quite similar to reflective writing. This type of writing explores possibilities and asks questions without necessarily expecting an answer. The purpose is to stimulate readers to further consider and reflect on the topic.

## Strategic arrangement

The order of the elements in a writing project can be organized in the following ways:

Logical order – There is a coherent pattern in the presentation of information, such as inductive or deductive reasoning or a division of a topic into its parts.

Hierarchical order – There is a ranking of material from most to least important or least to most important, depending on whether the writer needs a strong start or a sweeping finish. It can also involve breaking down a topic from a general form into specifics.

Chronological order – This is an order that follows a sequence. In a narrative, the sequence will follow the time order of beginning to middle to end. In a "how to," the sequence will be step 1, step 2, step 3, and so on.

Order defined by genre – This is a pre-determined order structured according to precedent or professional guidelines, such as the order required for a specific type of research or lab report, a resume, or an application form.

Order of importance – This method of organization relies on a ranking determined by priorities. For example, in a persuasive paper, the writer usually puts the strongest argument in the last body paragraph so that readers will remember it. In a news report, the most important information comes first.

Order of interest – This order is dependent on the level of interest the audience has in the subject. If the writer anticipates that reader knowledge and interest in the subject will be low, normal order choices need to be changed. The piece should begin with something very appealing. This will hook the reader and make for a strong opening.

## Beginning stages of writing

The following are the beginning stages of learning to write:
- Drawing pictures is the first written attempt to express thoughts and feelings. Even when the picture is unrecognizable to the adult, it means something to the child.
- The scribble stage begins when the child attempts to draw shapes. He or she may also try to imitate writing. The child may have a story or explanation to go with the shapes.
- Children have the most interest in learning to write their own names, so writing lessons usually start with that. Children will soon recognize that there are other letters too.
- Children are learning the alphabet and how to associate a sound with each letter. Reversing letters is still common, but instruction begins with teaching children to write from left to right.
- Written words may not be complete, but will likely have the correct beginning and end sounds/letters. Children will make some attempt to use vowels in writing.
- Children will write with more ease, although spelling will still be phonetic and only some punctuation will be used.

## Journals

Writing in a journal gives students practice in writing, which makes them more comfortable with the writing process. Journal writing also gives students the opportunity to sort out their thoughts, solve problems, examine relationships and values, and see their personal and academic growth when they revisit old entries. The advantages for the teacher are that the students become more experienced with and accustomed to writing. Through reading student journals, the teacher can also gain insight into the students' problems and attitudes, which can help the teacher tailor his or her lesson plans.

A journal can be kept in a notebook or in a computer file. It shouldn't be just a record of daily events, but an expression of thoughts and feelings about everything and anything. Grammar and punctuation don't matter since journaling is a form of private communication. Teachers who review journals need to keep in mind that they should not grade journals and that comments should be encouraging and polite.

## Revising

Revising a paper involves rethinking the choices that were made while constructing the paper and then rewriting it, making any necessary changes or additions to word choices or arrangement of points. Questions to keep in mind include:

- Is the thesis clear?
- Do the body paragraphs logically flow and provide details to support the thesis?
- Is anything unnecessarily repeated?
- Is there anything not related to the topic?
- Is the language understandable?
- Does anything need to be defined?
- Is the material interesting?

Another consideration when revising is peer feedback. It is helpful during the revision process to have someone who is knowledgeable enough to be helpful and will be willing to give an honest critique read the paper.

## Paragraph coherence

Paragraph coherence can be achieved by linking sentences by using the following strategies:

Repetition of key words – It helps the reader follow the progression of thought from one sentence to another if key words (which should be defined) are repeated to assure the reader that the writer is still on topic and the discussion still relates to the key word.

Substitution of pronouns – This doesn't just refer to using single word pronouns such as I, they, us, etc., but also alternate descriptions of the subject. For example, if someone was writing about Benjamin Franklin, it gets boring to keep saying Franklin or he. Other terms that describe him, such as that notable American statesman, this printer, the inventor, and so forth can also be used.

Substitution of synonyms – This is similar to substitution of pronouns, but refers to using similar terms for any repeated noun or adjective, not just the subject. For example, instead of constantly using the word great, adjectives such as terrific, really cool, awesome, and so on can also be used.

## Verbs

In order to understand the role of a verb and be able to identify the verb that is necessary to make a sentence, it helps to know the different types of verbs. These are:

Action verbs – These are verbs that express an action being performed by the subject. An example is: The outfielder caught the ball (outfielder = subject and caught = action).

Linking verbs – These are verbs that link the subject to words that describe or identify the subject. An example is: Mary is an excellent teacher (Mary = subject and "is" links Mary to her description as an excellent teacher). Common linking verbs are all forms of the verb "to be," appear, feel, look, become, and seem.

Helping verbs – When a single verb cannot do the job by itself because of tense issues, a second, helping verb is added. Examples include: should have gone ("gone" is the main verb, while "should" and "have" are helping verbs), and was playing ("playing" is the main verb, while "was" is the helping verb).

## Conjunctions

There are different ways to connect two clauses and show their relationship.

A coordinating conjunction is one that can join two independent clauses by placing a comma and a coordinating conjunction between them. The most common coordinating conjunctions are and, but, or, nor, yet, for, and so. Examples include: "It was warm, so I left my jacket at home" and "It was warm, and I left my jacket at home."
A subordinating conjunction is one that joins a subordinate clause and an independent clause and establishes the relationship between them. An example is: "We can play a game after Steve finishes his homework." The dependent clause is "after Steve finishes his homework" because the reader immediately asks, "After Steve finishes, then what?" The independent clause is "We can play a game." The concern is not the ability to play a game, but "when?" The answer to this question is dependent on when Steve finishes his homework.

## Run-ons and comma splices

A run-on sentence is one that tries to connect two independent clauses without the needed conjunction or punctuation and makes it hard for the reader to figure out where one sentence ends and the other starts. An example is: "Meagan is three years old she goes to pre-school." Two possible ways to fix the run-on would be: "Meagan is three years old, and she goes to pre-school" or "Meagan is three years old; however, she goes to pre-school."

A comma splice occurs when a comma is used to join two independent clauses without a proper conjunction. The comma should be replaced by a period or one of the methods for coordination or subordination should be used. An example of a comma splice is: "Meagan is three years old, she goes to pre-school."

## Fragment

A fragment is an incomplete sentence, which is one that does not have a subject to go with the verb, or vice versa. The following are types of fragments:

Dependent clause fragments – These usually start with a subordinating conjunction. An example is: "Before you can graduate." "You can graduate" is a sentence, but the subordinating conjunction "before" makes the clause dependent, which means it needs an independent clause to go with it. An example is: "Before you can graduate, you have to meet all the course requirements."

Relative clause fragments – These often start with who, whose, which, or that. An example is: "Who is always available to the students." This is a fragment because the "who" is not identified. A complete sentence would be: "Mr. Jones is a principal who is always available to the students."

The "ing" fragment lacks a subject. The "ing" form of a verb has to have a helping verb. An example is: "Walking only three blocks to his job." A corrected sentence would be: "Walking only three blocks to his job, Taylor has no need for a car."

Prepositional phrase fragments are ones that begin with a preposition and are only a phrase, not a complete thought. An example is: "By the time we arrived." "We arrived" by itself would be a complete sentence, but the "by" makes the clause dependent and the reader asks, "By the time you arrived, what happened?" A corrected sentence would be: "By the time we arrived, all the food was gone."

Infinitive phrase fragments have the same problem as prepositional phrase ones. An example is: "To plant the seed." A corrected sentence would be: "To plant the seed, Isaac used a trowel."

## Speaking skills children should have

Children of elementary/intermediate school age should be able to:
- Speak at an appropriate volume, tone, and pace that is understandable and appropriate to the audience
- Pronounce most words accurately
- Use complete sentences
- Make eye contact
- Use appropriate gestures with speech
- Exhibit an awareness of audience and adjust content to fit the audience (adjust word choices and style to be appropriate for peers or adults)
- Ask relevant questions
- Respond appropriately when asked questions about information or an opinion, possibly also being able to provide reasons for opinions
- Speak in turn, not interrupt, and include others in conversations
- Provide a summary or report orally
- Participate in small and large group discussions and debates
- Read orally before an audience
- Conduct short interviews
- Provide directions and explanations orally, including explanations of class lessons

## Viewing skills children should have

Children of elementary school age should be developing or have attained the ability to understand the importance of media in people's lives. They should understand that television, radio, films, and the Internet have a role in everyday life. They should also be able to use media themselves (printing out material from the Internet or making an audio or video tape, for example). They should also be aware that the purpose of advertising is to sell.

Children of intermediate school age should be developing or have attained the ability to obtain and compare information from newspapers, television, and the Internet. They should also be able to judge its reliability and accuracy to some extent. Children of this age should be able to tell the difference between fictional and non-fictional materials in media. They should also be able to use a variety of media, visuals, and sounds to make a presentation.

## Listening skills children should have

Through the elementary/intermediate school years, children should develop the following listening skills:
- Follow oral instructions consistently
- Actively listen to peers and teachers
- Avoid creating distracting behavior or being distracted by the behavior of others most of the time
- Respond to listening activities and exhibit the ability to discuss, illustrate, or write about the activity and show knowledge of the content and quality of the listening activity
- Respond to listening activities and exhibit the ability to identify themes, similarities/differences, ideas, forms, and styles of activities
- Respond to a persuasive speaker and exhibit the ability to analyze and evaluate the credibility of the speaker and form an opinion describing whether they agree or disagree with the point made
- Demonstrate appropriate social behavior while part of an audience

## Teaching viewing skills

Viewing skills can be sharpened by having students look at a single image, such as a work of art or a cartoon, and simply asking students what they see. The teacher can ask what is happening in the image, and then elicit the details that clue the students in to what is happening. Of course, there may be more than one thing happening. The teacher should also question the students about the message of the image, its purpose, its point of view, and its intended audience. The teacher should ask for first impressions, and then provide some background or additional information to see if it changes the way students look at or interpret the image. The conclusion of the lesson should include questions about what students learned from the exercise about the topic, themselves, and others.

Students are exposed to multiple images every day. It is important for them to be able to effectively interpret these images. They should be able to make sense of the images and the spoken and print language that often accompany them. Learning can be enhanced with images because they allow for quicker connections to prior knowledge than verbal information. Visuals in the classroom can also be motivational, can support verbal information, and can express main points, sometimes resulting in instant recognition.

Some of the common types of images that students see every day include: bulletin boards, computer graphics, diagrams, drawings, illustrations, maps, photographs, posters, book covers, advertisements, Internet sites, multimedia presentations, puppet shows, television, videos, print cartoons, models, paintings, animation, drama or dance performances, films, and online newscasts and magazines.

Activities at school that can be used to strengthen the viewing skills of students of varying ages include:
- Picture book discussions – Students can develop an appreciation of visual text and the language that goes with it through guided discussions of picture books that focus on the style and color of the images and other details that might capture a child's attention.
- Gallery walks – Students can walk around a room or hallway viewing the posted works of other students and hear presentations about the works. They can also view a display prepared by the teacher. Students are expected to take notes as they walk around, have discussions, and perhaps do a follow-up report.

- Puppet theater and drama presentations – Students can learn about plots, dialogue, situations, characters, and the craft of performance from viewing puppet or drama presentations, which also stimulate oral communication and strengthen listening skills. Discussions or written responses should follow performances to check for detail acquisition.

## Classroom viewing center

A classroom viewing center should contain magazines, CD-ROMs, books, videos, and individual pictures (photographs or drawings).

Students should have a viewing guide that explains expectations related to the viewing center (before, during, and after using the center). For younger students, the teacher can ask questions that guide them through the viewing rather than expecting them to read the guidelines and write responses.
- Before viewing, students should think about what they already know about the subject and what they want to learn from the viewing.
- During the viewing, students should make notes about whatever interests them or is new to them.
- After viewing, students could discuss or individually write down what they found to be the most interesting idea or striking image and explain why it caught their attention.

## Important questions pertaining to viewing a narrative

A teacher should make students responsible for gaining information or insight from the viewing. Setting expectations increases student attention and critical thinking. As with any viewing, the students should consider what they already know about the topic and what they hope to gain by watching the narrative before viewing it. During the viewing, the students should take notes (perhaps to answer questions provided by the teacher).
After the viewing, students should be able to answer the following questions:
- What was the time period and setting of the story?
- Who were the main characters?
- How effective was the acting?
- What was the problem or goal in the story?
- How was the problem solved or the goal achieved?
- How would you summarize the story?
- What did you learn from the story?
- What did you like or dislike about the story or its presentation?
- Would you recommend this viewing to others?
- How would you rate it?

## Learning by listening difficulties

It is difficult to learn just by listening because the instruction is presented only in spoken form. Therefore, unless students take notes, there is nothing for them to review. However, an active listener will anticipate finding a message in an oral presentation and will listen for it, interpreting tone and gestures as the presentation progresses. In group discussions, students are often too busy figuring out what they will say when it is their turn to talk to concentrate on what others are saying. Therefore, they don't learn from others, but instead come away knowing only what they already knew. Students should be required to respond directly to the previous speaker before launching into their own comments. This practice will force students to listen to each other and learn that their own responses will be better because of what can be added by listening to others.

## Speaking

Volume – Voice volume should be appropriate to the room and adjusted according to whether or not a microphone is used. The speaker should not shout at the audience, mumble, or speak so softly that his or her voice is inaudible.

Pace and pronunciation – The speaker shouldn't talk so fast that his or her speech is unintelligible, nor should the speaker speak so slowly as to be boring. The speaker should enunciate words clearly.

Body language and gestures – Body language can add to or distract from the message, so annoying, repetitive gestures such as waving hands about, flipping hair, or staring at one spot should be avoided. Good posture is critical.

Word choice – The speaker should use a vocabulary level that fits the age and interest level of the audience. Vocabulary may be casual or formal depending on the audience.

Visual aids – The speaker should use whatever aids will enhance the presentation, such as props, models, media, etc., but should not use anything that will be distracting or unmanageable.

## Listening and new language

Listening is a critical skill when learning a new language. Students spend a great deal more time listening than they do speaking, and far less time reading and writing than speaking. Two ways to encourage ESL students to listen are to:
- Talk about topics that are of interest to the ESL learner. Otherwise, students may tune out the speaker because they don't want to put in that much effort to learn about a topic they find boring.
- Talk about content or give examples that are easy to understand or are related to a topic that is familiar to ESL students. Culturally relevant materials will be more interesting to
- ESL students, will make them feel more comfortable, and will contain vocabulary that they may already be familiar with.

Listening is not a passive skill, but an active one. Therefore, a teacher needs to make the listening experience as rewarding as possible and provide as many auditory and visual clues as possible. Three ways that the teacher can make the listening experience rewarding for ESL students are:
- Avoid colloquialisms and abbreviated or slang terms that may be confusing to the ESL listener, unless there is enough time to define them and explain their use.
- Make the spoken English understandable by stopping to clarify points, repeating new or difficult words, and defining words that may not be known.

Support the spoken word with as many visuals as possible. Pictures, diagrams, gestures, facial expressions, and body language can help the ESL learner correctly interpret the spoken language more easily and also leaves an image impression that helps them remember the words.

## Top down and bottom up

ESL students need to be given opportunities to practice both top-down and bottom-up processing. If they are old enough to understand these concepts, they should be made aware that these are two processes that affect their listening comprehension.

In top-down processing, the listener refers to background and global knowledge to figure out the meaning of a message. For example, when asking an ESL student to perform a task, the steps of the task should be explained and accompanied by a review of the vocabulary terms the student already understands so that the student feels comfortable tackling new steps and new words. The teacher should also allow students to ask questions to verify comprehension.

In bottom-up processing, the listener figures out the meaning of a message by using "data" obtained from what is said. This data includes sounds (stress, rhythm, and intonation), words, and grammatical relationships. All data can be used to make conclusions or interpretations. For example, the listener can develop bottom-up skills by learning how to detect differences in intonation between statements and questions.

**Listening lesson steps**

All students, but especially ESL students, can be taught listening through specific training. During listening lessons, the teacher should guide students through three steps:
- Pre-listening activity – This establishes the purpose of the lesson and engages students' background knowledge. This activity should ask students to think about and discuss something they already know about the topic. Alternatively, the teacher can provide background information.
- The listening activity – This requires the listener to obtain information and then immediately do something with that information. For example, the teacher can review the schedule for the day or the week. The students are being given information about a routine they already know, but need to be able to identify names, tasks, and times.

Post-listening activity – This is an evaluation process that allows students to judge how well they did with the listening task. Other language skills can be included in the activity. For example, this activity could involve asking questions about who will do what according to the classroom schedule (Who is the lunch monitor today?) and could also involve asking students to produce whole sentence replies.

**Helping ESL students by speaking**

To help ESL students better understand subject matter, the following teaching strategies using spoken English can be used:
- Read aloud from a textbook, and then ask ESL students to verbally summarize what was read. The teacher should assist by providing new words as needed to give students the opportunity to practice vocabulary and speaking skills. The teacher should then read the passage again to students to verify accuracy and details.
- The teacher could ask ESL students to explain why the subject matter is important to them and where they see it fitting into their lives. This verbalization gives them speaking practice and helps them relate to the subject.

Whenever small group activities are being conducted, ESL students can be placed with English-speaking students. It is best to keep the groups to two or three students so that the ESL student will be motivated by the need to be involved. English-speaking students should be encouraged to include ESL students in the group work.

**Helping ESL students by reading**

There are supplemental printed materials that can be used to help ESL students understand subject matter. The following strategies can be used to help ESL students develop English reading skills.

- Make sure all ESL students have a bilingual dictionary to use. A thesaurus would also be helpful.
- Try to keep content area books written in the ESL students' native languages in the classroom. Students can use them side-by-side with English texts. Textbooks in other languages can be ordered from the school library or obtained from the classroom textbook publisher.

If a student lacks confidence in his/her ability to read the textbook, the teacher can read a passage to the student and have him or her verbally summarize the passage. The teacher should take notes on what the student says and then read them back. These notes can be a substitute, short-form, in-their-own-words textbook that the student can understand.

## Helping ESL students with general strategies

Some strategies can help students develop more than one important skill. They may involve a combination of speaking, listening, and/or viewing. Others are mainly classroom management aids. General teaching strategies for ESL students include:
- Partner English-speaking students with ESL students as study buddies and ask the English-speaking students to share notes.
- Encourage ESL students to ask questions whenever they don't understand something. They should be aware that they don't have to be able to interpret every word of text to understand the concept.
- Dictate key sentences related to the content area being taught and ask ESL students to write them down. This gives them practice in listening and writing, and also helps them identify what is important.
- Alternate difficult and easy tasks so that ESL students can experience academic success.
- Ask ESL students to label objects associated with content areas, such as maps, diagrams, parts of a leaf, or parts of a sentence. This gives students writing and reading experience and helps them remember key vocabulary.

# Mathematics

## Representation in mathematical processes

Representations are the tools of symbols and materials. They are used to help students understand mathematics by giving them visual guides in their thinking. For example, the conventional symbols that indicate addition, subtraction, equality, and so on (into the higher realms of symbols used in geometry, algebra, and calculus) tell students, at a glance, the process that is being calculated.

Materials that are used as representations are called manipulatives. These can be small plastic objects or pictures for the students to count, line up, or otherwise use to solve a problem. Representations make abstract concepts become concrete. They put mathematics into the students,' hands as well as heads, and the result is improved learning. Using familiar manipulatives with new problems helps the student to make connections and feel more confident and capable of expanding their skills.

## Kindergarten concepts

In kindergarten, children can be prepared for the study of mathematics by practicing certain concepts such as:

- position – top, middle, bottom, above, below, before, after, between, under, inside, outside, left, and right
- visual attributes – same and different colors, shapes, and sizes; identifying items that are out-of-place or don't belong
- sorting – by size, color, type, or shape; identifying an equal number, more, or fewer of a given item
- graphing – the use of picture graphs and using data from graphs
- patterns – identifying, copying, extending, and making patterns; finding patterns that are different or alike, making predictions from patterns
- measurements – longer and shorter; how much they weigh, heavier and lighter; how much an item can hold

## Mathematical properties

The properties of mathematical operations include:

- Commutative property – The product is the same regardless of the order of the factors. For example: $2 * 5 = 5 * 2$.
- Associative property – The product is the same regardless of grouping. For example: $(2 * 5) * 3 = 2 * (5 * 3)$.
- Distributive property – Multiplying a sum by a number is the same as multiplying each addend by the number and then adding the products. For example, $2 * (3 + 4) = (2 * 3) + (2 * 4) = 14$.
- Zero property – The sum of a number and 0 is that number. In multiplication, the product of a number and 0 is 0. For example, $3 + 0 = 3$ and $3 * 0 = 0$.

## Arithmetic terms specific to numbers

Numbers are the basic building blocks of mathematics. Specific features of numbers are identified by the following terms:

- Integers – The set of positive and negative numbers, including zero. Integers do not include fractions (1/3), decimals (0.56), or mixed numbers (7¾).
- Prime number – A whole number greater than 1 that has only two factors, itself and 1; that is, a number that can be divided evenly only by 1 and itself.
- Composite number – A whole number greater than 1 that has more than two different factors. In other words, any number that is not a prime number. For example: The composite number 8 has the factors of 1, 2, 4, and 8.
- Even number – Any integer that can be divided by 2 without leaving a remainder. For example: 2, 4, 6, 8, and so on.
- Odd number – Any integer that cannot be divided evenly by 2. For example: 3, 5, 7, 9, and so on.

## Rational, irrational, and real numbers

Rational, irrational, and real numbers can be described as follows:

- Rational numbers are the set of whole numbers, integers, decimals, and fractions. Rational numbers can be expressed as either a negative or positive value. Any terminating decimal that can be expressed as a fraction is a rational number. For example, 45.6 can be written as 456/10.
- Irrational numbers are numbers that are not rational. That is, like the square root of 2, they cannot be written as fractions or decimals because the number of decimal places is infinite and a recurring pattern does not exist within the number. For example, Pi ($\pi$) begins with 3.141592653 and continues without end, so Pi is an irrational number.
- Real numbers are the set of all rational and irrational numbers and are used in all applications of measuring, comparing, counting, or determining quantities.

## Factors

Factors are numbers that are multiplied together to obtain a product. For example, in the equation 2 * 3 = 6, the numbers 2 and 3 are factors. A prime number has only two factors (1 and itself), but other numbers can have many factors.

A "common" factor is a number that divides exactly into two or more other numbers. For example, the factors of 12 are 1, 2, 3, 4, 6, and 12, while the factors of 15 are 1, 3, 5, and 15. The common factors of 12 and 15 are 1 and 3.

A "prime" factor is also a prime number. Therefore, the prime factors of 12 are 2 and 3. For 15, the prime factors are 3 and 5.

## Fractions, numerators, and denominators

A fraction is a way to compare equal parts with a whole. For example, the fraction 5/8 shows there are 5 equal parts out of 8 equal parts. A fraction is expressed as one integer written above another, with a dividing line between them (x/y).

The top number of a fraction is called the numerator, and it represents the number of parts under consideration. For example, ¼ means that 1 part out of 4 is being considered in the calculation.

The bottom number of a fraction is called the denominator, and it represents the total number of equal parts. For example, ¼ means that the whole consists of 4 parts.

Note: A fraction with zero in the denominator is called "undefined."

## Decimal system

The decimal system is a number system that uses ten digits to help us with counting (0, 1, 2, 3, 4, 5, 6, 7, 8, 9), as opposed to the binary or base two number system, used by computers, that uses only the numbers 0 and 1. It is thought that the base ten (i.e. decimal) system originated when people had only their 10 fingers and 10 toes for counting.

Decimal – a number that uses a decimal point to show tenths, hundredths, thousandths, and so on. For example: 1.234

Decimal point – a symbol used, in the United States, to separate the ones place from the tenths place in decimals or dollars from cents in currency. Many countries use the decimal point to separate the one thousands place from the hundreds place.

Decimal place – the position of a number to the right of the decimal point. In the decimal 0.123, the 1 is in the first decimal place indicating tenths, the 2 is in the second decimal place indicating hundredths, and the 3 is in the third decimal place indicating thousandths.

## Basic mathematical operations

The four basic mathematical operations are:

- Addition – increasing one number by adding one or more other numbers to attain a sum. For example: 2 + 4 = 6 or 8 + 9 + 10 = 27. Addition is the opposite operation to subtraction. Addition follows the associative and commutative laws.
- Subtraction – finding the difference between two numbers or reducing one number by another. For example: 6 – 4 = 2. Subtraction is the opposite operation to addition. Subtraction does not follow the associative or commutative laws.
- Multiplication – a form of repeated addition in which two numbers are combined to give a product. For example: 3 * 2 = 6. In other words, add 2 three times: 2 + 2 + 2 = 6. Multiplication is the opposite operation to division. Multiplication follows the associative and commutative laws.
- Division – a form of repeated subtraction achieved by dividing one number by another number. For example: 20 ÷ 4 = 5. Division is the opposite operation to multiplication. Division does not follow the associative and commutative laws.

## PEMDAS

PEMDAS stands for the order in which mathematical operations should be performed in an expression involving multiple operations. Some teachers use the phrase "Please Excuse My Dear Aunt Sally" to help the students remember PEMDAS, which stands for

Parentheses, Exponents, Multiplication, Division, Addition, Subtraction.

For example, to solve the problem $5 + 20 \div 4 * (2 + 3)^2 - 6$ using PEMDAS:

P: First, perform the operations inside the parentheses, $(2 + 3) = 5$.

E: Then, solve the exponents, $(5)^2 = 25$.
At this point, the equation looks like this: $5 + 20 \div 4 * 25 - 6$.

M & D: Next, perform the multiplication and division from left to right, $20 \div 4 = 5$; then $5 * 25 = 125$.

A & S: Finally, do the addition and subtraction from left to right, $5 + 125 = 130$; then $130 - 6 = 124$.

## Cardinal and ordinal numbers

Cardinal numbers are the numbers we use for counting. They are, therefore, also called counting numbers or natural numbers.
Ordinal numbers are used to show position, 1st, 2nd, 3rd, 10th, 25th, and so on.

There is more to the concept of numbers than just sequence and order. There is also magnitude to consider. For example, two is not only the number after one in order, but it is also twice as big as one. Order and magnitude are the two essential properties of numbers.
In the place value system, a number represents a quantity, a numeral is the written representation of that number, and a digit is a single-place numeral (0, 1, 2, 3, 4, 5, 6, 7, 8, 9). A digit has value based not only upon its magnitude but also on its place or position in the numeral (units, tens, hundreds, and so on). Elementary school students should be able to read numbers into the billions (12 digits).

## Least common denominator, greatest common factor, and least common multiple

Least or lowest common denominator (LCD) – the lowest multiple of one or more denominators of a fraction. For example, the lowest common denominator for 2/3 and 4/9 is 9, so the fractions can be expressed as 6/9 and 4/9 for easier computation or comparison.

Greatest common factor (GCF) – the largest number that is a factor of two or more numbers. For example, the factors of 15 are 1, 3, 5, and 15; the factors of 35 are 1, 5, 7, and 35. Therefore, the greatest common factor of 15 and 35 is 5.

Least or lowest common multiple (LCM) – the smallest number that is a multiple of two or more numbers. For example, the multiples of 3 include 3, 6, 9, 12, 15, etc.; the multiples of 5 include 5, 10, 15, 20, etc. Therefore, the least common multiple of 3 and 5 is 15.

## Equivalent fractions, common or simple fraction, and mixed number

Equivalent fractions – two fractions that have the same value, but are expressed differently. For example, 1/5 = 20/100 = 2/10 = 4/20.

Simplifying a fraction – the numerator and denominator of a fraction are reduced to the smallest possible integers. For example, 4/8 simplified equals 1/2.
Common or simple fraction – a fraction that has integers for both its numerator and denominator; this is the most commonly seen type of fraction. For example, 1/2, 4/3, 5/7.

- 129 -

Mixed number – a number containing both an integer and a fraction. For example, 5¼.

## Bar graph, line graph, and pictograph

A bar graph is a graph that uses bars to compare data, as if each bar were a ruler being used to measure the data. The graph is made on grid paper and includes a scale of numbers that identify the units being measured.

A line graph is a graph that connects points to show how data increases or decreases over time. The time line is the horizontal axis. The connecting lines between data points on the graph are a way to more clearly show how the data changes.

A pictograph is a graph that uses pictures or symbols to show data. The pictograph will have a key to identify what each symbol represents. Each symbol stands for one or more objects.

The data in these types of graphs are the information that will be used in calculations.

## Problem-solving strategies

For any problem, the following strategies can be used according to their appropriateness to the type of problem or calculation: i) Use manipulatives or act out the problem, ii) draw a picture, iii) look for a pattern, iv) guess and check, v) use logical reasoning, vi) make an organized list, vii) make a table, viii) solve a simpler problem, and ix) work backward.

In order to solve a word problem, the following steps can be used:

- Achieve an understanding of the problem by reading it carefully, finding and separating the information needed to solve the problem, and discerning the ultimate question in the problem.
- Make a plan as to what needs to be done to solve the problem.
- Solve the problem using the plan from step 2.
- Review the word problem to make sure that the answer is the correct solution to the problem and makes sense.

## Relationship of fractions and decimals

Decimals are fractions that are based on a whole of 100 instead of a whole of 1; that is, one whole is equal to 100%. The word "percent" means "for every hundred."

Fractions can be expressed as percents by finding equivalent fractions with a denomination of 100. For example: $7/10 = 70/100$ or 70%; $1/4 = 25/100$ or 25%.

To express a fraction as a percent, use the formula % = 100 * (numerator/denominator). For example: 3/5 expressed as a percent would calculate as % = 100 * 3/5 = 300/5 = 60; therefore, 3/5 = 60%.

To express a percent as a common fraction, divide the percent number by 100 and reduce to lowest terms. For example: $96\% = 96/100 = 24/25$.

To convert decimals to fractions and fractions to decimals, just remember that percent means hundredths, that is, 0.23 = 23%, 5.34 = 534%, 0.007 = 0.7%, 700% = 7.0, 86% = 0.86, and so on.

## Percentage

To find a percent of a number, the percent must first be changed to a decimal number. So 30% becomes 0.3. Then, 0.3 is multiplied by the number in question. For example: to find 30% of 33, multiply 0.3 * 33; the product is 9.9; that is, 9.9 is 30% of 33.

To find the percentage, you need to know the number of the part and the number of the whole. If you know only the separate numbers, you will have to add them to get the whole. For example: In the school cafeteria, 7 students from your class chose pizza, 9 chose hamburgers, and 4 chose tacos. To find any percentage, you first add 7 + 9 + 4 = 20. The percentages can be found by dividing 7, 9, and 4 each by the whole (20). Four out of 20 students chose tacos, and 4/20 = 1/5. Changing 1/5 to a percentage tells us that 20% of the students chose tacos.

## Average, mean, median, and mode

Average is the overall term for the central tendencies of numbers that are found by determining the mean, median, and mode. An average is a single value used to represent a collection of data.

Mean is a measure of the general size of the data. The formula is: sum of values ÷ number of values. For example: given any six numbers that add up to 30, the mean of this distribution is 30 ÷ 6 = 5.

Median is the middle value of a distribution that is arranged in size order. The formula is: median = 1/2 (n + 1), where n is the number of values. However, if there is an even number of values, just add the two middle values and divide by two.

Mode is the value(s) that occur most often in a distribution. For example, in the list of 21, 23, 23, 25, 27, 27, 27, 28, 30, the value 27 occurs most often and is, therefore, the mode.

## Absolute value and positive and negative integers

The Absolute Value of a number is its distance from zero. Therefore, -3 and +3 have the same absolute value of 3.

The addition of two positive quantities results in a positive quantity. For example: 4 + (+7) = +11. The addition of two negative quantities results in a negative quantity. For example: -6 + (-8) = -14.

The addition of a positive quantity and a negative quantity requires assessing which addend has the larger absolute value. Subtract the smaller absolute value from the larger one, and give to the answer the sign of the larger absolute value. For example: -8 + (+12) = (+4); 11 + (-15) = -4.

If there are three or more negative and positive numbers to be added, first combine all the like-signs, and then add the two groups. Then, determine the larger absolute value of the summed groups, and write the appropriate sign. Given the calculation -8 + (-9) + (-10) + (+12), group and add the three negative terms, leaving the positive term separated: -27 + (+12). Since the larger absolute value of the two terms is 27 (versus 15), give a negative sign to the sum, and the answer becomes -15.

## Subtracting, multiplying, and dividing positive and negative integers

Subtracting a positive is the same as adding a negative and follows the rule of adding with two different signs: subtract the absolute value and give the sum the sign of the larger addend. For example: +7 – (+3) is the same as 7 – 3 = 4; or -5 – (+9) is the same as 9 – 5 = 4.

Subtracting a negative follows the same rule as the double negative in English: two negatives make a positive. Therefore, 9 – (-3) is the same as 9 + 3 or 12.

Multiplying and dividing integers with like signs follow the same rules as adding and subtracting integers: if both factors are positive, the product will be positive; if both factors are negative, the product will be positive. Multiplying or dividing a positive number by a negative one, or a negative number by a positive one, will result in a negative product; that is, multiplying or dividing integers with unlike signs always results in a negative.

## Exponent

An exponent is the superscript number placed next to another number at the top right to indicate how many times the number is multiplied by itself. Exponents provide a shorthand way to write a mathematical problem.

If the exponent is 2, then the number is multiplied by itself twice, or squared; that is $a^2 = a * a$. For example: $2^2 = 2 * 2 = 4$; $3^2 = 3 * 3 = 9$

If the exponent is 3, then the number is multiplied by itself three times, or cubed, that is $a^3 = a * a * a$. For example: $2^3 = 2 * 2 * 2 = 8$; $3^3 = 3 * 3 * 3 = 27$.

The value of a number raised to an exponent is called its "power." So, $8^4$ is said to be 8 to the 4th power, or 8 is raised to the power of 4.

## Laws of exponents

The laws of exponents are:

- Any number to the power of 1 is equal to itself; that is, $a^1 = a$.
- The number 1 raised to any power is equal to 1; that is, $1^n = 1$.
- Any number raised to the power of 0 is equal to 1; that is $a^0 = 1$.
- Add exponents to multiply powers of the same base number; that is, $a^n * a^m = a^{n+m}$ with $a$ as the base number and $n$ and $m$ representing any exponent value.
- Subtract the exponents to divide powers of the same number; that is $a^n \div a^m = a^{n-m}$.
- Multiply the exponent to raise a power to a power; that is $(a^n)^m = a^{n*m}$.
- Raise each number in the expression to the power to raise a multiplication or division expression to a power; that is, $(a * b)^n = a^n * b^m$ and $(a/b^m) = a^m / b^m$.
- Fractional exponents can be multiplied and divided like other exponents; for example, $5^{¼} * 5^{¾} = 5^{¼ + ¾} = 5^1 = 5$.

## Building number sense

It is important to think flexibly to develop number sense. Therefore, it is imperative to impress upon students that there is more than one right way to solve a problem. Otherwise, students will try to learn only one method of computation, rather than think about what makes sense or contemplate the possibility of an easier way. Some strategies for helping students develop number sense include the following:

- Frequently asking students to make their calculations mentally and rely on their reasoning ability. Answers can be checked manually afterwards, if needed.
- Having a class discussion about solutions the students found using their minds only and comparing the different approaches to solving the problem. Have the students explain their reasoning in their own words.
- Modeling the different ideas by tracking them on the board as the discussion progresses.
- Presenting problems to the students that can have more than one answer.

## Using manipulative materials

As with all classroom supplies, the students must understand that there are rules for their use, including how to store the materials when they are not in use.

In addition the teacher should discuss with the students the purpose of the manipulatives and how they will help the students to learn.

The students should understand that the manipulatives are intended for use with specific problems and activities; however, time for free exploration should be made available so students are less tempted to play when assigned specific tasks.

A chart posted in the classroom of the manipulatives with their names will help the students to gain familiarity with them and develop mathematical literacy skills, and loans of manipulatives for home use with a letter of explanation to the parents about the purpose and value of the manipulatives will encourage similar strategies with homework.

## Square roots

A number multiplied by itself two times is squared, or raised to the power of 2; for example 4 * 4 = 16, 5 * 5 = 25, etc. The number that is squared is the square root; therefore, 4 is the square root of 16, 5 is the square root of 25. The square root of a number is indicated by a "radical" sign: $\sqrt{\ }$. For example: $2^2 = 4$; $\sqrt{4} = 2$ or the square root of 4 equals 2.

A perfect square is a number that has an integer for a square root. There are 10 perfect squares from 1 to 100: 1, 4, 9, 16, 25, 36, 49, 64, 81, 100 (the squares of integers 1, 2, 3, 4, 5, 6, 7, 8, 9, and 10).

Every number has both a positive and a negative square. For example, the square root of 9 is +3 and -3 because 3 * 3 = 9 and -3 * -3 = 9.

## Algorithms and estimates

Algorithms result in an exact answer, while an estimate gives an approximation.

Algorithms are systematic, problem-solving procedures used to find the solution to a mathematical computation in a finite number of steps. Algorithms are used for recurring types of problems, thus saving mental time and energy because they provide a routine, unvaried method, like a standard set of instructions or a recipe. A computer program could be considered an elaborate algorithm.

An estimate attempts only to find a value that is close to an exact answer. A multidigit multiplication problem such as 345 * 12 can be calculated on paper or with a calculator but would be difficult to do mentally. However, an estimation of the answer based on something simpler *can* be done mentally, such as 350 * 10 = 3500 + 700 = 4200. This estimate is close to the actual answer of 4140. Students can practice their number sense by computing estimations.

## Standard systems of measurements

There are two standard systems of measurement used for a variety of types of measurement:
- US customary units – A system used in many English-speaking countries, particularly the United States, although it has been replaced by the metric system in a number of areas. The units of measurement in this system are the inch, foot, yard, mile for length; fluid ounce, cup, pint, quart, gallon for capacity; and ounce, pound, and ton for mass.
- Metric system – A system used in many countries around the world that is based on decimals (e.g. tens, hundreds, thousands). The units of measurement in this system are the millimeter, centimeter, meter, kilometer for length; milligram, gram, kilogram, and metric tonne for mass; and milliliter, centiliter, and liter for capacity.

Length is the distance between two points. Mass is the amount of matter that an object contains, and capacity is the internal volume of an object or container.

## Measures of motion

There are three measures of motion:
- Speed – the measure of distance moved over time. Speed is often measured in miles per hour, kilometers per hour, or meters per second. The formula for measuring the rate of speed is rate = distance ÷ time. Therefore, if 150 miles are traveled in 3 hours, the rate of speed is 150 ÷ 3 or 50 miles per hours.
- Velocity – the measure of distance moved in a particular direction over a period of time. Velocity is a vector quantity, meaning it has both magnitude (size) and direction. Often measured in mph or kph, velocity is expressed, for example, as 150 mph on a bearing of 45 degrees.
- Acceleration – the rate of change of velocity. Also a vector quantity, acceleration is most often measured in meters per second. The formula for calculating acceleration equals change of velocity divided by time taken. For example, a sports car is considered fast if it can accelerate from 0-100 kph in 4 seconds.

## Measures of time

The standard measures of time are:
- Millisecond (ms) – there is 1,000 milliseconds in a second; this unit is useful for computing the rate of speed of computer processing.
- Second (s) – the smallest unit of time on a standard clock; there are 60 seconds in 1 minute.
- Minute (min) – 60 seconds; there are 60 minutes in one hour.
- Hour (hr) – 60 minutes; there are 24 hours in a day.
- Day – the time it takes the Earth to rotate once, or 24 hours.
- 12-hour clock – most time is expressed in two 12-hour groups: the time between midnight and noon or a.m. (**a**nte **m**eridian or before noon), and the time between noon and midnight, or p.m. (**p**ost **m**eridian or after noon). Time on this system is written with the minutes after a colon, so 3:15 p.m. means fifteen minutes after 3 p.m.
- 24-hour clock – used by the military and on some digital clocks. There is no a.m. or p.m. since time, expressed in 4 figures, runs from 0000 h to 2359 h; for example 3:40 p.m. = 1540 h.

## Scientific notation

Scientific notation, also known as exponential notation, is a way of writing large numbers in a shorter form. The form $a * 10^n$ is used in scientific notation, where $a$ is greater than or equal to 1 and less than 10 and $n$ is the number of places the decimal must move to obtain this form.

For example, the number 234,000,000 is cumbersome to write, with all those zeroes. So, to write the value in scientific notation, place a decimal point between the first and second numbers (2.34). Then, to find the appropriate power of 10, count the number of digits to the right of the decimal point (to the left if the number is less than one). Therefore, $234,000,000 = 2.34*10^8$ and $0.0000234 = 2.34*10^{-5}$. This method is also a quick way to compare very large and very small numbers. By comparing exponents, it is easy to see that $3.28 * 10^4$ is smaller than $1.51*10^7$ (because 4 is less than 7). Calculators often use scientific notation to express numbers that are too long to fit in the display.

## Ratio and proportion

A ratio is a comparison of two quantities in a particular order. For example, if there are 14 computers in a lab, but the class has 20 students, there is a ratio of 14 to 20. Ratios can be written with a colon, so the ratio of students to computer would be 20:14, or as a fraction, 20/14.

A proportion is the relationship of change in two quantities. A direct proportion describes a quantity that increases with an increase in another quantity or decreases with a decrease in the other quantity. For example, if a sheet cake can be cut to serve 18 people and 2 sheet cakes can serve 36 people, the number served is directly proportional to the number of cakes.

Inverse proportion describes a quantity that increases as the other quantity decreases (or vice versa). For example, the time of a car trip decreases as the speed increases, so the time is inversely proportional to the speed.

## Interest

Interest is the amount of money earned in savings (loaned to a bank) or paid for the use of borrowed money (bank gives loan). The rate of interest is set by the bank and varies according to economic conditions.

Principal is the amount originally loaned or borrowed.

Simple interest is the interest that is earned or paid only on the principal; it does not change.

Compound interest is the interest that is earned or paid on the principal and the interest already earned; thus, the amount of money that earns interest is cumulative and increases each year.

A multiplier is a number multiplied by the principal that gives the total amount earned or borrowed at the end of a given period, usually a year. The multiplier is 1 plus the rate of interest. So, an interest rate of 5% per annum results in a multiplier of 1.05.

## Calculating interest

The following formula is used to calculate simple interest:

Simple interest = Principle * Rate of interest * Time ÷ 100.

For example, if a person invests $1,000 at an interest rate of 5% per annum, that would be 1,000 * 5 * 1 ÷ 100 or 5,000 ÷ 100 = $50.

The following formula is used to calculate compound interest:

Compound interest = Principle * (1 + interest rate [i.e. the multiplier])$^{Time}$ – Principle.

For example, $1,000 invested for 3 years at 5% interest would be 1,000 * (1.05)$^3$ - $1,000 = 1157.63 – 1,000 = $157.63.  Using simple interest, the same account would have earned only $150.

## Probability

Probability is a branch of statistics that calculates the ratio of the number of ways an event can occur to the total number of possible outcomes; in other words, the calculation shows how likely something is to happen.  The classic example is a coin toss.  There are only two possible results:  heads or tails.  The likelihood that the coin will land as one or the other is 1 out of 2, or 1/2 (or 0.5, or 50%).  When there are equally likely outcomes, such as in a coin toss, the events are called equiprobable.

Other terms used in probability include:  Outcome – a possible result in an experiment or event; Sample – a selected part of a large group (large samples tend to be more accurate than smaller samples); Success – the desired result (for example, if you want the coin toss to come up heads and it does, you have had a successful outcome).

## Probability scale

A probability scale is one that measures the likelihood of an outcome.  Certainty is if something is certain to happen, such as growing older each minute, and has a probability of 1.  Impossibility is if something has no possibility of happening (such as turning into a frog without an evil spell), and the probability assigned is 0.  The values of 0 and 1 are the extremes of probability.  Thus, the probability of an event happening between certainty and impossibility can be anything between 0 and 1.  If the probability number is closer to 0, then the event is less likely to happen; if closer to 1, it is more likely to happen.

Probabilities are affected by the frequency of an event (2 out 3 tosses), how many items are involved (more than one coin), and whether the event can be altered by other factors (rain, loaded dice).  Two or more events that cannot have a successful outcome at the same time are called mutually exclusive events.

## Dividend, division, remainder, divisor, and quotient

Dividend is the number to be divided.  For example, if 18 is divided by 6 (18 ÷ 6), then 18 is the dividend.

Division is the process that tells how many items are in a group, or how many groups exist.

Remainder is the surplus value when one number cannot be evenly divided by another; that is, the number less than the divisor that remains after dividing.  For example, 36 divided by 5 is 7 with a remainder of 1.

Divisor is the number by which a dividend is divided.  For example, if 18 is divided by 6 (18 ÷ 6), then 6 is the divisor.

Quotient is the number, other than the remainder, that is the result of the division operation. For example, if 18 is divided by 6, the outcome is 3 and is called the quotient.

## Vertical axis, horizontal axis, scale, interval, and coordinates

Vertical Axis is the up-and-down number line on a graph.
Horizontal Axis is the left-to-right number line on a graph.

Scale is the marked intervals on the vertical or horizontal axis of a graph that represent the units being measured. For example, a common scale is from 1 to 10, with intervals of 1 (1, 2, 3, 4, 5, 6, 7, 8, 9, and 10).

Interval is the fixed distance between the numbers on the scale of a graph. For example, if the axis reads 2001, 2002, 2003, 2004, then the graph represents one year intervals of data.

Coordinates are the points on the graph that indicate the intersection of two data numbers. For example, a graph that shows 60% of a goal was reached in November would have a point placed where 60 and November meet on the graph.

## Roman numerals

In ancient Rome, a system of numerals was devised that is still being used today. The system consists of 7 letters or symbols to represent numbers: I = 1, V = 5, X = 10, L = 50, C = 100, D = 500, and M = 1,000.

To represent numbers in between these 7 main numbers, a system of addition and subtraction was devised. If the symbol to the right is of equal or lesser value, add its value to the value of the symbol to the left; for example, VI = 5 + 1 = 6 or CC = 100 + 100 = 200. If the symbol to the right is of greater value, subtract the left symbol from the right one; for example, IV = 5 – 1 = 4 or XC = 100 – 10 = 90.

## Rounding

Rounding is the approximation of a figure by reducing or increasing a number to the nearest integer (ten, hundred, etc.). The amount of approximation depends on the degree of accuracy of the number itself, and the amount of rounding often depends on what is being measured. For example, a person's height would be rounded to the nearest inch, but the national debt might be rounded to the nearest trillion.

To round a number, determine the digit place to which the number will be rounded, and then look at the digit to the right – if it is 5 or greater, increase the digit being rounded by 1. If it is less than 5, the digit being rounded remains the same. For example, 346 rounded to the nearest 10 would be 350, but 342 would be rounded to 340. The number 8,766 rounded to the nearest 1,000 would be 9,000 and to the nearest 100 would be 8800.

## Temperature

Temperature is the measure of the degree of hotness or coldness of a substance according to a standard scale.

The Celsius temperature scale (once called Centigrade because the scale is divided into 100 parts) is one in which water boils at 100°C and freezes at 0°C. It was devised by Anders Celsius, a Swedish astronomer, in 1742.

The Fahrenheit temperature scale is one in which water boils at 212°F and freezes at 32°F. It was devised by Daniel Gabriel Fahrenheit, a German physicist who invented the alcohol thermometer in 1709 and the mercury thermometer in 1714. This scale is commonly used in the United States, but many other countries use the Celsius scale. To convert a temperature from Fahrenheit to Celsius, use the following formula: F = 9/5C + 32, where F is the temperature in Fahrenheit and C is the temperature in Celsius. If you are given the temperature in Fahrenheit, you can always rearrange the formula and solve for C.

## Algebraic expressions and formulas

An algebraic expression is a mathematical statement written in a form that uses letters and symbols to represent numbers and the relationships between them. Letters from the beginning of the alphabet are used to represent known values (for example, $a^2 = a * a$), and letters from the end of the alphabet are used to represent unknown values (for example, $3x + 4y = 18$). An algebraic expression can contain any combination of letters or numbers and usually involves arithmetic operations, such as addition, subtraction, multiplication, or division.

A formula is the algebraic expression of a general rule. For example, the formula for finding the area of a parallelogram is a = bh or area = base * height.

## Variable, dependent variable, constant, and coefficient

A variable is an unknown number or quantity represented by a letter. Sometimes the letter will represent the word it is replacing (for example, d for distance, h for height, t for time), but ordinarily the variable is indicated by a general letter, like "x."

A dependent variable is a variable with a value that is calculated from other values. For example, the area of a parallelogram is dependent on the values of the base and the perpendicular height, that is, a = bh, with "a" as the dependent variable. Since the base and height are predetermined, they are independent variables.

A constant is a number with a value that is always the same. For example, in the algebraic expression y = ¾x – 5, 5 is the constant.

A coefficient is a constant that is placed before a variable in an algebraic expression. For example, in the expression 3y + 1, 3 is the coefficient of y.

## Term

A term can be a variable, a constant, or a coefficient separated from the rest of the mathematical expression by an algebraic sign, such as a "+" or "-" sign. For example, in the expression ¾x – 5, there are two terms: ¾x and 5. The variable is "x," 5 is the constant, and ¾ is the coefficient.

Terms that contain the same letter or combination of letters and the same exponents are "like" terms (for example, xy and 2xy are like terms); terms that contain different letters or combinations of letters or different exponents are "unlike" terms (for example, 2y and $y^2$ are unlike terms).

Any algebraic expression containing two terms is called a binomial expression. An algebraic expression containing three terms is a trinomial expression (for example, 3x + y – xy); however, any algebraic expression containing two or more terms can also be called a polynomial or multinomial expression (for example, 2 + 3y + 4x – 1).

## Parentheses, substitution, and simplification

Parentheses are used to group terms together. A term directly in front of a set of parentheses can be multiplied by each term in the parentheses; that is, $3(x - y) = 3x - 3y$.

Substitution is the replacement of the letters in an algebraic expression with known values. For example, given the formula for the area of a parallelogram, $a = bh$, if it is known that the base is 4 cm and the height is 5 cm, then these numbers can be substituted into the formula to calculate the area: $a = 4 * 5 = 20$ cm$^2$.

Simplification is the process of combining like terms in an algebraic expression to reduce the expression to the minimum number of terms.

## Simplification

When like terms are added or subtracted, for example, $2x + 3y + 2y - x$ can be simplified to $(2x - x) + (3y + 2y) = x + 5y$.

When like terms are multiplied, simplification involves multiplying all terms; for example, $2a * 3b = 2 * a * 3 * b = 6 * a * b = 6ab$.
When like terms are divided, simplification involves canceling the common terms; for example, $6xy^3 \div 2y = 6 * x * y * y * y \div 2 \div y = 3xy^2$ ($6 \div 2 = 3$ and cancel out 1 y which is common in the numerator and denominator).

When like terms involve fractions, find a common denominator, collect like terms, and simplify as usual.

## Factor an expression

An expression is factored when it is rewritten as a product of its factors. For example, to factor $4x - 16$:
- Find the common factor of 4 and 16, and write it outside a set of parentheses 4 ( ).
- Divide each term by the common factor, $4x \div 4 = x$ and $-16 \div 4 = -4$.
- Write the result in the parentheses, $4(x - 4)$.
- Check the answer by applying the distributive property, $4(x-4) = 4x - 16$.

## Equation and solution

An algebraic equation is a mathematical statement that two expressions are equal. An equation is solved by finding the value of the unknown variable or variables.

A solution is any value of a variable that satisfies the equation; in other words, makes the equation true.

Rearranging an equation means moving around the terms until one of the terms is alone on one side of the equal sign. The equation can then be solved for that one term.
For example, to solve $3y = 6x - 9$ for x:

- Rearrange the terms so that the $x$ term will be separated on one side of the equation. This can be accomplished by adding 9 to both sides of the equation, resulting in $6y + 9 = 3x$.
- Divide both sides by 3 to solve for the value of x, $(6y + 9) \div 3 = 3x \div 3 = 2y + 3 = x$.
- Therefore, the final answer is $x = 2y + 3$.

- 139 -

## Quadratic equation

A quadratic equation includes a variable that is squared, and the standard form is $ax^2 + bx + c = 0$, where "a" does not equal 0.

The solutions of a quadratic equation are called its "roots." The following steps are used when a quadratic equation can be solved by factoring:

1. If not in standard form, rearrange the equation to equal zero.

2. Factor the left side of the equation to give two expressions in parentheses.

a) Find the factors of the "$x^2$" term, and place these terms first in each of the parentheses. If the factors were 2 and 1, we would have $(2x + \ )(x + \ ) = 0$.

b) Now, find all factors of the "c" constant.

c) If the coefficient of $x^2$ is one, find two factors of "c" that, when multiplied, are equal to "c" and when added are equal to "b." For example, the equation $x^2 + 6x + 8 = 0$ factors to $(x + 2)(x + 4) = 0$. [If the coefficient of $x^2$ is not one, the terms in the parentheses will be a combination of the factors from $x^2$ and "c."]

3. Set each pair of parentheses equal to zero. That is, $(x + 2) = 0$ or $(x + 4) = 0$
4. Solve these two equations for x to obtain the roots of $x = -2$ or $x = -4$.

## Completing the square

"Completing the square" means converting the left side of a quadratic equation into a perfect square: $(x + y)^2 = z$. This method can be used to solve any quadratic equation.
Starting with the standard quadratic form, $ax^2 + bx + c = 0$, move the number represented by c to the right side of the equation.
For example: $x^2 - 6x + 5 = 0$ becomes $x^2 - 6x = -5$.

To complete the square on the left, half the coefficient of x and square the result: $(6/2)^2 = 3^2 = 9$. Then add the result to both sides: $x^2 - 6x + 9 = -5 + 9$.

Factor the left side using the form $(x + y)^2 = z$: $(x - 3)^2 = 4$

To solve for x, take the square root of both sides: $x - 3 = \pm 2$ or $x = 5$ or $1$.

Note: Remember that there is a positive and negative value when taking a square root. If you only use the positive value, you will be missing one of the solutions of the quadratic.

## Quadratic formula

The quadratic formula can be used to solve any quadratic equation in the form:
$ax^2 + bx + c = 0$.

The quadratic formula is:

$$x = \frac{-b \pm \sqrt{b^2 - 4ac}}{2a}$$

A, b, and c from the given equation.

If the equation is $2x^2 + 4x - 6 = 0$, then a = 2, b = 4, and c = -6.

Solve the equation by substituting the values for a, b, and c into the quadratic formula.

In our example above, the roots will be x = 1 and x = -3.

If your answer is correct, the sum of the roots should be equal to $-b \div a$. For example, the solutions summed equal 1 + (-3) = -2, which gives the same result as $-4 \div 2 = -2$.

## Simultaneous equations

Simultaneous equations are pairs of equations in which the variables represent the same numbers in each equation. To solve, find a solution that makes both equations true.

One method to solve simultaneous equations is through the use of substitution. In this process, we substitute one of the expressions in the other equation to find the value of one variable. The value of this variable can then be substituted into the first equation to find the remaining variable. For example, given the two equations 5x – y =13 and 2x + y = 15, find the solution for x and y that makes both equations true.

First, solve one equation for the y variable: y = 5x – 13.

Substitute the re-written expression for the same variable in the other equation: 2x + 5x – 13 = 15.

Collect like terms and simplify: 7x – 13 = 15, so 7x = 28, and x = 4.

Substitute the known value into the other equation: 2(4) + y = 15, so y = 15 – 8, and y = 7.

Therefore, the solution to this set of simultaneous equations is x = 4 and y = 7.

If the same or opposite terms appear in two equations, the method of elimination can easily be used to solve the simultaneous equations. If the terms are the same (for example 2x and 2x) subtract one equation from the other. If the terms are opposite (for example -2x and 2x), add the equations, then simplify.

To solve the equations 2x – 3y = 5 and x + 3y = 16, add the two equations to eliminate the y term: 3x = 21, so x = 7.

Then substitute the value of the known variable into either equation to find the value of the unknown variable:     2(7) – 3y = 5 or 3y = 14 – 5 or 3y = 9, and y = 3.

Therefore, the solution to this set of simultaneous equations is x = 7 and y = 3.

## Eliminating terms

First, find the least common multiple of one pair of coefficients, and multiply one or both equations by the required number to make those coefficients equal. For example, given the equations $2x + 3y = 0$ and $3x + 2y = 5$, multiply the first equation by 2 and the second by 3 to get $4x + 6y = 0$ and $9x + 6y = 15$. (Don't forget to multiply through both sides of the equation!)

Now two terms are the same, and we can subtract one equation from the other. (If the terms had been opposite, we would have added the equations.) Subtracting the equations in the example... $(4x + 6y) - (9x + 6y) = 0 - 15$ or $-5x = -15$ or $5x = 15$, so $x = 3$.

Lastly, substitute the value of the known variable in either of the equations to find the value of the remaining variable. For example: $4(3) + 6y = 0$ or $12 + 6y = 0$ or $6y = -12$, so $y = -2$. Therefore, the solution to these simultaneous equations is $x = 3$ and $y = -2$.

## Inequalities

Opposite of an equation, an inequality is a mathematical statement that shows two algebraic expressions are not equal. An inequality, nonetheless, can be solved in a way similar to an equation.

The symbols for an inequality are given by the following:

a) < means "less than"; b) > means "greater than"; and c) ≠ means "not equal to."

A conditional inequality is one that is true only for certain values of the variable.

An unconditional inequality is one that is true for all values of the variables.

A double inequality is one in which a variable has to satisfy two inequalities.

Inequalities can be solved by rearranging the inequality and solving for an unknown variable. To keep the inequality true, any term added to or subtracted from one side of the inequality must be added to or subtracted from the other side. The same is true for multiplying or dividing. Although, if multiplying or dividing by a negative number, the inequality sign is reversed.

## Domain, range, composite function, and inverse function

A function is a relationship in which two sets are linked by a rule that pairs each element of the first set with exactly one element of the second set. A function is represented by the letter "f." Functions are used in every-day situations. For example, the relationship between the cost of an item and the amount of sales tax is a function.

Result: a value that is obtained when a function is applied to a value x; represented as $f(x)$ [pronounced "f of x"].

Domain: The set of values to which a function is applied.

Range: The set of values to which the results belong.

Composite function: a combination of two or more functions; the second and subsequent functions are represented by different letters. For example: f∘g(x) means "f of g of x;" g is calculated first and that answer is used in the function, f.

Inverse function: An operation or series of operations that reverses a function; usually written as $f^{-1}(x)$.

## Value of algebra

Algebra serves as the basic language of mathematics. As such, it provides a means of condensing large amounts of data into efficient mathematical statements. Through algebra, we are also able to create a mathematical model of a situation. Further, algebra provides the structure for solving mathematical problems and links numerical and graphical representations of data.

A perpetual debate exists about the value of studying algebra for the average person because it is felt that few people actually use algebra in the workplace. While that is not necessarily true, it is a fact that studying algebra teaches a style of thinking that is important to competent functioning, including the concepts of patterns, functions, and quantitative relationships.

## History of variables

Variables are the heart of algebra. Historically, algebra in its earliest stages used ordinary language. In the period from 250-1600 A.D., mathematicians began to use symbols to represent unknown quantities and solve problems for these unknowns. Since 1600 A.D., symbols have been used in all algebraic operations, starting with Francoise Viète, who used letters for mathematical notations. Soon afterward, René Descarte developed the system of using a, b, c for constants and x, y, z for unknowns.

Today, the particular use of a variable is determined by the mathematical context. The most common uses are as specific unknowns, as generalizers, and as varying quantities. The challenge for students is to learn how values are represented symbolically and to understand the various meanings for letters or shapes in equations, inequalities, formulas, and functions.

## Fibonacci sequence

Patterns are an important aspect of mathematics. Italian mathematician Leonardo de Pisa (1175-1245), nicknamed Fibonacci, discovered a unique sequence of numbers with several amazing relationships. The sequence begins with 1, 1, and each following number is the sum of the two preceding numbers. The result is 1, 1, 2, 3, 5, 8, 13, 21, 34, 55, 89, 144, and so on.

Interestingly, the sum of the first 3 numbers is 4, which is one less than the fifth number (5). The sum of the first 4 numbers is 7, one less than the sixth number (8). The relationship holds throughout the sequence.

The Fibonacci sequence describes a variety of phenomena in the world. In music, the keys of a piano have 5 black and 8 white keys in each octave of 13 notes. In nature, the number of spirals on pinecones, pineapples, and in the center of a sunflower is in a Fibonacci sequence, as are the leaves on the stems of many types of plants.

## Fibonacci numbers and the golden ratio

Fibonacci ratios are a comparison of two Fibonacci numbers, usually adjacent numbers in the sequence. These ratios, if expressed as decimals, hover around 1.6 to 1.618 and are irrational numbers. Oddly enough, this 1.6 ratio is found in many shapes and objects. The Greeks called it the golden ratio (or golden proportion) and represented it with the letter phi. The Egyptians may have used this ratio in the construction of the pyramids.

Rectangles whose length-to-width ratio is 1.6 are called golden rectangles. Psychologists have discovered that people find golden rectangles more aesthetically pleasing than other rectangles. It is this knowledge that has determined the shape of common objects, such as cereal boxes and picture frames.

The human body has golden proportions, which helps artists to draw figures accurately. For example, the length of an index finger compared with the length from the fingertip to the big knuckle is a ratio of 1.6, as is the length of the arm from the shoulder in relation to the length from the fingertips to the elbow.

## Equality and balance scales

Equality is a fundamental concept of algebra, but many students find it difficult to understand. Students may misinterpret the use of the equal sign by thinking it is telling them to perform an operation, as in + or – signs. However, students seem to understand that a balance scale remains balanced if equal amounts are on both sides but becomes unbalanced if items are added or subtracted. Therefore, performing activities with balance scales is often a good hands-on practice for the concept of equality.

Using manipulatives of various shapes on the balance scale can also help with the understanding of different letters in an algebraic equation. If three triangular-shaped objects are equal in weight to two cylinders, the students should be able to make the connection to $3x = 2y$. Adding or taking away different shapes also helps with grasping the use of symbols in longer equations.

## Representation in algebra

Representation is the display of mathematical relationships graphically, symbolically, pictorially, or verbally.

Graphical representations include bar graphs, line graphs, histograms, line plots, and circle graphs.

Symbolic representations involve the use of symbols and include equations, formulas, and rules.

Pictorial representations include two- and three-dimensional drawings, maps, balance scales, and scale drawings.
Verbal representations are the use of words to express mathematical relationships in speech or writing.

Even though any of these representations can be used in a math problem, there is probably one way that is easier to use and provides more clarity about the situation than the others. Which representation to use should be evaluated for each individual problem. For example, working with numbers in an organized way, such as putting them on a table, often makes patterns more obvious.

## Field properties, closure, and denseness

Field properties are the same as those learned in foundational mathematics; however, for algebra, these properties can be expressed using symbols. The basic rules for using symbols are… (1) a, b, and c are real numbers and (2) multiplication is implied when there is no symbol between two variables; that is, $ab = a * b$. Multiplication can also be indicated by a raised dot (`).

The rule of closure states that the sum or product of two real numbers is a real number; that is, if a and b are real numbers, then a + b is a real number, and ab is a real number.

Denseness is a rule that says, between any pair of rational numbers, there is at least one rational number. For example, between 4.2 and 4.3, there is the rational number of 4.25. However, the set of natural numbers in not dense because, between two consecutive natural numbers, there may not exist another natural number. For example, between 3 and 4 there exists no other natural number.

## Associative, commutative, and distributive

The commutative property shows that the order of the addends, or factors, does not affect the sum or product: $a + b = b + a$ and $ab = ba$.

The associative property states that the grouping of the addends, or factors, does not affect the sum or product: $(a + b) + c = a + (b + c)$ and $(ab)*c = a*(bc)$.

The distributive property states that multiplying a sum by a number is equal to multiplying each addend by that number: $a(b+c) = ab + ac$.

## Additive identity, multiplicative identity, additive inverse, and multiplicative inverse

The additive identity property states that the sum of any number and zero is that number: $a + 0 = a$.

The multiplicative identity, or the property of one, says that the product of any number and one is that number: $a * 1 = a$.

Additive inverse, or the property of opposites, states that the sum of any number and its opposite is zero and is represented by the following statement: $a + (-a) = 0$.

Multiplicative inverse, or the property of reciprocals, says that the product of any number and its reciprocal is one and is represented by the following statement: $a/b * b/a = 1$.

## Point, line segment, transversal, horizontal, vertical, perpendicular, parallel, collinear, plane, coplanar, and solid

The following terms are commonly used in geometric studies:

- Point – a location found by its coordinates; usually represented on diagrams by a small dot or two crossed lines
- Line segment – the part of a straight line between two points, thus having a fixed length
- Transversal – a line that crosses two or more other lines
- Horizontal – a line or plane that follows the horizon, at a right angle to the vertical
- Vertical – a line or plane that is at a right angle to the horizon
- Perpendicular – a line or plane that is at a right angle to another line or plane
- Parallel – a set of lines or curves that never cross and are the same distance apart at every point along the lines
- Collinear – points that lie in a straight line or share a common straight line
- Plane (or plane figure) – a two-dimensional object, with length and width
- Coplanar – points that lie on the same plane, or share a common plane

- Solid – a three-dimensional object, with a length, width, and thickness

## Cartesian coordinate system

The Cartesian coordinate system describes the position of points on a plane or in a space in terms of their distance from lines called axes. The two lines, or axes, are the horizontal x-axis and the vertical y-axis, which are at right angles to each other and thus form a rectangular coordinate system. The point at which the two axes meet is the "origin."

Points along the x-axis and to the right of the origin have a positive value, while those to the left of the origin are negative. Points along the y-axis above the origin are positive, while those below the origin are negative.

The position of a point, labeled (x,y), is described in terms of its distance from the origin. The x-coordinate is the distance of the point from the origin, parallel to the x-axis. The y-coordinate is the distance of the point from the origin, parallel to the y-axis. The x-coordinate is always written first.

## Quadrant and dimensions

A quadrant is any of the four regions formed on a plane by the x-axis and the y-axis (not to be confused with the use of the term quadrant for a part of a circle). The 1st quadrant is to the right of the y-axis and above the x-axis. The 2nd quadrant is to the left of the y-axis and above the x-axis. The 3rd quadrant is to the left of the y-axis and below the x-axis. The 4th quadrant is to the right of the y-axis and below the x-axis.

Dimensions are determined by the number of coordinates needed to fix a point in space. If the position of a point on a line or line segment can be described by one coordinate, then the line is one-dimensional. If two coordinates are needed to describe the position of a point in a plane, the plane is two-dimensional. If three coordinates are needed, then the plane is three-dimensional.

## Angles

Each type of angle has a distinctive feature:

- Null or zero angle – No rotation ( 0° )
- Whole turn, or full turn, or round angle, or perigon – A complete turn, or revolution, equal to 360°
- Right angle – A quarter of a full turn, equal to 90°
- Straight or flat angle – half a full turn, equal to 180°
- Acute angle – Any angle smaller than a right angle (< 90°)
- Obtuse angle – Any angle greater than a right angle (> 90°), but smaller than a straight angle (< 180°)
- Reflex angle – Any angle greater than a straight angle (> 180°)
- Positive angle – An angle that is constructed or measured in a counter-clockwise direction
- Negative angle – An angle that is constructed or measure in a clockwise direction

## Polygons, vertices, sides, interior and exterior angles, a cyclic, and a diagonal

A polygon is a shape formed from three or more points called vertices (each point is called a vertex) joined by three or more straight lines called sides. The name of most polygons is determined by the number of angles or sides it has.

An interior angle is any of the angles inside a polygon where two sides meet at a vertex. The sum of the interior angles of a polygon is equal to the sum of the interior angles of any other polygon with the same number of sides.

An exterior or external angle is any of the angles formed between a side of a polygon and the extension of the side next to it.

A cyclic is a polygon that can have a circle drawn around it such that each vertex of the polygon lies on the circle's circumference.

A diagonal is a line that joins two vertices of a polygon that are not next to each other.

## Polygons

The following list presents several different types of polygons:

> Triangle – 3 sides
> Quadrilateral – 4 sides
> Pentagon – 5 sides
> Hexagon – 6 sides
> Heptagon or septagon – 7 sides
> Octagon – 8 sides
> Nonagon – 9 sides
> Decagon – 10 sides
> Hendecagon – 11 sides
> Dodecagon – 12 sides
> Quindecagon – 15 sides
> Icosagon – 20 sides

N-gon – a polygon that has "n" angles and "n" sides, where n represents any number.

The sum of the interior angles of an n-sided polygon is $180°(n-2)$. For example, in a triangle, n is 3, so the sum of the interior angles is $180°(3-2) = 180°$. In a quadrilateral, n is 4, and the sum of the angles is $180°(4-2) = 360°$. The sum of the interior angles of a polygon is equal to the sum of the interior angles of any other polygon with the same number of sides.

An equiangular polygon is one in which all the interior angles are equal.

An equilateral polygon is one in which all sides are equal.

Note: An equiangular polygon does not have to be equilateral, and an equilateral polygon does not have to be equiangular.

A convex polygon is one in which all interior angles are less than 180°.

A concave polygon is one in which one or more interior angles are greater than 180°.

A regular polygon is one in which all the sides and interior angles are equal; it is both equilateral and equiangular. Examples of regular polygons are squares, equilateral triangles, regular pentagons, and regular hexagons.

Upper-case letters (A, B, C, etc.) are used to label the vertices of a polygon, while the sides are labeled using lower-case letter (a, b, c, etc.).

## Tessellation

Tessellation is the combination of one or more shapes such that, when repeated, the pattern covers a surface plane without leaving any gaps or overlaps. Shapes that fit together in this way are said to tessellate. Another word for tessellation is tiling. For example, a group of squares can tessellate because they fit together completely; however, a group of circles does not tessellate because there are gaps at the curves.

A regular polygon has 3 or more sides and angles, all equal. A regular tessellation includes only one type of congruent (all the same size and shape), regular polygon. Only three regular polygons tessellate in the Euclidean plane: triangles (in a pyramid shape), squares (in a block), and hexagons.

Semi-regular tessellation is a tessellation made up of more than one type of regular polygon. The pattern formed at each vertex where the polygons meet is the same. There are eight semi-regular tessellations. These use a combination of equilateral triangles, squares, hexagons, octagons, and dodecagons.

## Triangles

A triangle is a polygon with three sides and three angles. A triangle can be classified according to the length of its sides or magnitude of its angles.

Scalene – The sides are all different lengths, so all three angles are different as well.

Isosceles – Has two equal sides; the angles opposite these sides are also equal. An isosceles triangle has one line of symmetry that divides the triangle into two identical right-angled triangles.

Equilateral –Has three equal sides; each angle measures 60°. An equilateral triangle has three lines of symmetry, each of which divides the triangle into two identical right-angled triangles.
Acute-angled – All three interior angles are less than 90°.

Obtuse-angled – One interior angle is greater than 90°.

Right-angled – One interior angle is equal to 90°; the other two angles are complementary, meaning they sum to 90°.

## Congruent, SSS, SAS, AAS, RHS, and similar triangles

Pairs of triangles can have unique features and names. The following pairs are congruent triangles that are exactly the same shape and size.

Side-side-side (SSS) triangles are two triangles in which all three sides of one are equal to all t̶ of another, but positioned differently.

Side-angle-side (SAS) triangles are two triangles in which two sides and the included angle of one triangle are the same as the other, but positioned differently.

Angle-angle-side (AAS) triangles are two triangles in which two angles and any side on one triangle are the same as that of the other, but positioned differently.

Right-angle-hypotenuse-side (RHS) triangles are two triangles in which the hypotenuse and one side of a right-angled triangle are the same as the other, but positioned differently.

Similar triangles are the same shape but not necessarily the same size; corresponding angles are equal and corresponding sides are in the same ratio.

## Pythagorean theorem

Named after the sixth-century Greek mathematician Pythagoras, this theorem states that, for a right-angled triangle, the square of the hypotenuse (the longest side of a right-angled triangle and always opposite the right (90°) angle) is equal to the sum of the squares of the other two sides. Written in symbols, the Pythagorean theorem has the following formula: $a^2 + b^2 = c^2$, where "c" is the hypotenuse and "a" and "b" are the remaining two sides. The theorem proves that when one side of a triangle is equal to the sum of the squares of the other two sides, the triangle must contain a right angle.

The theorem can be used to find the length of the third side of a right-angled triangle, given the lengths of any two sides. For example, given that the hypotenuse of a right-triangle is 25 and one side is 9, the other side can be found using the formula: $a^2 + b^2 = c^2$, $9 + b^2 = 25$, or $b^2 = 25 - 9$, or $b^2 = 16$, so b = 4.

## Quadrilaterals

A quadrilateral is a four-sided polygon, and all quadrilaterals tessellate. Each quadrilateral has special properties:

- Square – All sides are equal and all angles are right angles. The opposite sides are parallel, and there are four lines of symmetry. The rotation symmetry is of order 4.
- Rectangle (or oblong) – Opposite sides are equal and parallel, and all interior angles are right angles. There are two lines of symmetry and a rotation symmetry of order 2. The diagonals of a rectangle are of equal length.
- Kite – Two pairs of sides are equal, and one pair of opposite angles are equal. There is only one line of symmetry and no rotation symmetry.
- Parallelogram – Opposite sides are parallel and of equal length, and opposite angles are equal. Most have no lines of symmetry, but do have a rotation symmetry of order 2. The exceptions are rectangles, squares, and rhombuses, which are special types of parallelograms.
- Rhombus – All four sides are equal in length, and opposite angles are equal. There are two lines of symmetry and a rotation symmetry of order 2. A square is a special type of rhombus that has four right angles.
- Trapezoid – One pair of sides is parallel. Most trapezoids have no symmetry, unless the sloping sides, a and b, are the same length. In this case, the trapezoid has one line of symmetry and is called an isosceles trapezoid.

- Arrowhead (or delta) – This concave quadrilateral has two pair of equal adjacent sides. There is one interior angle greater than 180°, and one line of symmetry. There is no rotation symmetry.

## Polyhedron

A polyhedron is a solid that has a surface area made of a series of polygons. The polygons are called "faces," and the lines where they meet are called "edges." The corners where three or more faces meet are called "vertices."

A dihedral angle is the angle formed inside a polyhedron where two faces meet.

Euler's theorem, named after 18th-century Swiss mathematician Leonard Euler, is expressed as $V - E + F = 2$, where V is the number of vertices, E is the number of edges and F is the number of faces. For example, a cube has 8 vertices, 12 edges, and 6 faces, so $8 - 12 + 6 = 2$.

The name of a polyhedron is determined by the number of faces it has.

Tetrahedron – 4 faces
Pentahedron – 5 faces
Hexahedron – 6 faces
Heptahedron – 7 faces
Octahedron – 8 faces
Nonahedron – 9 faces
Decahedron – 10 faces
Dodecahedron – 12 faces
Icosahedron – 20 faces

## Polyhedra

Convex: Each dihedral angle is less than 180° (for example, a cube).

Concave: At least one dihedral angle is greater than 180°, such that at least one vertex points toward the middle of the solid.
Regular: The faces are identical polygons, and the angles at the vertices are equal. There are five regular polyhedra, called Platonic solids (named after the Greek philosopher, Plato):

Cube – six square faces

Regular Dodecahedron – twelve faces, all of which are regular pentagons

Regular Tetrahedron – four faces, all of which are equilateral triangles

Regular Octahedron – eight faces, all of which are equilateral triangles

Regular Icosahedron – twenty faces, all of which are equilateral triangles

Semi-regular: The faces are more than one type of polygon. For example, an icosidodecahedron is a semi-regular polyhedron with 32 faces, consisting of 20 triangles and 12 pentagons.

## Solid

A solid is a three-dimensional object that can be any shape or size. Many solids, such as polyhedra, spheres, cylinders, and cones, have particular properties.

Plan – a two-dimensional drawing of a solid as if viewed directly from above

Elevation – a two-dimensional drawing of a solid as if viewed directly from the front (front elevation) or the side (side elevation); the front is the side nearest the viewer

Diagonal – a line drawn between two vertices that are not on the same edge of the solid

Short diagonals – those that lie across the surface

Long diagonals – those that run through the middle of the solid

Plane section – a flat or plane surface formed by cutting through a solid at any angle

Cross section – a flat or plane surface formed by cutting through a solid at right angles to the axis of rotation symmetry

Frustum – the part below the cross section.

Net – a flat or plane shape composed of polygons that represents the faces of a polyhedron and can be folded to make a polyhedron

## Reflection symmetry

Symmetry describes a property of a shape that can be halved and turned such that it fits exactly onto itself. One of two types of symmetry is reflection, also called reflective or line symmetry. This type occurs when a shape can be divided into two parts by a line or plane and each part of the shape is a mirror image of the other. The wings of a butterfly are an example of reflection symmetry.

A line of symmetry, or mirror line, divides a plane into two parts, and each part is a mirror image of the other. A plane can have more than one line of symmetry.

A plane of symmetry divides a solid into two parts, and each part is a mirror image of the other. A solid can have more than one plane of symmetry.

## Rotation symmetry

Symmetry describes a property of a shape that can be halved and turned such that it fits exactly onto itself. One of two types of symmetry is rotations, also called rotational symmetry. This type of symmetry occurs when a shape can be turned about a fixed point or line and fit exactly onto itself.

Order of rotation symmetry is the number of times within a revolution (360°) that a shape can be turned to fit exactly onto itself. For example, a four-pointed star has rotation symmetry of order 4 because it can fit onto itself in four different positions.

Center of rotation symmetry is the point around which a plane can be rotated to fit exactly onto itself.

Axis of rotation symmetry is the line around which a solid can be rotated to fit exactly onto itself. For example, a rectangular prism has rotation symmetry of order 4.

## Calculating the area of a given shape

The following formulas are used to calculate the area of the given shape:

- Rectangle: area = length * width, a = lw
- Square: area = (side)$^2$, a = s$^2$
- Triangle: area = ½ * (base * perpendicular height), a = ½bh. The perpendicular height is a line from the apex of the triangle that meets the base at a right angle. Any side of the triangle can be the base.
- Parallelogram: area = base * perpendicular height, a = bh. In this case, perpendicular height is a line from a vertex that meets the base at a right angle.
- Trapezoid: area = ½ * (a + b) * h. In this formula, a and b are the lengths of the parallel sides, and h is the perpendicular distance between them.
- Circle: area = π * r$^2$ or πr$^2$, where π (Pi) is approximately 3.14 and r is the radius of the circle. The radius is the distance from the center of the circle to any point on the circumference (edge).

## Volume, capacity, and density

Volume is the amount of space that a solid, liquid, or gas occupies. This space is measured by the number of unit cubes that can fit inside it. Common units of measuring volume are based on the units of length, such as cubic centimeters (cm$^3$) or cubic meters (m$^3$).

Capacity is the amount that a container can hold. Capacity is often measured in milliliters (ml) or liters (l). Volume and capacity are closely related. A container with a volume of 1 cm$^3$ holds 1 milliliter of liquid, and a container with a volume of 1000 cm$^3$ holds 1 liter.

Density is the mass of one unit volume of a material from which an object is made. The shorthand expression is "mass per unit volume." Density is often measured in grams per cubic centimeter (g/cm$^3$) or kilograms per cubic meter (kg/m$^3$). The following formula is used to calculate density: Density = mass/volume or D = m/V.

## Bimodal and multimodal distribution

One of the three commonly used types of measures of central tendency (average) is mode, which is the value or values that occur most often in a distribution.

Bimodal distribution is one that has two modes. For example, in the distribution of 20, 21, 21, 22, 25, 25, 26, 28, the values of 21 and 25 occur most often, both twice, and are therefore both modes.

Multimodal distribution is one that has three or more modes.

Mode of a frequency distribution is the value with the highest frequency of an item in a group of items. For example, in a group of shoes, a store may have 88 in size 6, 376 in size 7, 255 in size 8, and 142 in size 9. The category with the highest frequency, 376, is size 7, so the mode of this frequency is size 7.

## Median and mean of a distribution

Median is the middle value of a distribution that is arranged in size order. The formula used for determining median is ½ (n + 1), where n is the number of values. To find the median of the following distribution, first arrange the distribution in size order: 25, 21, 24, 21, 26, 27, 22, 29, 25 → 21, 21, 22, 24, 25, 25, 26, 27, 29. Then, calculate the median position: median = ½ (9 + 1) = ½ * 10 = 5. The value that is in the 5th position on this distribution list is 25.

Mean, or arithmetic mean, of a distribution is a measure of the general size of the data. The following formula is used to find the mean: sum of values ÷ number of values. For the distribution 1, 6, 8, 4, 7, 10, the sum is 36. There are 6 numbers in the distribution. Therefore, the mean of this distribution is 6 (36 ÷ 6).

## Range and quartiles

Range is the difference between the highest and lowest values in a distribution list. For example, in the distribution 3, 1, 6, 4, 7, 12, 9, 5, 8, twelve is the high value and one is the low value; therefore, 12 − 1 = 11, so the range is 11.

The lower, or first quartile (Q₁), is the value that lies one quarter of the way through a distribution arranged in ascending order. The formula for finding the lower quartile position is (n + 1) ÷ 4, where n is the number of values in the distribution.

The upper, or third quartile (Q₃), is the value that lies three-quarters of the way through a distribution arranged in ascending order. The formula for finding the upper quartile position is 3(n + 1) ÷ 4.

## Standard deviation

Standard deviation from the mean expresses how spread out the values of a distribution are from its mean, while taking into account every value of a distribution. Standard deviation is given in the same units as the original data and is represented by a lower case sigma (σ).
A high standard deviation means that the values are very spread out.

A low standard deviation means that the values are close together.
If every value in a distribution is increased or decreased by the same amount, the mean is increased or decreased by that amount, but the standard deviation stays the same.

If every value in a distribution is multiplied or divided by the same number, the standard deviation and the mean will both be multiplied or divided by that amount.

## Pie chart

A pie chart or circle graph is a diagram used to compare parts of a whole. The frequency of a distribution is represented by the area of the sectors within the circle. The diagram has a title to explain what it is showing. Each "slice" or sector of the pie is labeled to tell what it represents or is explained on a key. The size of the slice is determined by the amount of frequency; that is, something that happens 30% of the time is going to get a larger slice than something that happens 20% of the time.

The size of an angle or area can be calculated by the formula: angle = f * (360° ÷ Σf), where f is the frequency.

The sum of the angles must always be 360°.

## Bar charts

A bar chart uses vertical or horizontal bars of equal width to show the frequency of a distribution. For example, a bar chart can show the frequency distribution of car sales according to model.

A compound, or multiple, bar chart uses multiple bars within a category to illustrate more than one set of date. For example, the data on car sales can be separated to show the number of each model sold to men and the number sold to women.
A component bar chart, also known as a composite, sectional, or stacked bar chart, is one that divides each bar into sections to illustrate more than one set of data. That is, the bar can represent total sales, with sections of the bar showing the number sold by model. A component chart could also have bars for each model, but with each bar divided into two sections showing the numbers bought by men and the number by women.

## Theoretical and experimental probability

Theoretical probability is a way of calculating the odds of a certain event occurring without actually performing the event. It is based on equally likely outcomes, with no bias or error involved.

The following formula is used to calculate theoretical probability: P (the probability of success for the required or desired outcome) = total successful outcomes ÷ total possible outcomes. For example, given 20 marbles in a bag, 5 red, 8 blue, 4 green, and 3 yellow, the odds of choosing a red one are 5 in 20 or 5 ÷ 20 = 1/4 or 0.25 or 25%.

Experimental probability, or relative frequency, is the number of times an outcome occurs in an experiment or a certain number of events.

The formula, or rule, for calculating experimental probability is: P = total successful outcomes ÷ total events. For example, if a die is thrown 100 times and lands showing the number 5 a total of 10 times, then P = 10 ÷ 100 = 1/10 = 0.2 = 20%. This can be compared to the theoretical probability of 1/6 or 17% (there are 6 sides on a die, each with an equal theoretical probability of rolling face up).

## Events

Single event – one that involves only one item, such as tossing a coin

Compound or multiple event – one that involves more than one item, such as a pair of dice

Independent or random event – one that has an outcome that is not affected by any other event; that is, when repeatedly throwing a pair of dice, no throw is affected by any other throw

Dependent or conditional event – one that has an outcome that is affected by another event; for example, once a bag of 20 marbles is reduced by one red marble (originally having 5 red marbles), the odds of getting another red one are changed to 4 out of 19 or 21%.

Mutually exclusive events – two or more events that cannot have a successful outcome at the same time; for example, choosing a spade from a deck of cards is one event and choosing a club is another event. When choosing a card, it cannot be both a club and a spade, so these events are mutually exclusive.

## Histogram

A histogram is a special type of bar graph where the data are grouped in intervals (for example 20-29, 30-39, 40-49, etc.). The frequency, or number of times a value occurs in each interval, is indicated by the height of the bar and is called the frequency density. Frequency density can be calculated with the following formula: frequency ÷ class width (the size of the interval). For example, if measuring how much time it takes 20 different people to walk a mile, the frequency would be 20 and the class width would be groups of minutes from the first to finish to the last to finish. Similarly, frequency can be calculated with the formula: class width * frequency density. The total frequency should be the sum of the frequencies in the table.

The intervals do not have to be the same amount but usually are (all data in ranges of 10 or all in ranges of 5, for example). The smaller the intervals, the more detailed the information.

## Permutation and combination

Permutation and combination involve the arrangement of items. Use a permutation when order is important and a combination when order has no importance.

For example: It does not matter in what order one picks up pens, pencils, and markers; that's combination. However, it matters in what order numbers are entered into a combination lock; that's permutation. (Maybe it should be renamed a "permutation" lock.)

Two types of permutations and combinations exist within mathematics, those with repetition and those without, as demonstrated in the following examples:
- Permutation with repetition – The same number could repeat in the lock combination, such as 444512.
- Permutation without repetition – Contest results are given by 1st, 2nd, and 3rd place, and two objects cannot be in the same place.
- Combination with repetition – When sorting change according to nickels, dimes, and pennies, order does not matter, but more than one of a particular coin can exist within the quantity of change.
- Combination without repetition – Finding the total number of two-letter combinations that can be made from a three-letter word is an example of a combination with repetition (cat = ca, ct, at, ac, tc, ta).

## Stem-and-leaf plot

A stem-and-leaf plot is a method where data is organized visually so that the information is easier to understand. A stem-and-leaf plot is very easy to construct because a simple line separates the stem (the part of the plot listing the tens digit, if displaying two-digit data) from the leaf (the part that shows the ones digit). Thus, the number 45 would appear as 4 | 5. The stem-and-leaf plot for test scores of a group of 11 students might look like the following:

```
9 | 5
8 | 1, 3, 8
```

| 7 | 6, 0, 2, 4, 7 |
|---|---|
| 6 | 2, 8 |

A stem-and-leaf plot is similar to a histogram or other frequency plot, but, with a stem-and-leaf plot, all the original data is preserved. In this example, it can be seen at a glance that nearly half the students scored in the 70's, yet all the data has been maintained. These plots can be used for larger numbers, as well. However, they do tend to work best for small sets of data and can become unwieldy with larger sets.

## Addition Principle of Counting

The Addition Principle of Counting, or Addition Rule, is used to find the probability of one of any number of outcomes occurring. Expressed symbolically, let $E_1$ and $E_2$ be mutually exclusive events (that is, no common outcomes can occur), and let event $E$ describe the situation where either event $E_1$ or event $E_2$ will occur. The number of times event $E$ will occur can be expressed as: $n(E) = n(E_1) + n(E_2)$. The addition principle can be generalized for more than two events. In a simple example, there are two types of meat on the cafeteria menu: beef and chicken. Within those two categories, there are 3 beef dishes (3 outcomes) and 4 chicken dishes (4 outcomes). Therefore, $n(E) = 3 + 4 = 7$.

## Multiplication Principle of Counting

The Multiplication Principle of Counting, or Multiplication Rule, is used to find the probability of a combination of outcomes occurring, both independent (one event does not affect the other's outcome) or dependent (one event does affect the other) events. For two independent events, the number of possible outcomes for event $E$, if both $E_1$ and $E_2$ must occur, is expressed by: $n(E) = n(E_1) * n(E_2)$. For example: If there are two major highway routes from Houston to St. Louis and three from St. Louis to Cleveland, then there are $2 * 3 = 6$ different ways to drive from Houston to Cleveland. For two dependent events, calculate any changes in probability following each outcome, and then multiply the results. For example: Given 20 marbles in a bag, 5 of which are red, the probability of choosing a red one is 5 in 20 on the first draw, but 4 in 19 on the second. Therefore, the calculation becomes $n(E) = 5/20 * 4/19 = 1/19$ or 0.0525.

## Data and statistics

- Quantitative data – measurements (such as length, mass, and speed) that provide information about quantities in numbers
- Qualitative data – information (such as colors, scents, tastes, and shapes) that cannot be measured using numbers
- Discrete data – information that can be expressed only by a specific value, such as whole or half numbers; For example, since people can be counted only in whole numbers, a population count would be discrete data.
- Continuous data – information (such as time and temperature) that can be expressed by any value within a given range
- Primary data – information that has been collected directly from a survey, investigation, or experiment, such as a questionnaire or the recording of daily temperatures; Primary data that has not yet been organized or analyzed is called raw data.
- Secondary data – information that has been collected, sorted, and processed by the researcher
- Ordinal data – information that can be placed in numerical order, such as age or weight
- Nominal data – information that cannot be placed in numerical order, such as names or places

# Science

## Atoms

All matter consists of atoms. Atoms consist of a nucleus and electrons. The nucleus consists of protons and neutrons. The properties of these are measurable; they have mass and an electrical charge. The nucleus is positively charged and consists of protons and neutrons. Electrons are negatively charged and orbit the nucleus. An atom is held together by electromagnetic force between the nucleus and the electrons. The nucleus, which contains protons and neutrons, has considerably more mass than the surrounding electrons. The forces that hold the nucleus of an atom together are usually stronger than the electric forces trying to break it apart. Protons and neutrons are formed from hadrons, which are composed of quarks. Atoms bond together to make molecules. Atoms that have an equal number of protons and electrons are neutral. If the number of protons and electrons is not equal, atoms have positive or negative charges and are known as ions.

## Atom, nucleus, electrons, and protons

An atom is one of the most basic units of matter. An atom consists of a central nucleus surrounded by electrons.

The nucleus of an atom consists of protons and neutrons. It is positively charged, dense, and heavier than the surrounding electrons. The plural form of nucleus is nuclei.

Electrons are atomic particles that are negatively charged and orbit the nucleus of an atom.

Along with neutrons, protons make up the nucleus of an atom. The number of protons in the nucleus usually determines the atomic number of an element. Carbon atoms, for example, have six protons. The atomic number of carbon is 6. The number of protons also indicates the charge of an atom.

## Atomic number, neutrons, nucleon, and element

The atomic number of an element, also known as the proton number, refers to the number of protons in the nucleus of an atom. It is a unique identifier. It can be represented as "Z." Atoms with a neutral charge have an atomic number that is equal to the number of electrons. The number of protons in the atomic nucleus also determines its electric charge, which in turn determines the number of electrons the atom has in its non-ionized state.

Neutrons are the uncharged atomic particles contained within the nucleus. The number of neutrons in a nucleus can be represented as "N."

Nucleon refers to the collective number of neutrons and protons.

An element is matter with one type of atom. It can be identified by its atomic number. There are 117 elements, 94 of which occur naturally on Earth.

## Difference between atoms and molecules

Elements from the periodic table such as hydrogen, carbon, iron, helium, mercury, and oxygen are atoms. Atoms combine to form molecules. For example, two atoms of hydrogen (H) and one atom of oxygen (O) combine to form water ($H_2O$). Atoms are made up of subatomic particles. Atoms consist of electrons and a nucleus containing at least one proton and one neutron. The one exception to this rule is the hydrogen isotope hydrogen-1, which does not contain a neutron. Protons have a positive charge, while neutrons have no charge. Electrons have a negative charge and orbit the nucleus. The atomic number refers to the number of protons in the nucleus. This number is used to sort elements in the periodic table.

## Molecular formation

Electrons in an atom can orbit different levels around the nucleus. They can absorb or release energy, which can change the location of their orbit or even allow them to break free from the atom. The outermost layer is the valence layer, which contains the valence electrons. The valence layer tends to have or share eight electrons. Molecules are formed by a chemical bond between atoms, a bond which occurs at the valence level. Two basic types of bonds are covalent and ionic. A covalent bond is formed when atoms share electrons. An ionic bond is formed when an atom transfers an electron to another atom. A hydrogen bond is a weak bond between a hydrogen atom of one molecule and an electronegative atom (such as nitrogen, oxygen, or fluorine) of another molecule. The Van der Waals force is a weak force between molecules. This type of force is much weaker than actual chemical bonds between atoms.

## Atomic model

Atoms are extremely small. A hydrogen atom is about $5 \times 10^{-8}$ mm in diameter. According to some estimates, five trillion hydrogen atoms could fit on the head of a pin. Atomic radius refers to the average distance between the nucleus and the outermost electron. Models of atoms that include the proton, nucleus, and electrons typically show the electrons very close to the nucleus and revolving around it, similar to how the Earth orbits the sun. However, another model relates the Earth as the nucleus and its atmosphere as electrons, which is the basis of the term "electron cloud." Another description is that electrons swarm around the nucleus. It should be noted that these atomic models are not to scale. A more accurate representation would be a nucleus with a diameter of about 2 cm in a stadium. The electrons would be in the bleachers. This model is similar to the not-to-scale solar system model.

## Compounds

Atoms interact by transferring or sharing the electrons furthest from the nucleus. Known as the outer or valence electrons, they are responsible for the chemical properties of an element. Bonds between atoms are created when electrons are paired up by being transferred or shared. If electrons are transferred from one atom to another, the bond is ionic. If electrons are shared, the bond is covalent. Atoms of the same element may bond together to form molecules or crystalline solids. When two or more different types of atoms bind together chemically, a compound is made. The physical properties of compounds reflect the nature of the interactions among their molecules. These interactions are determined by the structure of the molecule, including the atoms they consist of and the distances and angles between them.

## Periodic table

The periodic table groups elements with similar chemical properties together. The grouping of elements is based on atomic structure. It shows periodic trends of physical and chemical properties and identifies families of elements with similar properties. It is a common model for organizing and understanding elements. In the periodic table, each element has its own cell that includes varying amounts of information presented in symbol form about the properties of the element. Cells in the table are arranged in rows (periods) and columns (groups or families). At minimum, a cell includes the symbol for the element and its atomic number. The cell for hydrogen, for example, which appears first in the upper left corner, includes an "H" and a "1" above the letter. Elements are ordered by atomic number, left to right, top to bottom.

## Matter

Matter refers to substances that have mass and occupy space (or volume). The traditional definition of matter describes it as having three states: solid, liquid, and gas. These different states are caused by differences in the distances and angles between molecules or atoms, which result in differences in the energy that binds them. Solid structures are rigid or nearly rigid and have strong bonds. Molecules or atoms of liquids move around and have weak bonds, although they are not weak enough to readily break. Molecules or atoms of gases move almost independently of each other, are typically far apart, and do not form bonds. The current definition of matter describes it as having four states. The fourth is plasma, which is an ionized gas that has some electrons that are described as free because they are not bound to an atom or molecule.

## Conservation of matter and atomic theory

Atomic theory is concerned with the characteristics and properties of atoms that make up matter. It deals with matter on a microscopic level as opposed to a macroscopic level. Atomic theory, for instance, discusses the kinetic motion of atoms in order to explain the properties of macroscopic quantities of matter. John Dalton (1766-1844) is credited with making many contributions to the field of atomic theory that are still considered valid. This includes the notion that all matter consists of atoms and that atoms are indestructible. In other words, atoms can be neither created nor destroyed. This is also the theory behind the conservation of matter, which explains why chemical reactions do not result in any detectable gains or losses in matter. This holds true for chemical reactions and smaller scale processes. When dealing with large amounts of energy, however, atoms can be destroyed by nuclear reactions. This can happen in particle colliders or atom smashers.

## Mass, weight, volume, density, and specific gravity

Mass is a measure of the amount of substance in an object.

Weight is a measure of the gravitational pull of Earth on an object or between two bodies.

Volume is a measure of the amount of cubic space occupied. There are many formulas to determine volume. For example, the volume of a cube is the length of one side cubed ($a^3$) and the volume of a rectangular prism is length times width times height ($l \cdot w \cdot h$). The volume of an irregular shape can be determined by how much water it displaces.

Density is a measure of the amount of mass per unit volume. The formula to find density is mass divided by volume ($D=m/V$). It is expressed in terms of mass per cubic unit, such as grams per cubic centimeter ($g/cm^3$).
Specific gravity: This is a measure of the ratio of a substance's density compared to the density of water.

## Physical and chemical properties

Both physical changes and chemical reactions are everyday occurrences. The physical properties of a substance refer to attributes such as appearance, color, mass, and volume. Physical changes do not result in different substances. For example, when water becomes ice it has undergone a physical change, but not a chemical change. It has changed its form, but not its composition. It is still $H_2O$. Chemical properties are concerned with the constituent particles that make up the physicality of a substance. Chemical properties are apparent when chemical changes occur. The chemical properties of a substance are influenced by its electric charge, which is determined in part by the number of protons in the nucleus (the atomic number). The number of electrons is the same as an atom's atomic number. Carbon, for example, has 6 protons and 6 electrons. It is an element's outermost valence electrons that mainly determine its chemical properties. Chemical changes are when a change in a substance results in a different substance. Chemical reactions may release or consume energy.

## Elements, compounds, solutions, and mixtures

These are substances that consist of only one type of atom.

These are substances containing two or more elements. Compounds are formed by chemical reactions and frequently have different properties than the original elements. Compounds are decomposed by a chemical reaction rather than separated by a physical one.

These are homogeneous mixtures composed of two or more substances that have become one.

Mixtures contain two or more substances that are combined but have not reacted chemically with each other. Mixtures can be separated using physical methods, while compounds cannot.

Some chemical properties of elements include: atomic number, category, group, period, block, weight, electron configuration, electrons per shell, phase, density, sublimation point (the temperature at which elements change from solids to gases without going through a liquid phase), specific heat capacity, oxidation states, electronegativity, ionization energy, atomic radius, and isotopes.

## Chemical reactions

Chemical reactions measured in human time can take place quickly or slowly. They can take fractions of a second or billions of years. The rates of chemical reactions are determined by how frequently reacting atoms and molecules interact. Rates are also influenced by the temperature and various properties (such as shape) of the reacting materials. Catalysts accelerate chemical reactions, while inhibitors decrease reaction rates. Some types of reactions release energy in the form of heat and light. Some types of reactions involve the transfer of either electrons or hydrogen ions between reacting ions, molecules, or atoms. In other reactions, chemical bonds are broken down by heat or light to form reactive radicals with electrons that will readily form new bonds. Processes such as the formation of ozone and greenhouse gases in the atmosphere and the burning and processing of fossil fuels are controlled by radical reactions.

## Most abundant elements

Aside from dark energy and dark matter, which are thought to account for all but four percent of the universe, the two most abundant elements in the universe are hydrogen (H) and helium (He). After hydrogen and helium, the most abundant elements are oxygen, neon, nitrogen, carbon, silicon, and magnesium. The most abundant isotopes in the solar system are hydrogen-1 and helium-4.

Measurements of the masses of elements in the Earth's crust indicate that oxygen (O), silicon (Si), and aluminum (Al) are the most abundant on Earth. Hydrogen in its plasma state is the most abundant chemical element in stars in their main sequences, but is relatively rare on planet Earth.

## Past atomic models and theories

There have been many revisions to theories regarding the structure of atoms and their particles. Part of the challenge in developing an understanding of matter is that atoms and their particles are too small to be seen. It is believed that the first conceptualization of the atom was developed by Democritus in 400 B.C. Some of the more notable models are the solid sphere or billiard ball model postulated by John Dalton, the plum pudding or raisin bun model by J.J. Thomson, the planetary or nuclear model by Ernest Rutherford, the Bohr or orbit model by Niels Bohr, and the electron cloud or quantum mechanical model by Louis de Broglie and Erwin Schrodinger. Rutherford directed the alpha scattering experiment that discounted the plum pudding model. The shortcoming of the Bohr model was the belief that electrons orbited in fixed rather than changing ecliptic orbits.

## Heat, energy, work, thermal energy, and heat engine

Heat is the transfer of energy from a body or system as a result of thermal contact. Heat consists of random motion and the vibration of atoms, molecules, and ions. The higher the temperature is, the greater the atomic or molecular motion will be.

Energy is the capacity to do work.
Work is the quantity of energy transferred by one system to another due to changes in a system that is the result of external forces, or macroscopic variables. Another way to put this is that work is the amount of energy that must be transferred to overcome a force. Lifting an object in the air is an example of work. The opposing force that must be overcome is gravity. Work is measured in joules (J). The rate at which work is performed is known as power.

Thermal energy is the total kinetic and potential energy present in a system.

Heat engine refers to a machine that converts thermal energy to mechanical energy that can be used to do work.

## Thermal contact, entropy, conservation of energy, and perpetual motion

Thermal contact refers to energy transferred to a body by a means other than work. A system in thermal contact with another can exchange energy with it through the process of heat. Thermal contact does not necessarily involve direct physical contact.

Entropy refers to the amount of energy in a system that is no longer available for work. Entropy is also a term used to describe the amount of disorder in a system.

Conservation of energy is a concept that refers to the fact that the total amount of energy in a closed system is constant.

Perpetual motion is the misguided belief that a system can continuously produce more energy than it consumes. Since the law of conservation of energy states that energy cannot be created or destroyed, a true perpetual motion machine is not possible.

## Kinetic and potential energy

Kinetic and potential energy are two commonly known types of energy. Kinetic energy refers to the energy of an object in motion. The following formula is used to calculate kinetic energy: $KE = \frac{1}{2}mv^2$, where "KE" stands for kinetic energy, "m" stands for mass, and "v" stands for velocity. Even though an object may appear to be motionless, its atoms are always moving. Since these atoms are colliding and moving, they have kinetic energy. Potential energy refers to a capacity for doing work that is based upon position or configuration. The following formula can be used to calculate potential energy: $PE = mgh$, where "PE" stands for potential energy, "m" stands for mass, "g" stands for gravity, and "h" stands for height.

## Laws of thermodynamics

The zeroth laws of thermodynamics states that two objects in thermodynamic equilibrium with a third object are also in equilibrium with each other. Thermodynamic equilibrium basically means that different objects are at the same temperature.

The first law deals with conservation of energy. It states that heat is a form of energy that cannot be created or destroyed, only converted.

The second law is that entropy (the amount of energy in a system that is no longer available for work or the amount of disorder in a system) of an isolated system can only increase. The second law also states that heat is not transferred from a lower-temperature system to a higher-temperature one.

The third law of thermodynamics states that as temperature approaches absolute zero, entropy approaches a constant minimum. It also states that a system cannot be cooled to absolute zero.

## Energy

Some discussions of energy consider only two types of energy: kinetic energy (the energy of motion) and potential energy (which depends on relative position). There are, however, other types of energy. Electromagnetic waves, for example, are a type of energy contained by a field. Gravitational energy is a form of potential energy. Objects perched any distance from the ground have gravitational energy, or the potential to move. Another type of potential energy is electrical energy, which is the energy it takes to pull apart positive and negative electrical charges. Chemical energy refers to the manner in which atoms form into molecules, and this energy can be released or absorbed when molecules regroup. Solar energy comes in the form of visible light and non-visible light, such as infrared and ultraviolet rays. Sound energy refers to the energy in sound waves.

## Energy transformations

<u>Electric to mechanical</u>
Ceiling fan

<u>Chemical to heat</u>
A familiar example of a chemical to heat energy transformation is the internal combustion engine, which transforms the chemical energy (a type of potential energy) of gas and oxygen into heat. This heat is transformed into propulsive energy, which is kinetic. Lighting a match and burning coal are also examples of chemical to heat energy transformations.

## Chemical to light

Phosphorescence and luminescence (which allow objects to glow in the dark) occur because energy is absorbed by a substance (charged) and light is re-emitted comparatively slowly. This process is different from the one involved with glow sticks. They glow due to chemiluminescence, in which an excited state is created by a chemical reaction and transferred to another molecule.

## Heat to electricity

Examples include thermoelectric, geothermal, and ocean thermal.

## Nuclear to heat

Examples include nuclear reactors and power plants.

## Mechanical to sound

Playing a violin or almost any instrument

## Sound to electric

Microphone

## Light to electric

Solar panels

## Electric to light

Light bulbs

## Heat and temperature

Heat is energy transfer (other than direct work) from one body or system to another due to thermal contact. Everything tends to become less organized and less orderly over time (entropy). In all energy transfers, therefore, the overall result is that the energy is spread out uniformly. This transfer of heat energy from hotter to cooler objects is accomplished by conduction, radiation, or convection. Temperature is considered a measurement of heat or heat energy. More specifically, temperature is the average kinetic energy of an object's particles. When the temperature of an object increases and its atoms move faster, kinetic energy also increases. Temperature is not energy since it changes and is not conserved. Thermometers are used to measure temperature.

## Motion and force

A fundamental concept in physics is that objects can change their motion when a force is applied. Newton's laws, the laws of motion, describe how these forces behave and how they can be used to calculate the effects of forces on the motion of objects. Four basic forces are gravity, nuclear weak force, electromagnetic force, and nuclear strong force, with nuclear strong force being the strongest. Linear motion is caused by forces, while rotational motion is caused by torques. The magnitude of the change in motion can be calculated using the relationship $F = ma$, where "F" stands for force, "m" stands for mass, and "a" stands for acceleration of gravity. Another important concept related to force is that when one object exerts a force on another, a force equal in magnitude and opposite in direction is exerted on the first object.

## Gravitational force

Gravitational force is a universal force that causes masses to exert forces on other masses. The strength of the gravitational attractive force between two objects is proportional to their mass and inversely proportional to the square of the distance between them. Gravity is the weakest of the four fundamental forces. Gravity is an attractive force and acts along the imaginary line joining centers of masses. The formula for gravitational force, $F = G[(m_1*m_2)/r^2]$, follows Newton's third law, the law of universal gravitation. Newton's law is widely used to explain and calculate the effects of gravity, but Einstein's theory of general relativity is considered a better model and more accurate. Applying Newton's third law allowed scientists to predict the existence of Neptune.

Newton's formula, however, did not work with Mercury, but Einstein's theory of general relativity did.

## Newton's laws of motion

Newton's First Law: This is also known as the law of inertia. It states that a body in motion tends to stay in motion and a body at rest tends to stay at rest until another force acts upon it.

Newton's Second Law: This is expressed by the formula $F = ma$, where "F" is force, "m" is mass, and "a" is acceleration. In other words, force is equal to mass times acceleration. This is applicable when the objects encounter a net external force, but does not tend to be directly applicable to cases where mass varies. The formula is generally not suitable for calculations being made at an atomic level. Quantum mechanics is more suitable for these instances. The formula is also not suitable when objects are approaching the speed of light. Relativity is more suitable for these instances.

Newton's Third Law: This states that for every force there is an equal and opposite force. This also applies to the law of work, the law of energy, and the laws of power.

## Simple machines

Simple machines include the incline plane, lever, wheel and axle, and pulley. These simple machines have no internal source of energy. More complex or compound machines can be formed from them. Simple machines provide a force known as a mechanical advantage and make it easier to accomplish a task. The incline plane enables a force less than the object's weight to be used to push an object to a greater height. A lever enables a multiplication of force. The wheel and axle allows for less resistance and is similar to the force of a lever. Single or double pulleys allows for easier direction of force. A wedge is similar to an incline plane in that a smaller force working over a longer distance can produce a larger force. The wedge and screw are forms of the incline plane. The screw is similar to an incline that is wrapped around a shaft.

## Friction

Friction is the resistance to motion that occurs where two surfaces touch each other. Generally, the magnitude of the frictional force is affected by the material composition of the surfaces of the objects. Frictional force is independent of the area of contact between two surfaces. While the direction of motion occurs one way, frictional force occurs in the opposite direction. Frictional force is also proportional to the normal force between two surfaces. Two types of friction are static and kinetic. Static friction occurs when there is no relative motion between the surfaces. Kinetic friction occurs when there is relative motion between the surfaces.

## Electric charges

The attractive force between the electrons and the nucleus is called the electric force. A positive (+) charge or a negative charge (-) creates a field of sorts in the empty space around it, which is known as an electromagnetic field. The direction of a positive charge is away from it and the direction of a negative charge is towards it. An electron within the force of the field is pulled towards a positive charge because an electron has a negative charge. A particle with a positive charge is pushed away, or repelled. Like charges repel each other and opposite charges attract. Lines of force show the paths of charges. Electric force between two objects is proportional to the inverse square of the distance between the two objects. The electric charge can be negative, zero, or positive. An electric charge is measured with the unit Coulomb (C). It is the amount of charge moved in one second by a steady current of one ampere (1C = 1A * 1s).

## Circuits and potential

Electric current is the sustained flow of electrons that are part of an electric charge along a path. This differs from a static electric charge, which is characterized by a discharge or change of charge rather than a continuing flow. The rate of flow of electric charge is expressed using the ampere (amp or A) and can be measured using an ammeter. Movement of electric charge along a path between areas of high electric potential and low electric potential is the definition of a simple circuit. It is a closed conducting path between the high and low points, or the positive and negative charges. An energy supply is required to do the work necessary to move the charge from an area of low electric potential to one of high electric potential. Once at the area of high electric potential, the charge moves or flows back to an area of low electric potential.

## Examples of circuits

Current is the measurement of the rate at which charge flows through a circuit point. The formula used to measure current is 1 amp = 1 coulomb/1 second. In other words, a current of 1 ampere means that 1 coulomb of charge passes through a cross section of a wire every second. One example of a circuit is the flow from one terminal of a car battery to the other. The electrolyte solution of water and sulfuric acid provides work in chemical form to start the flow. A frequently used classroom example of circuits involves using a D cell (1.5 V) battery, a small light bulb, and a piece of copper wire to create a circuit to light the bulb. In this example, the light bulb is the load, a device that uses energy. A bell or light could also be used.

## Electric charge

Models that can be used to explain the flow of electric current, potential, and circuits include water, gravity, and roller coasters. For example, just as gravity is a force and a mass can have a potential for energy based on its location, so can a charge within an electrical field. Just as a force is required to move an object uphill, a force is also required to move a charge from a low to high potential. Another example is water. Water does not flow when it is level. If it is lifted to a point and then placed on a downward path, it will flow. A roller coaster car requires work to be performed to transport it to a point where it has potential energy (the top of a hill). Once there, gravity provides the force for it to flow (move) downward. If either path is broken, the flow or movement stops or is not completed.

## Magnet

A magnet is a piece of metal, such as iron, steel, or magnetite (loadstone) that can affect another substance within its field of force that has like characteristics. Magnets can either attract or repel other substances. Magnets have two poles: north and south. Like poles repel and opposite poles (pairs of north and south) attract. The magnetic field is a set of invisible lines representing the paths of attraction and repulsion. Magnetism can occur naturally, or ferromagnetic materials can be magnetized. Matter that is magnetized can retain its magnetic properties indefinitely and become a permanent magnet. Other matter may lose its magnetic properties, and is considered a temporary magnet. For example, an iron nail can be temporarily magnetized by stroking it repeatedly in the same direction using one pole of another magnet. Once magnetized, it can attract or repel other magnetically inclined materials, such as paper clips. Dropping the nail will cause it to lose its charge.

## Magnetic fields

A magnetic field can be formed not only by a magnetic material, but also by electric current flowing through a wire. When a coiled wire is attached to the two ends of a battery, for example, an electromagnet can be formed by inserting a ferromagnetic material such as an iron bar within the coil. When electric current flows through the wire, the bar becomes a magnet. If there is no current, the magnetism is lost. A magnetic domain is when the magnetic fields of atoms are grouped and aligned. These groups form what can be thought of as miniature magnets within a material. This is what happens when an object like an iron nail is temporarily magnetized. Prior to magnetization, the organization of atoms and their various polarities are somewhat random with respect to where the north and south poles are pointing. After magnetization, many of the poles are lined up in one direction, which is what causes the magnetic force exerted by the material.

The motions of subatomic structures (nuclei and electrons) produce a magnetic field. It is the direction of the spin and orbit that indicate the direction of the field. The strength of a magnetic field is known as the magnetic moment. As electrons spin and orbit a nucleus, they produce a magnetic field. Pairs of electrons that spin and orbit in opposite directions cancel each other out, creating a net magnetic field of zero. Materials that have an unpaired electron are magnetic. Those with a weak attractive force are referred to as paramagnetic materials, while ferromagnetic materials have a strong attractive force. A diamagnetic material has electrons that are paired, and therefore does not typically have a magnetic moment. There are, however, some diamagnetic materials that have a weak magnetic field.

## Waves

Waves have energy and can transfer energy when they interact with matter. Although waves transfer energy, they do not transport matter. They are a disturbance of matter that transfers energy from one particle to an adjacent particle. There are many types of waves, including sound, seismic, water, light, micro, and radio waves. The two basic categories of waves are mechanical and electromagnetic. Mechanical waves are those that transmit energy through matter. Electromagnetic waves can transmit energy through a vacuum. A transverse wave provides a good illustration of the features of a wave, which include crests, troughs, amplitude, and wavelength. The crest is the maximum upward disturbance of a wave, while the trough is the maximum downward displacement of a wave. Both of these measurements use the wave in its resting position (the position of the wave when there is no disturbance) as the starting point. Amplitude refers to the maximum amount of displacement from the rest position. The wavelength is one complete cycle, which is determined by measuring the distance from a point on the first wave to the corresponding point on the next wave (from crest to crest, for example).

## Sound

Sound is a pressure disturbance that moves through a medium in the form of mechanical waves, which transfer energy from one particle to the next. Sound requires a medium to travel through, such as air, water, or other matter since it is the vibrations that transfer energy to adjacent particles, not the actual movement of particles over a great distance. Sound is transferred through the movement of atomic particles, which can be atoms or molecules. Waves of sound energy move outward in all directions from the source. Sound waves consist of compressions (particles are forced together) and rarefactions (particles move farther apart and their density decreases). A wavelength consists of one compression and one rarefaction. Different sounds have different wavelengths. Sound is a form of kinetic energy.

## Pitch, loudness, sound intensity, timbre, and oscillation

Pitch is the quality of sound determined by frequency. For example, a musical note can be tuned to a specific frequency. A, for instance, has a frequency of 440 Hz, which is a higher frequency than middle C. Humans can detect frequencies between about 20 Hz to 20,000 Hz.

Loudness is a human's perception of sound intensity.

Sound intensity is measured as the sound power per unit area, and can be expressed in decibels.

Timbre is a human's perception of the type or quality of sound.

Oscillation is a measurement, usually of time, against a basic value, equilibrium, or rest point.

## Electromagnetic spectrum

The electromagnetic spectrum is defined by frequency (f) and wavelength ($\lambda$). Frequency is typically measured in hertz and wavelength is usually measured in meters. Frequency is inversely proportional to wavelength, a relationship expressed by the formula $f = v/\lambda$, where "f" is frequency, "v" is phase speed or phase velocity, and "$\lambda$" is wavelength. Frequency refers to the number of occurrences of an event in a given time period. Frequency multiplied by wavelength always equals the speed of light, which is $3.0 \times 10^8$. Electromagnetic waves occur when a charged object is accelerated or decelerated. Electromagnetic waves include radio waves (which have the longest wavelength), microwaves, infrared radiation (radiant heat), visible light, ultraviolet radiation, x-rays, and gamma rays. The energy of electromagnetic waves is carried in packets that have a magnitude that is inversely proportional to the wavelength. Radio waves have a range of wavelengths, from about $10^{-1}$ to $10^{-5}$ meters, while their frequencies range from $10^5$ to about $10^{-1}$.

## Visible light

Light is the portion of the electromagnetic spectrum that is visible because of its ability to stimulate the retina. It is absorbed and emitted by electrons, atoms, and molecules that move from one energy level to another. Visible light interacts with matter through molecular electron excitation (which occurs in the human retina) and through plasma oscillations (which occur in metals). Visible light is between ultraviolet and infrared light on the spectrum. Wavelengths of visible light range from 380 nanometers (nm) to 760 nm. Different wavelengths correspond to different colors. The color red has the longest wavelength, while the wavelength of violet is on the short end of the spectrum. The human brain interprets or perceives visible light, which is emitted from the sun and other stars, as color. For example, when the entire wavelength reaches the retina, the brain perceives the color white. When no part of the wavelength reaches the retina, the brain perceives the color black.

## Doppler effect

The Doppler effect refers to the effect the relative motion of the source of the wave and the location of the observer has on waves. The Doppler effect is easily observable in sound waves. What a person hears when a train approaches or a car honking its horn passes by are examples of the Doppler effect. The pitch of the sound is different not because the emitted frequency has changed, but because the received frequency has changed. The frequency is higher (as is the pitch) as the train approaches, the same as emitted just as it passes, and lower as the train moves away. This is because the wavelength changes. The Doppler effect can occur when an observer is stationary, and can also occur when two trains approach and pass each other. Electromagnetic waves are also affected in this manner. The motion of the medium can also affect the wave. For waves that do not travel in a medium, such as light waves, it is the difference in velocity that determines the outcome.

## Kinetic theory of gases

The kinetic theory of gases assumes that gas molecules are small compared to the distances between them and that they are in constant random motion. The attractive and repulsive forces between gas molecules are negligible. Their kinetic energy does not change with time as long as the temperature remains the same. The higher the temperature is, the greater the motion will be. As the temperature of a gas increases, so does the kinetic energy of the molecules. In other words, gas will occupy a greater volume as the temperature is increased and a lesser volume as the temperature is decreased. In addition, the same amount of gas will occupy a greater volume as the temperature increases, but pressure remains constant. At any given temperature, gas molecules have the same average kinetic energy. The ideal gas law is derived from the kinetic theory of gases.

## Inorganic compounds

The main trait of inorganic compounds is that they lack carbon. Inorganic compounds include mineral salts, metals and alloys, non-metallic compounds such as phosphorus, and metal complexes. A metal complex has a central atom (or ion) bonded to surrounding ligands (molecules or anions). The ligands sacrifice the donor atoms (in the form of at least one pair of electrons) to the central atom. Many inorganic compounds are ionic, meaning they form ionic bonds rather than share electrons. They may have high melting points because of this. They may also be colorful, but this is not an absolute identifier of an inorganic compound. Salts, which are inorganic compounds, are an example of inorganic bonding of cations and anions. Some examples of salts are magnesium chloride ($MgCl_2$) and sodium oxide ($Na_2O$). Oxides, carbonates, sulfates, and halides are classes of inorganic compounds. They are typically poor conductors, are very water soluble, and crystallize easily. Minerals and silicates are also inorganic compounds.

## Organic compounds

Two of the main characteristics of organic compounds are that they include carbon and are formed by covalent bonds. Carbon can form long chains, double and triple bonds, and rings. While inorganic compounds tend to have high melting points, organic compounds tend to melt at temperatures below 300° C. They also tend to boil, sublimate, and decompose below this temperature. Unlike inorganic compounds, they are not very water soluble. Organic molecules are organized into functional groups based on their specific atoms, which helps determine how they will react chemically. A few groups are alkanes, nitro, alkenes, sulphides, amines, and carbolic acids. The hydroxyl group (-OH) consists of alcohols. These molecules are polar, which increases their solubility. By some estimates, there are more than 16 million organic compounds.

## Reading chemical equations

Chemical equations describe chemical reactions. The reactants are on the left side before the arrow and the products are on the right side after the arrow. The arrow indicates the reaction or change. The coefficient, or stoichiometric coefficient, is the number before the element, and indicates the ratio of reactants to products in terms of moles. The equation for the formation of water from hydrogen and oxygen, for example, is $2H_2$ (g) + $O_2$ (g) → $2H_2O$ (l). The 2 preceding hydrogen and water is the coefficient, which means there are 2 moles of hydrogen and 2 of water. There is 1 mole of oxygen, which does not have to be indicated with the number 1. In parentheses, g stands for gas, l stands for liquid, s stands for solid, and aq stands for aqueous solution (a substance dissolved in water). Charges are shown in superscript for individual ions, but not for ionic compounds. Polyatomic ions are separated by parentheses so the ion will not be confused with the number of ions.

## Balancing equations

An unbalanced equation is one that does not follow the law of conservation of mass, which states that matter can only be changed, not created. If an equation is unbalanced, the numbers of atoms indicated by the stoichiometric coefficients on each side of the arrow will not be equal. Start by writing the formulas for each species in the reaction. Count the atoms on each side and determine if the number is equal. Coefficients must be whole numbers. Fractional amounts, such as half a molecule, are not possible. Equations can be balanced by multiplying the coefficients by a constant that will produce the smallest possible whole number coefficient. $H_2 + O_2$ → $H_2O$ is an example of an unbalanced equation. The balanced equation is $2H_2 + O_2$ → $2H_2O$, which indicates that it takes two moles of hydrogen and one of oxygen to produce two moles of water.

## Water

The important properties of water ($H_2O$) are high polarity, hydrogen bonding, cohesiveness, adhesiveness, high specific heat, high latent heat, and high heat of vaporization. It is essential to life as we know it, as water is one of the main if not the main constituent of many living things. Water is a liquid at room temperature. The high specific heat of water means it resists the breaking of its hydrogen bonds and resists heat and motion, which is why it has a relatively high boiling point and high vaporization point. It also resists temperature change. In its solid state, water floats. Most substances are heavier in their solid forms. Water is cohesive, which means it is attracted to itself. It is also adhesive, which means it readily attracts other molecules. If water tends to adhere to another substance, the substance is said to be hydrophilic. Water makes a good solvent. Substances, particularly those with polar ions and molecules, readily dissolve in water.

## Hydrogen bonds

Hydrogen bonds are weaker than covalent and ionic bonds, and refer to the type of attraction in an electronegative atom such as oxygen, fluorine, or nitrogen. Hydrogen bonds can form within a single molecule or between molecules. A water molecule is polar, meaning it is partially positively charged on one end (the hydrogen end) and partially negatively charged on the other (the oxygen end). This is because the hydrogen atoms are arranged around the oxygen atom in a close tetrahedron. Hydrogen is oxidized (its number of electrons is reduced) when it bonds with oxygen to form water. Hydrogen bonds tend not only to be weak, but also short-lived. They also tend to be numerous. Hydrogen bonds give water many of its important properties, including its high specific heat and high heat of vaporization, its solvent qualities, its adhesiveness and cohesiveness, its hydrophobic qualities, and its ability to float in its solid form. Hydrogen bonds are also an important component of proteins, nucleic acids, and DNA.

## Solutions

A solution is a homogeneous mixture. A mixture is two or more different substances that are mixed together, but not combined chemically. Homogeneous mixtures are those that are uniform in their composition. Solutions consist of a solute (the substance that is dissolved) and a solvent (the substance that does the dissolving). An example is sugar water. The solvent is the water and the solute is the sugar. The intermolecular attraction between the solvent and the solute is called solvation. Hydration refers to solutions in which water is the solvent. Solutions are formed when the forces of the molecules of the solute and the solvent are as strong as the individual molecular forces of the solute and the solvent. An example is that salt (NaCl) dissolves in water to create a solution. The $Na^+$ and the $Cl^-$ ions in salt interact with the molecules of water and vice versa to overcome the individual molecular forces of the solute and the solvent.

## Mixtures, suspensions, colloids, emulsions, and foams

A mixture is a combination of two or more substances that are not bonded. Suspensions are mixtures of heterogeneous materials. Particles are usually larger than those found in true solutions. Dirt mixed vigorously with water is an example of a suspension. The dirt is temporarily suspended in water, but the two separate once the mixing is ceased. A mixture of large (1 nm to 500 nm) particles is called a colloidal suspension. The particles are termed dispersants and the dispersing medium is similar to the solvent in a solution. Sol refers to a liquid or a solid that also has solids dispersed through it, such as milk or gelatin. An aerosol spray is a colloid suspension of gas and the solid or liquid being dispersed. An emulsion refers to a liquid or a solid that has a liquid dispersed through it. A foam is a liquid that has gas dispersed through it.

## Acids

When they are dissolved in aqueous solutions, some properties of acids are that they conduct electricity, change blue litmus paper to red, have a sour taste, react with bases to neutralize them, and react with active metals to free hydrogen. A weak acid is one that does not donate all of its protons or disassociate completely. Strong acids include hydrochloric, hydroiodic, hydrobromic, perchloric, nitric, and sulfuric. They ionize completely. Superacids are those that are stronger than 100 percent sulfuric acid. They include fluoroantimonic, magic, and perchloric acids. Acids can be used in pickling, a process used to remove rust and corrosion from metals. They are also used as catalysts in the processing of minerals and the production of salts and fertilizers. Phosphoric acid ($H_3PO_4$) is added to sodas and other acids are added to foods as preservatives or to add taste.

## Bases

When they are dissolved in aqueous solutions, some properties of bases are that they conduct electricity, change red litmus paper to blue, feel slippery, and react with acids to neutralize their properties. A weak base is one that does not completely ionize in an aqueous solution, and usually has a low pH. Strong bases can free protons in very weak acids. Examples of strong bases are hydroxide compounds such as potassium, barium, and lithium hydroxides. Most are in the first and second groups of the periodic table. A superbase is extremely strong compared to sodium hydroxide and cannot be kept in an aqueous solution. Superbases are organized into organic, organometallic, and inorganic classes. Bases are used as insoluble catalysts in heterogeneous reactions and as catalysts in hydrogenation.

## Salts

Some properties of salts are that they are formed from acid base reactions, are ionic compounds consisting of metallic and nonmetallic ions, dissociate in water, and are comprised of tightly bonded ions. Some common salts are sodium chloride (NaCl), sodium bisulfate, potassium dichromate ($K_2Cr_2O_7$), and calcium chloride ($CaCl_2$). Calcium chloride is used as a drying agent, and may be used to absorb moisture when freezing mixtures. Potassium nitrate ($KNO_3$) is used to make fertilizer and in the manufacture of explosives. Sodium nitrate ($NaNO_3$) is also used in the making of fertilizer. Baking soda (sodium bicarbonate) is a salt, as are Epsom salts [magnesium sulfate ($MgSO_4$)]. Salt and water can react to form a base and an acid. This is called a hydrolysis reaction.

## pH

The potential of hydrogen (pH) is a measurement of the concentration of hydrogen ions in a substance in terms of the number of moles of $H^+$ per liter of solution. All substances fall between 0 and 14 on the pH scale. A lower pH indicates a higher $H^+$ concentration, while a higher pH indicates a lower $H^+$ concentration. Pure water has a neutral pH, which is 7. Anything with a pH lower than water (0 to 6) is considered acidic. Anything with a pH higher than water (8 to 14) is a base. Drain cleaner, soap, baking soda, ammonia, egg whites, and sea water are common bases. Urine, stomach acid, citric acid, vinegar, hydrochloric acid, and battery acid are acids. A pH indicator is a substance that acts as a detector of hydrogen or hydronium ions. It is halochromic, meaning it changes color to indicate that hydrogen or hydronium ions have been detected.

## Earth's life-sustaining system

Life on earth is dependent on:

- All three states of water – gas (water vapor), liquid, and solid (ice)
- A variety of forms of carbon, the basis of life (carbon-based units)
- In the atmosphere, carbon dioxide in the forms of methane and black carbon soot produce the greenhouse effect that provides a habitable atmosphere.
- The earth's atmosphere and electromagnetic field, which shield the surface from harmful radiation and allow useful radiation to go through
- The earth's relationship to the sun and the moon, which creates the four seasons and the cycles of plant and animal life
- The combination of water, carbon, and nutrients, which provides sustenance for life and regulates the climate system in a habitable temperature range with non-toxic air.

## Earth system science

The complex and interconnected dynamics of the continents, atmosphere, oceans, ice, and life forms are the subject of earth system science. These interconnected dynamics require an interdisciplinary approach that includes chemistry, physics, biology, mathematics, and applied sciences in order to study the Earth as an integrated system and determine (while considering human impact and interaction) the past, present, and future states of the earth. Scientific inquiry in this field includes exploration of:

- Extreme weather events as they pertain to a changing climate
- Earthquakes and volcanic eruptions as they pertain to tectonic shifts
- Losses in biodiversity in relation to the changes in the earth's ecosystems
- Causes and effects in the environment
- The sun's solar variability in relation to the earth's climate
- The atmosphere's increasing concentrations of carbon dioxide and aerosols
- Trends in the earth's systems in terms of changes and their consequences

## Earth science disciplines

Modern science is approaching the study of the earth in an integrated fashion that sees the earth as an interconnected system that is impacted by humankind and, therefore, must include social dimensions. Traditionally, though, the following were the earth science disciplines:

- Geology is the study of the origin and structure of the earth and of the changes it has undergone and is in the process of undergoing. Geologists work from the crust inward.
- Meteorology is the study of the atmosphere, including atmospheric pressure, temperature, clouds, winds, precipitation, etc. It is also concerned with describing and explaining weather.
- Oceanography is the study of the oceans, which includes studying their extent and depth, the physics and chemistry of ocean waters, and the exploitation of their resources.
- Ecology is the study of living organisms in relation to their environment and to other living things. It is the study of the interrelations between the different components of the ecosystem.

## Geological eras

Geologists divide the history of the earth into units of time called eons, which are divided into eras, then into periods, then into epochs and finally into ages. Dates are approximate of course, and there may be variations of a few million years. (Million years ago is abbreviated as Ma.) Some of the most commonly known periods are:
- Hadean Period – About 4.5 to 3.8 billion years ago
- Archaean Period – 3.8 to 2.5 billion years ago
- Proterozoic Period – 2.5 billion to 542 Ma
- Cambrian Period – 542 to 488 Ma
- Ordovician Period – 488 to 443 Ma
- Silurian Period – 443 to 416 Ma
- Devonian Period – 416 to 359 Ma
- Carboniferous Period – 359 to 290 Ma
- Permian Period – 290 to 248 Ma
- Triassic Period – 251 to 200 Ma
- Jurassic Period – 200 to 150 Ma
- Cretaceous Period – 150 to 65 Ma
- Paleogene Period – 65 to 28 Ma
- Neogene Period – 28 to 2 Ma
- Quaternary Period – about 2 Ma to the present

## Development of life on earth

The evolution of life on earth is believed to have occurred as follows:

- Igneous rocks formed. (Hadean)
- The continents formed. (Archaean Eon)
- One-celled creatures such as hydras, jellyfish, and sponges appeared about 600 Ma.
- Flatworms, roundworms, and segmented worms appeared about 550 Ma.
- Moss, arthropods, octopus, and eels appeared. (Cambrian Period)
- Mushrooms, fungi, and other primitive plants appeared; sea animals began to use calcium to build bones and shells. (Ordovician Period)
- Fish with jaws appeared. (Silurian Period)
- Fish developed lungs and legs (frogs) and went on land; ferns appeared. (Devonian period)
- Reptiles developed the ability to lay eggs on land and pine trees appeared. (Carboniferous Period)
- Dinosaurs dominated the land during the Triassic and Jurassic Periods.
- Flying insects, birds, and the first flowering plants appeared; dinosaurs died out. (Cretaceous Period)
- Mammals evolved and dominated; grasses became widespread. (50 Ma)
- Hominids appeared more than 2 Ma.

## Planets

In order of their distance from the sun (closest to furthest away), the planets are: Mercury, Venus, Earth, Mars, Jupiter, Saturn, Uranus, Neptune, and Pluto (there is debate about whether Pluto should be classified as a planet). All the planets revolve around the sun, which is an average-sized star in the spiral Milky Way galaxy. They revolve in the same direction in nearly circular orbits. If the planets were viewed by looking down from the sun, they would rotate in a counter-clockwise direction. Pluto's orbit is so highly inclined at 18 degrees that at times its ellipse is nearer to the sun than to its neighbor, Neptune. All the planets are in or near the same plane, called the ecliptic, and the axis of rotation is nearly perpendicular to the ecliptic. The exceptions are Uranus and Pluto, which are tipped on their sides.

## Terrestrial and Jovian Planets

The Terrestrial Planets are: Mercury, Venus, Earth, and Mars. These are the four planets closest to the sun. They are called terrestrial because they all have a compact, rocky surface similar to the Earth's. Venus, Earth, and Mars have significant atmospheres, but Mercury has almost no atmosphere.

The Jovian Planets are: Jupiter (the largest planet), Saturn, Uranus, and Neptune. They are called Jovian (Jupiter-like) because of their huge sizes in relation to that of the Earth, and because they all have a gaseous nature like Jupiter. Although gas giants, some or all of the Jovian Planets may have small, solid cores.

Pluto does not have the characteristics necessary to fit into either the Terrestrial or the Jovian group.

The sun represents 99.85% of all the matter in our solar system. Combined, the planets make up only 0.135% of the mass of the solar system, with Jupiter having twice the mass of all the other planets combined. The remaining 0.015% of the mass comes from comets, planetary satellites, asteroids, meteoroids, and interplanetary medium.

## Hydrosphere

The hydrosphere is anything on earth that is related to water, whether it is in the air, on land, or in a plant or animal system. A water molecule consists of only two atoms of hydrogen and one of oxygen, yet it is what makes life possible. Unlike the other planets, earth is able to sustain life because its temperature allows water to be in its liquid state most of the time. Water vapor and ice are of no use to living organisms.

The hydrologic cycle is the journey water takes as it assumes different forms. Liquid surface water evaporates to form the gaseous state of a cloud, and then becomes liquid again in the form of rain. This process takes about 10 days if water becomes a cloud. Water at the bottom of the ocean or in a glacier is not likely to change form, even over periods of thousands of years.

## Aquifers

An aquifer is an underground water reservoir formed from groundwater that has infiltrated from the surface by passing through the soil and permeable rock layers (the zone of aeration) to a zone of saturation where the rocks are impermeable.

There are two types of aquifers. In one, the water is under pressure (confined) as the supply builds up between layers of impermeable rocks and has to move back towards the surface, resulting in a spring or artesian well. The second type of aquifer is called "unconfined" because it has room to expand and contract, and the water has to be pumped out. The highest level of the aquifer is called the water table. If water is pumped out of the aquifer such that the water table dips in a specific area, that area is called a cone of depression.

## Freshwater biomes, estuaries, intertidal zones, and subtidal zones

Freshwater biomes are areas of relatively slow-moving water, such as rivers, lakes, and ponds. Since the water is not moving so quickly as to move life forms along, insects and fish have time to grow, and plants have time to attach themselves to the soil.

Estuaries are coastline regions where the fresh water from rivers mixes with the salt water of the ocean. This mix is attractive to numerous types of marine life (and birds). It is especially suitable for laying eggs because the water is quite still and its brackishness hides newborn fish.

The intertidal zone is the space on the coastline that is under water during high tide and dry during low tide. It is usually rocky, and contains abundant amounts of algae, small marine life, and many birds looking for food.

The subtidal zone, which may have large sandy plains, is always under water near the coast. Coral reefs and most of the world's fish are here because the waves create abundant life-sustaining oxygen in the water.

## Euphotic , bathyal, and abyssal zone

Beyond the subtidal zone, the ocean floor drops away to the deep ocean biome, which has three layers:

- The euphotic zone is the surface area of deep ocean water where there is a lot of sunshine and oxygen and therefore many small photosynthetic organisms. However, there are few nutrients because they fall to the bottom.
- The bathyal zone is the area further down that has dim light and no little organisms. It does, however, have some fish that go to feed on the organisms on the surface.

- The abyssal zone is the bottom of the ocean where it is pitch black. There are no producers and little oxygen. This zone is very cold and has high pressure. There are predator fish and living organisms that feed on whatever falls from the surface.

## Biosphere

Biosphere is the term used by physical geographers to describe the living world of trees, bugs, and animals. It refers to any place where life exists on earth, and is the intersection of the hydrosphere, the atmosphere, the land, and the energy that comes from space. The biosphere includes the upper areas of the atmosphere where birds and insects can travel, areas deep inside caves, and hydrothermal vents at the bottom of the ocean. Factors that affect the biosphere include:
- The distance and tilt between the earth and the sun – This produces temperatures that are conducive to life and causes the seasons.
- Climate, daily weather, and erosion – These change the land and the organisms on and in it.
- Earthquakes, tornadoes, volcanoes, tsunamis, and other natural phenomena – These all change the land.
- Chemical erosion – This changes the composition of rocks and organic materials, as well as how bacteria and single-celled organisms break down organic and inorganic materials.

## Ecological system and biome

An ecological system, or ecosystem, is the community of all the living organisms in a specific area interacting with non-living factors such as temperature, sunlight, atmospheric pressure, weather patterns, wind, types of nutrients, etc. An ecosystem's development depends on the energy that passes in and out of it. The boundaries of an ecosystem depend on the use of the term, whether it refers to an ecosystem under a rock or in a valley, pond, or ocean.

A biome is a general ecosystem type defined by the plants and animals that live there and the local climate patterns. Examples include tropical rainforests or savannas, deserts, grasslands, deciduous forests, tundra, woodlands, and ice caps. There can be more than one type of biome within a larger climate zone. The transition area between two biomes is an ecotone, which may have characteristics of both biomes.

## Erosion

Erosion is the process that breaks down matter, whether it is a rock that is broken into pebbles or mountains that are rained on until they become hills. Erosion always happens in a downhill direction. The erosion of land by weather or breaking waves is called denudation. Mass wasting is the movement of masses of dirt and rock from one place to another. This can occur in two ways: mechanical (such as breaking a rock with a hammer) or chemical (such as pouring acid on a rock to dissolve it). If the material changes color, it indicates that a break down was chemical in nature. Whatever is broken down must go somewhere, so erosion eventually builds something up. For example, an eroded mountain ends up in a river that carries the sediment towards the ocean, where it builds up and creates a wetland or delta at the mouth of the river.

## Climates

Climate is the atmospheric condition in a certain location near the surface of the earth. Scientists have determined the following different types of climates:

- Polar (ice caps)
- Polar (tundra)
- Subtropical (dry summer)
- Subtropical (dry winter)
- Subtropical (humid)
- Subtropical (marine west coast)
- Subtropical (Mediterranean)
- Subtropical (wet)
- Tropical (monsoon)
- Tropical (savannah/grasslands)
- Tropical (wet)

Several factors make up and affect climates. These include:
- Temperature
- Atmospheric pressure
- The number of clouds and the amount of dust or smog
- Humidity
- Winds

The moistest and warmest of all the climates is that of the tropical rainforest. It has daily convection thunderstorms caused by the surface daytime heat and the high humidity, which combine to form thunderclouds.

## Layers of the earth

The earth has several distinct layers, each with its own properties:

- Crust is the outermost layer of the earth that is comprised of the continents and the ocean basins. It has a variable thickness (35-70 km in the continents and 5-10 km in the ocean basins) and is composed mostly of alumino-silicates.
- Mantle is about 2900 km thick, and is made up mostly of ferro-magnesium silicates. It is divided into an upper and lower mantle. Most of the internal heat of the earth is located in the mantle. Large convective cells circulate heat, and may cause plate tectonic movement.
- Core is separated into the liquid outer core and the solid inner core. The outer core is 2300 km thick (composed mostly of nickel-iron alloy), and the inner core (almost entirely iron) is 12 km thick. The earth's magnetic field is thought to be controlled by the liquid outer core.

## Earth's atmosphere

The earth's atmosphere is 79% nitrogen, 20% oxygen, and 1% other gases. The oxygen was originally produced almost entirely by algae-type plants. The atmosphere has four layers:

- Troposphere – This is the layer closest to the earth where all weather takes place. It is the region that contains rising and falling packets of air. Air pressure at sea level is 0.1 atmospheres, but the top of the troposphere is about 10% of that amount.
- In the stratosphere, air flow is mainly horizontal. The upper portion has a thin layer of concentrated ozone (a reactive form of oxygen) that is largely responsible for absorbing the sun's ultraviolet rays.
- Mesosphere is the coldest layer. Temperatures drop to -100°C at the top.

- Thermosphere is divided into the lower ionosphere and the higher exosphere. This layer is very thin and has many ionized atoms with a net electrical charge. The aurora and Van Allen Belts are here. This layer also absorbs the most energetic photons from the sun and reflects radio waves, enabling long distance radio communication.

## Paleontology

Paleontology is the study of prehistoric plant and animal life through the analysis of fossil remains. These fossils reveal the ecologies of the past and the path of evolution for both extinct and living organisms. A historical science, paleontology seeks information about the identity, origin, environment, and evolution of past organisms and what they can reveal about the past of the earth as a whole. Paleontology explains causes as opposed to conducting experiments to observe effects. It is related to the fields of biology, geology, and archaeology, and is divided into several sub-disciplines concerned with the types of fossils studied, the process of fossilization, and the ecology and climate of the past. Paleontologists also help identify the composition of the earth's rock layers by the fossils that are found, thus identifying potential sites for oil, mineral, and water extraction.

## Rock record

The Law of Superposition logically assumes that the bottom layer of a series of sedimentary layers is the oldest, unless it has been overturned or older rock has been pushed over it.

In addition, since igneous intrusions can cut through or flow above other rocks, these other rocks are older. For example, molten rock (lava) flows out over already present, older rocks.

Another guideline for the rock record is that rock layers are older than the folds and faults in them because the rocks must exist before they can be folded or faulted.

If a rock contains atomic nuclei, reference tables of the half lives of commonly used radio isotopes can be used to match the decay rate of known substances to the nuclei in a rock, and thereby determine its age.

Ages of rocks can also be determined from contact metamorphism, the re-crystallization of pre-existing rocks due to changes in physical and chemical conditions, such as heat, pressure, and chemically active fluids that might be present in lava or polluted waters.

## Matching rocks and geologic events

Geologists physically follow rock layers from one location to another by a process called "walking the outcrop." Geologists walk along the outcropping to see where it goes and what the differences and similarities of the neighboring locations they cross are.

Similar rock types or patterns of rock layers that are similar in terms of thickness, color, composition, and fossil remains tell geologists that two locations have a similar geologic history.

Fossils are found all over the earth, but are from a relatively small time period in earth's history. Therefore, fossil evidence helps date a rock layer, regardless of where it occurs.

Volcanic ash is a good time indicator since ash is deposited quickly over a widespread area. Matching the date of an eruption to the ash allows for a precise identification of time. Similarly, the meteor impact at the intersection of the Cretaceous and Tertiary Periods left a time marker. Wherever the meteor's iridium content is found, geologists are able to date rock layers.

## Fossil and rock record

Reference tables are used to match specimens and time periods. For example, the fossil record has been divided into time units of the earth's history. Rocks can therefore be dated by the fossils found with them. There are also reference tables for dating plate motions and mountain building events in geologic history.

Since humans have been around for a relatively short period of time, fossilized human remains help to affix a date to a location.

Some areas have missing geologic layers because of erosion or other factors, but reference tables specific to a region will list what is complete or missing.

The theory of uniformitarianism assumes that geologic processes have been the same throughout history. Therefore, the way erosion or volcanic eruptions happen today is the same as the way these events happened millions of years ago because there is no reason for them to have changed. Therefore, knowledge about current events can be applied to the past to make judgments about events in the rock record.

Fossils can show how animal and plant life have changed or remained the same over time. For example, fossils have provided evidence of the existence of dinosaurs even though they no longer roam the earth, and have also been used to prove that certain insects have been around forever.

Fossils have been used to identify four basic eras: Proterozoic, the age of primitive life; Paleozoic, the age of fishes; Mesozoic, the age of dinosaurs; and Cenozoic, the age of mammals.

Most ancient forms of life have disappeared, and there are reference tables that list when this occurred. Fossil records also show the evolution of certain life forms, such as the horse from the eohippus. However, the majority of changes do not involve evolution from simple to complex forms, but rather an increase in the variety of forms.

## Mountains

A mountain is a portion of the earth that has been raised above its surroundings by volcanic action or tectonic plate movement. Mountains are made up of igneous, metamorphic, and sedimentary rocks, and most lie along active plate boundaries. There are two major mountain systems. The Circum-Pacific encircles the entire Pacific Ocean, from New Guinea up across Japan and the Aleutians and down to southern South America. The Alpine-Himalaya stretches from northern Africa across the Alps and to the Himalayas and Indonesia.

Orogeny is the term for the process of natural mountain formation. Therefore, physical mountains are orogens.

Folded mountains are created through the folding of rock layers when two crustal plates come together. The Alps and Himalayas are folded mountains. The latter was formed by the collision of India with Asia.

Fault-block mountains are created from the tension forces of plate movements. These produce faults that vertically displace one section to form a mountain.

Dome mountains are created from magma pushing up through the earth's crust.

## Volcanoes

Volcanoes are classified according to their activity level. An active volcano is in the process of erupting or building to an eruption; a dormant volcano has erupted before and may erupt again someday, but is not currently active; and an extinct volcano has died out volcanically and will not erupt ever again. Active volcanoes endanger plant and animal life, but lava and ash add enriching minerals to the soil. There are three types of volcanic mountains:

- Shield volcanoes are the largest volcanic mountains because of a repeated, viscous lava flow from small eruptions over a long period of time that cause the mountain to grow.
- Cinder cone volcanoes, or linear volcanoes, are small in size, but have massive explosions through linear shafts that spread cinders and ash around the vent. This results in a cone-shaped hill.
- Composite volcanoes get their name from the mix of lava and ash layers that build the mountain.

## Major subdivisions

The three major subdivisions of rock are:

- Igneous (magmatites) – This type is formed from the cooling of liquid magma. In the process, minerals crystallize and amalgamate. If solidification occurs deep in the earth (plutonic rock), the cooling process is slow. This allows for the formation of large crystals, giving rock a coarse-grained texture (granite). Quickly cooled magma has a glassy texture (obsidian).
- Metamorphic – Under conditions of high temperature and pressure within the earth's crust, rock material melts and changes structure, transitioning or metamorphosing into a new type of rock with different minerals. If the minerals appear in bands, the rock is foliated. Examples include marble (unfoliated) and slate (foliated).
- Sedimentary – This is the most common type of rock on earth. It is formed by sedimentation, compaction, and then cementation of many small particles of mineral, animal, or plant material. There are three types of sedimentary rocks: clastic, clay, and sand that came from disintegrated rocks; chemical (rock salt and gypsum), formed by evaporation of aqueous solutions; and biogenic (coal), formed from animal or plant remnants.

## Glaciers

Glaciers start high in the mountains, where snow and ice accumulate inside a cirque (a small semicircular depression). The snow becomes firmly packed into masses of coarse-grained ice that are slowly pulled down a slope by gravity. Glaciers grow with large amounts of snowfall and retreat (diminish) if warm weather melts more ice than can be replaced. Glaciers once covered large areas of both the northern and southern hemispheres with mile-thick ice that carved out valleys, fjords, and other land formations. They also moved plants, animals, and rocks from one area to another. There were two types of glaciers: valley, which produced U-shaped erosion and sharp-peaked mountains; and continental, which moved over and rounded mountain tops and ridges. These glaciers existed during the ice ages, the last of which occurred from 2.5 million years ago to 12,000 years ago.

## Planet definition

On August 24, 2006, the International Astronomical Union redefined the criteria a body must meet to be classified as a planet, stating that the following conditions must be met:

- "A planet orbits around a star and is neither a star nor a moon."
- "Its shape is spherical due to its gravity."
- "It has 'cleared' the space of its orbit."

A dwarf planet such as Pluto does not meet the third condition. Small solar system bodies such as asteroids and comets meet only the first condition.

The solar system developed about 4.6 billion years ago out of an enormous cloud of dust and gas circling around the sun. Four rocky planets orbit relatively close to the sun. Their inside orbit is separated from the outside orbit of the four, larger gaseous planets by an asteroid belt. Pluto, some comets, and several small objects circle in the Kuiper belt outside Neptune's orbit. The Oort cloud, composed of icy space objects, encloses the planetary system like a shell.

## Moon

Earth's moon is the closest celestial body to earth. Its proximity has allowed it to be studied since the invention of the telescope. As a result, its landforms have been named after astronomers, philosophers, and other scholars. Its surface has many craters created by asteroids since it has no protective atmosphere. These dark lowlands looked like seas to early astronomers, but there is virtually no water on the moon except possibly in its polar regions. These impact craters and depressions actually contain solidified lava flows. The bright highlands were thought to be continents, and were named terrae. The rocks of the moon have been pounded by asteroids so often that there is a layer of rubble and dust called the regolith. Also because there is no protective atmosphere, temperatures on the moon vary widely, from 265°F to -255°F.

## Sun

A star begins as a cloud of hydrogen and some heavier elements drawn together by their own mass. This matter then begins to rotate. The core heats up to several million degrees Fahrenheit, which causes the hydrogen atoms to lose their shells and their nuclei to fuse. This releases enormous amounts of energy. The star then becomes stable, a stage called the main sequence. This is the stage our sun is in, and it will remain in this stage until its supply of hydrogen fuel runs out. Stars are not always alone like our sun, and may exist in pairs or groups. The hottest stars shine blue-white; medium-hot stars like our sun glow yellow; and cooler stars appear orange. The earth's sun is an average star in terms of mass, light production, and size. All stars, including our sun, have a core where fusion happens; a photosphere (surface) that produces sunspots (cool, dark areas); a red chromosphere that emits solar (bright) flares and shooting gases; and a corona, the transparent area only seen during an eclipse.